THE STATES AND THE NATION SERIES, of which this volume is a part, is designed to assist the American people in a serious look at the ideals they have espoused and the experiences they have undergone in the history of the nation. The content of every volume represents the scholarship, experience, and opinions of its author. The costs of writing and editing were met mainly by grants from the National Endowment for the Humanities, a federal agency. The project was administered by the American Association for State and Local History, a nonprofit learned society, working with an Editorial Board of distinguished editors, authors, and historians, whose names are listed below.

Virginia

A Bicentennial History

Louis D. Rubin, Jr.

W. W. Norton & Company, Inc.
New York

American Association for State and Local History
Nashville

F
226
R7

Library of Congress Cataloging in Publication Data

Rubin, Louis Decimus, Jr., 1923–
Virginia.

(The States and the Nation series)
Bibliography: p.
Includes index.
1. Virginia—History. I. Title. II. Series.
F226.R7   975.5   77–3250
ISBN 0–393–05630–9

Published and distributed by
W. W. Norton & Company, Inc.
500 Fifth Avenue
New York, New York 10036

Printed in the United States of America

1 2 3 4 5 6 7 8 9 0

Contents

Illustrations

45615

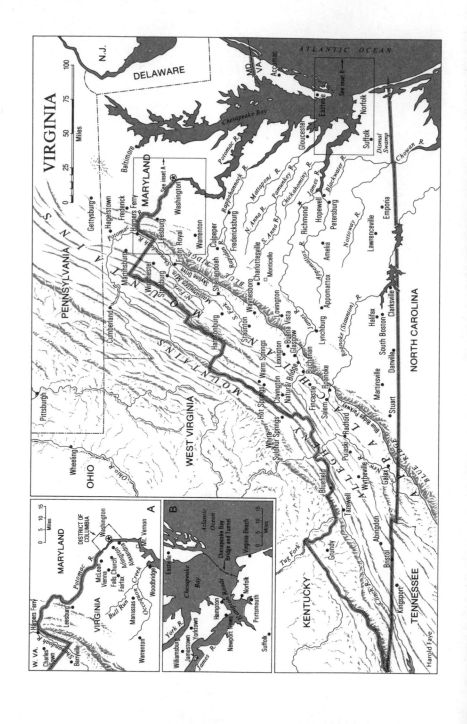

ᑌnvitation to the Reader

IN 1807, former President John Adams argued that a complete history of the American Revolution could not be written until the history of change in each state was known, because the principles of the Revolution were as various as the states that went through it. Two hundred years after the Declaration of Independence, the American nation has spread over a continent and beyond. The states have grown in number from thirteen to fifty. And democratic principles have been interpreted differently in every one of them.

We therefore invite you to consider that the history of your state may have more to do with the bicentennial review of the American Revolution than does the story of Bunker Hill or Valley Forge. The Revolution has continued as Americans extended liberty and democracy over a vast territory. John Adams was right: the states are part of that story, and the story is incomplete without an account of their diversity.

The Declaration of Independence stressed life, liberty, and the pursuit of happiness; accordingly, it shattered the notion of holding new territories in the subordinate status of colonies. The Northwest Ordinance of 1787 set forth a procedure for new states to enter the Union on an equal footing with the old. The Federal Constitution shortly confirmed this novel means of building a nation out of equal states. The step-by-step process through which territories have achieved self-government and national representation is among the most important of the Founding Fathers' legacies.

The method of state-making reconciled the ancient conflict between liberty and empire, resulting in what Thomas Jefferson called an empire for liberty. The system has worked and remains unaltered, despite enormous changes that have taken

place in the nation. The country's extent and variety now sur-
pass anything the patriots of '76 could likely have imagined.
The United States has changed from an agrarian republic into a
highly industrial and urban democracy, from a fledgling nation
into a major world power. As Oliver Wendell Holmes remarked
in 1920, the creators of the nation could not have seen completely how it and its constitution and its states would develop.
Any meaningful review in the bicentennial era must consider
what the country has become, as well as what it was.

The new nation of equal states took as its motto *E Pluribus
Unum*—"out of many, one." But just as many peoples have
become Americans without complete loss of ethnic and cultural
identities, so have the states retained differences of character.
Some have been superficial, expressed in stereotyped images—
big, boastful Texas, "sophisticated" New York, "hillbilly"
Arkansas. Other differences have been more real, sometimes instructively, sometimes amusingly; democracy has embraced
Huey Long's Louisiana, bilingual New Mexico, unicameral Ne-
braska, and a Texas that once taxed fortunetellers and spawned
politicians called "Woodpecker Republicans" and "Skunk
Democrats." Some differences have been profound, as when
South Carolina secessionists led other states out of the Union in
opposition to abolitionists in Massachusetts and Ohio. The result was a bitter Civil War.

The Revolution's first shots may have sounded in Lexington
and Concord; but fights over what democracy should mean and
who should have independence have erupted from Pennsylvania's Gettysburg to the "Bleeding Kansas" of John Brown,
from the Alamo in Texas to the Indian battles at Montana's
Little Bighorn. Utah Mormons have known the strain of isola-
tion; Hawaiians at Pearl Harbor, the terror of attack; Georgians
during Sherman's march, the sadness of defeat and devastation.
Each state's experience differs instructively; each adds under-
standing to the whole.

The purpose of this series of books is to make that kind of un-
derstanding accessible, in a way that will last in value far
beyond the bicentennial fireworks. The series offers a volume
on every state, plus the District of Columbia—fifty-one, in all.

Each book contains, besides the text, a view of the state through eyes other than the author's—a "photographer's essay," in which a skilled photographer presents his own personal perceptions of the state's contemporary flavor.

We have asked authors not for comprehensive chronicles, nor for research monographs or new data for scholars. Bibliographies and footnotes are minimal. We have asked each author for a summing up—interpretive, sensitive, thoughtful, individual, even personal—of what seems significant about his or her state's history. What distinguishes it? What has mattered about it, to its own people and to the rest of the nation? What has it come to now?

To interpret the states in all their variety, we have sought a variety of backgrounds in authors themselves and have encouraged variety in the approaches they take. They have in common only these things: historical knowledge, writing skill, and strong personal feelings about a particular state. Each has wide latitude for the use of the short space. And if each succeeds, it will be by offering you, in your capacity as a *citizen* of a state *and* of a nation, stimulating insights to test against your own.

James Morton Smith
General Editor

Preface

$\mathcal{T}$HE aim of this book is to set forth, within a very brief format, some notion of what the history of the Commonwealth of Virginia and its citizenry has meant for the United States of America.

As such the book has been written in accord with the objectives of The States And The Nation series as a whole, the editors of which have given the individual authors a fairly free hand to approach the task as each thinks best. My approach has been largely chronological. I could not envision an interpretation of some 350 years of well-recorded history being undertaken any other way, for the subject is too complex and has involved too many changes, shifts, and reversals to be separated from its chronological unfolding. How things happened helps to explain why they happened; Virginia *is* because Virginia *was*.

All the same, the interpretative narrative that follows is by no means a factual account of the Virginia historical experience. Both in what it includes and what it leaves out, it has been very much shaped and patterned to make certain emphases and develop certain points. Though remaining reluctant to go charging into the fray with much explicit generalizing, I have sought, as best I can, to set forth my own interpretation of how American history happened to Virginians, and vice versa, through my choice of form and direction.

Out of deference to non-Virginia readers I should like to

identify two geographical place names that are likely to cause confusion. "Northern Virginia" is that cluster of counties and cities centering on Alexandria and the District of Columbia, as far west as the line of the Blue Ridge and southward to Fredericksburg. "Southside" is that group of tobacco-growing counties lying between Suffolk in the Tidewater and Martinsville at the base of the mountains, and stretching roughly from the North Carolina line to Petersburg and Lynchburg. Thus not all of the northern area of Virginia is in "Northern Virginia," while the "Southside" includes only some of the territory along the state's southern border.

In writing this book I have drawn at all times upon the abundant availability of good historical scholarship on the subject. The overall stylistic format of the series, designed as it is for the nonspecialist, has prevented my giving detailed, annotated acknowledgement to my sources, but I feel sure that these will be readily identifiable by scholars in the particular field.

I should like to express my strong gratitude to certain persons who have read portions of what follows, and have made suggestions for improvement—though surely the shortcomings are mine alone. In particular I would acknowledge the help of Thad Tate, John Nelson, Parke Rouse, and Richard Beale Davis with the colonial chapters, and of Guy Friddell with the more recent political developments.

Finally, I should like to dedicate this book about Virginia to a community, past and present, of persons who to my mind constitute the very best that Virginia has been and can be, and who are known collectively as Hollins College. Those who have meant and mean most to me I need not name. The list would be too long, and besides, they know who they are.

LOUIS D. RUBIN, JR.

August 30, 1976

Virginia

1

The Colonial Era

*In which the English
come to Virginia, recognize their good fortune,
and become Virginians.*

N late April of the year 1607, three English sailing ships made their way into the body of water that is now called the Chesapeake Bay. They had come from London, by way of the Canary Islands and the West Indies, under the command of Captain Christopher Newport. There were 143 men aboard, and they were looking for a place to make a settlement in the New World.

The location they chose and on May 14 went ashore to claim was some thirty miles up the river they called the James, after their king. It was a peninsula, which at its narrowest point was only about three hundred yards wide, and so near the river channel that Captain Newport could moor his ships merely by securing lines to the trees. Unfortunately it was also low-lying, with considerable salt marsh, and they had been instructed to avoid "a low and moist place because it will prove unhealthful," [1] but the other advantages appeared to outweigh that.

1. Warren M. Billings, ed., *The Old Dominion in the Seventeenth Century: A Documentary History of Virginia, 1606–1689* (Chapel Hill: University of North Carolina Press, 1975), p. 21.

3

Unlike the Spanish settlement of the New World, their venture was not financed by the crown; it was the speculative affair of a stock company, and in the years ahead it was to suffer from lack of sufficient financial backing. There was hope of making a profit through discovery of precious metals or other minerals, through trade with the Indians, and through the development of agriculture. In its inception it was very much a patriotic venture—hitherto Spain had dominated both the ocean and the settlement of the new continent, but now the English had decided to establish a base and get in on the acquisition of new lands and strategic naval outposts. There would be ample tall trees for masts, and turpentine, hemp, timber, and tar for naval stores. There would be room in the new settlements for the excess of population that was already crowding into London and the other cities of England, now that profound changes in the English economy had broken up the accustomed feudal patterns of life on the land. Colonies abroad, too, would create a market for English woolens and other manufactures, which were still in a state of disruption following the religious wars and the rise of the modern nation states of Europe with their own goals of self-sufficiency.

By no means least among the motives that brought the English to Virginia was the desirability of carrying the true Gospel to heathen shores and saving the souls of resident savages who might otherwise live and die in complete spiritual darkness or, almost as bad, fall into the clutches of the Roman Catholicism that the Jesuit missionaries of Spain were forcefully promulgating further to the south. Like their fellow countrymen who would land in New England a full decade later, they considered themselves to be what a modern scholar has described as "an inspired band marching out, in a world disfigured by the ravages of sin, including their own, for the glory of God, in whose sign they are confident of conquering not only the wilderness but themselves." [2] That the heathen savages had a workable and reasonably stable society of their own, and were not barbarians

2. Perry Miller, "Religion and Society in the Early Literature of Virginia," in *Errand into the Wilderness* (New York: Harper and Row, 1964), p. 101.

but a people of considerable sophistication, never occurred to them.

Finally, encompassing all these motives and more besides, they were Europeans, living in an age when the ocean borders of the Old World had ceased to be barriers and had become portals of discovery, and who—like their Spanish, Portuguese, French, and Dutch neighbors—sought new lands and new adventures, and were willing to risk their fortunes and their lives aboard tiny ships upon the immense ocean in order to secure them.

The Jamestown venture was the culmination of more than three decades of English colonizing efforts along the Atlantic seaboard. Unlike the others, it was destined to survive, though for some years the issue seemed problematical. "Our men were destroyed with cruell diseases as Swellings, Flixes, Burning Fevers, and by warres," George Percy wrote, "and some departed suddenly, but for the most part they died of meere famine. There were never Englishmen left in a foreigne countrey in such miserie as wee were in this new discovered Virginia." [3]

Fortunately for the English, the heathen Indian savages decided to send emissaries with corn, bread, meat, and fish just when starvation threatened. The ineptness of the settlers' leadership also began to be remedied when a certain hard-nosed, willful, somewhat disputatious soldier of fortune, Captain John Smith, assumed greater importance in council. Showing no patience with malingerers and idlers, Smith forced upon his colleagues the ingenuity and efficiency needed if the enterprise was to survive. It was fortunate that he did so, for after a mild summer season the winter of 1608–1609 might have been even more disastrous than its predecessor. Near-tragedy came when it was discovered that the entire corn supply had been ruined, either from rotting or by rodents. Smith promptly stopped all work at Jamestown, divided the settlers into groups, and sent them to various places where food was available until the Jamestown supply could be replenished. That summer new settlers and provisions came from England, and all was well for a time.

3. Billings, ed., *The Old Dominion*, p. 25.

The following autumn Smith, wounded in an explosion, was replaced in command by George Percy, and he departed for England, never to return. Had he remained in charge through the winter, the dreadful ordeal of 1609–1610 might have been averted. As it was, however, poor management, disease, malnutrition, and a renewed series of Indian attacks all but wiped out the Jamestown colony. It was "the starving time"; the English died like flies. "Now we all found the losse of Captaine *Smith,*" a survivor wrote, "yea his greatest maligners could now curse his losse." Anything that could be eaten was devoured. One man was said to have killed his wife and eaten her, "for which hee was executed, as hee well deserved; now whether shee was better roasted, boyled or carbonado'd I know not. . . ." [4] When on May 23, 1610, two ships arrived in Virginia bringing Acting Governor Thomas Gates, hardly sixty settlers remained of the five hundred who had been there the previous fall.

Gates decided reluctantly that Jamestown would have to be abandoned, and on June 7 the remaining colonists went aboard ship and all sailed away. Fifteen miles downstream, they encountered a rowboat, its occupant bearing the news that Lord De La Warr had arrived in Virginia with three ships and three hundred men, and would soon be with them. Back to Jamestown the settlers went. In John Estèn Cooke's summation, "In the space of three days the Virginia colony had perished and come to life again." [5]

In early September of 1611 Lieutenant-Governor Sir Thomas Dale took 350 men up the James River and laid out a fortified town fifteen miles below the falls of the James, on the site of the present-day Farrar's Island, below Richmond. They called it Henrico, and its facilities included a church, warehouses, three streets with houses along them, blockhouse, and watchtowers. The colony was expanding its borders, though progress was slow at first and the merchant-adventurers and others in En-

4. Billings, ed., *The Old Dominion,* p. 28.

5. John Esten Cooke, *Virginia: A History of the People* (Boston: Houghton Mifflin, 1884), p. 83.

gland who had invested money in the Virginia Company were far from delighted with the return on their investment and increasingly reluctant to commit any more funds.

Thomas Dale remained in command until 1616, though Thomas Gates served as deputy governor during part of that time. Relations with the Indians improved notably after the marriage of Pocahontas, daughter of the emperor Powhatan, to John Rolfe in 1614. There was stability in government; no longer could a council elect and depose its own leaders. One of Dale's earliest recommendations to the company was that all settlers of whatever rank be allowed to grow food on land of their own, and in 1614 Dale secured permission to rent to each indentured settler, as his term of service expired, three acres of cleared land, in return for one month's work for the company and a supply of corn to go into the common store for consumption by new arrivals. Those still in indenture were given a month each year to farm for themselves. Furthermore, new emigrants with families were to receive, rent-free for at least a year, a house with twelve acres of fenced land, a year's provisions, tools, poultry, and livestock.

The nature of the Virginia venture was changing, although it would be a while before the fact was fully recognized. Instead of an exploitative enterprise of adventurers like the Spanish colonizers who would develop a trading post and build a colony from which minerals and agricultural goods could be sent back home to provide a quick return on investments, this venture would attract to the new land persons who would be going there primarily as farmers, to make permanent homes for themselves and their families.

In 1612 John Rolfe performed a notable experiment. Since their arrival in Jamestown the Virginia colonists had seen the Indians smoking tobacco, and had attempted to grow it themselves. Long before 1607, tobacco had been introduced into Europe by the Spanish and had become a profitable crop. The results in Virginia, however, had proved less than satisfactory, for tobacco produced there was small of leaf and exceedingly bitter to the taste. It was Rolfe who "partly for the love he hath a long time borne unto it, and partly to raise commodity to the

adventurers,'' [6] decided that the fault might lie not in the
method of cultivation, but in the plant itself, and so somehow
secured (probably illegally, by way of Trinidad), seeds from the
large-leaf *Nicotiana tabacum* plant of the West Indies, a much
more palatable variety. In 1612 or 1613 his first crop of
Virginia-grown Orinoco leaf was sent to England, and though
there would be need of refinement before the Virginia product
could compete successfully with Spanish tobacco, it quickly became apparent that the Virginia colony at last had a potentially
profitable item of export.

The settlement, though enjoying a respite from disaster, was
not attracting enough emigrants. What the colony needed was a
generally better sort of colonist—men and women of industry
and responsibility. If such English settlers were to stay in the
New World, however, it would be necessary to amend the terms
of their going there, and to give them more voice in their own
destiny. Men such as Gates, Dale, and, a little later, Samuel
Argall had provided iron-willed leadership, with swift and severe retribution for violations and no recourse from their judg-
ments. But now that the terrible early emergency was subsiding,
decent men and women were no longer willing to accept such
abridgement of their liberties.

It was for such reasons that Sir Thomas Smith, Alderman
Robert Johnson, Sir Edwin Sandys, and the other entrepreneurs
who were at the head of the Virginia Company were impelled to
draw up the "greate Charter" of 1618–1619. The system of
land grants was revised, rules were made for the location of new
plantations, and emigrants going to Virginia at their own expense would hold fifty acres of land of their own. The civil authority would take precedence over the military, and a "generall
Assemblie," including a council of burgesses chosen by the inhabitants themselves, would be convened. While the governor
of the colony was to have a veto over its actions, and continued
overall control would remain vested in London, the settlers were
now to have a say in their own government, and "No orders of
our Courte afterwarde shall bind the colony unless they bee rat-

6. Billings, ed., *The Old Dominion*, p. 36.

ified in like manner in ther generall Assembly." [7] Representative government was to be established—in form, at least—in
Virginia.

Thus it was that on June 30, 1619, the first legislative assembly in the new world convened for a six-day meeting at the
church on Jamestown Island. The House of Burgesses, chosen
by the settlers, met in company with what in effect served as an
"upper house," a council chosen by the Virginia Company to
give aid and advice to Sir George Yeardley, the new governor
sent to replace Samuel Argall.

Another event, which took place three weeks later in
Virginia, was to be of much consequence to the descendants of
those representatives. A ship sailed up the James River and
discharged a cargo of twenty blacks from Africa. According to
John Rolfe's account it was "a dutch man of warre that sold us
twenty Negars"; [8] but it may instead have been the *Treasurer,* a
vessel under the control of the Earl of Warwick.

The blacks were admitted not as slaves but as indentured servants; it would be a while before the chattel slavery status
would be formally evolved. No matter; in Virginius Dabney's
words, "the flow of Africans to America had begun, and there
would be no stopping it for more than two hundred years." [9] In
that single month of August 1619, therefore, both hope and
peril gained a foothold in the little seaboard colony of Jamestown.

More than 1,200 emigrants arrived in Virginia from England
during that momentous year of 1619. Not only did they include
men and their families, but also a shipload of young maids,
recruited by the company to go to the New World to find hus-
bands. A settler who wished to marry one of the new arrivals
was obligated to pay to the company the equivalent of a sum of
money in tobacco, to cover the cost of passage. Among the

7. Wesley Frank Craven, *The Southern Colonies in the Seventeenth Century,
1607–1689* (Baton Rouge: Louisiana State University Press, 1949), p. 135.

8. Billings, ed., *The Old Dominion,* p. 155.

9. Virginius Dabney, *Virginia: The New Dominion* (Garden City: Doubleday and
Co., 1971), p. 33.

projects begun that year was the locating of the site for a college at Henrico. Ten thousand acres were set aside for the purpose; in addition to educating the settlers, the college would instruct the Indians in the "true religion and civil course of life." [10]

The Emperor Powhatan was dead; his brother had been displaced by Opecancanough, a powerful, strong-willed man who had apparently brought his tribe all the way to Virginia from what is now known as the far Southwest, where he had been accepted by Powhatan as a werowance, or chief, under the emperor's regime. Opecancanough made strong professions of his friendship for the English. Yet all this time the crafty chieftain was plotting his strategy for the day when the Indians might rise up and strike a decisive blow that would drive the invading Europeans forever from Indian soil.

In the winter of 1621–1622 there was considerable illness among the colonists, and hundreds died. It was perhaps for this reason that Opecancanough decided that the hour was now propitious. At eight o'clock on the morning of March 22, 1622, Good Friday, the redmen attacked. From Henrico to Hampton Roads they fell upon the unsuspecting colonists. Some had arranged to be overnight guests in settlers' households. Some had borrowed boats, so that the settlers would be cut off from flight by water. Suddenly, without warning, men, women, and children were slain in fields or at home; only the blacks were spared.

The new town of Henrico and its college were both wiped out, and were never again recommenced. Of the twelve hundred settlers in the Virginia colony, close to four hundred were slaughtered that Good Friday morning. The effort to achieve annihilation of the whites through total surprise had failed, however, and now the colonists hit back. A series of attacks was launched against the Indians, with the objective of defeating them in battle whenever possible and, when they fled from battle, destroying their villages and their crops, since without corn the Indians would face starvation. Opecancanough had

10. Richard L. Morton, *Colonial Virginia*, 2 vols. 1: *The Tidewater Period, 1607–1710* (Chapel Hill: University of North Carolina Press, 1960), p. 60.

failed to drive the Europeans into the sea, and now his own weakened warriors were forced to withdraw from the area of the settlements.

The Indian attack, however, proved a fatal blow to the Virginia Company's fortunes. The bare mortality statistics were the most realistic argument against the stewardship of the company. Of more than four thousand settlers who went to Virginia during the years 1619–1624, less than twelve hundred survived. Disease was taking a ghastly toll; more than five hundred persons died from an epidemic in the winter of 1622–1623. Ships arriving from Europe often brought more ill persons than well ones, and periodically introduced new illnesses to the settlements. The colonists had to spend so much of their time fighting the Indians that they had little time to plant crops and improve their land. Thus agricultural harvests were scanty. Livestock had been driven off. There had been a rush to plant tobacco at all hazards, including the health of indentured servants, who were being cruelly exploited. The governor and council ruled arbitrarily and tolerated no dissent whatever. In London there was a factional struggle for power, and published accounts of affairs in Virginia brought new demands for intervention by the royal government.

The upshot was that in 1624 the charter of the Virginia Company was revoked and a new commission was established to take charge of the affairs of the colony. So after eighteen years the history of the Virginia Company's enterprise came to an end, though as a crown colony Virginia would grow and ultimately flourish. Measured by what the merchant-adventurers and others who had financed the expedition had expected to achieve in the way of profits, the venture cannot be said to have been much of a success—though some did profit handsomely from it. Compared to the riches that Spain was annually extracting from its possessions to the south, the return from Virginia thus far was meager indeed.

Many have wondered why it was that the settlers at Jamestown had had so wretched a time of it, and had failed for so long to prosper in the new land. Here, after all, was a region of temperate climate and rich soil, with fields and forests teeming with berries, fruits, edible plants of all sorts, with the finest timber for houses all around the settlements, with wild game of all kinds running in abundance in the woods and winging overhead and an inexhaustible supply of fish in the rivers and the bay. The native inhabitants of the land were few in number and without firearms. Yet Englishmen had starved, had gone naked and without decent shelter, had been for years unable to sustain themselves without importing provisions from across three thousand miles of ocean. Set ashore in a land of plenty, they had been barely able to keep from starving.

There are many explanations. For one thing, as many realized at the time, the men who first came to Virginia were after adventure, overnight wealth; many were gentlemen who had no taste for muscular labor and felt it beneath their station. To clear the forests and till and plant the fields and build farmhouses, men and women were needed who would view the colonial opportunity as the chance to make homes for themselves, with land of their own and the possibility of a better life for themselves and their children than would be their lot in England. Too many of the earliest settlers were primarily in search of quick profits from the boom in tobacco use in Europe, and all too willing to exploit indentured labor ruthlessly in order to produce large harvests of the weed.

It was land that was the attraction. To hold it, to live upon it, to make it productive was what finally brought Englishmen to Virginia to stay. Though ruinous at first, in the long run the experiment of John Rolfe with tobacco from the Indies gave the colony the stability of a lasting revenue crop, something it could produce to satisfy an urgent need in England. Land and tobacco, once these were made available and properly used instead of merely exploited, ultimately brought success to the venture, made the Jamestown enterprise the first permanent English settlement in the New World, and opened the way to possession of a continent.

In the early years of Virginia's existence as a royal colony, her settlements were concentrated in the area along the James River and Hampton Roads. Jamestown was still the principal center of activity. From there to the mouth of the river along each bank, away from the Indian menace, colonization proceeded unhindered. Other settlers were clearing land and laying out farms throughout the peninsula between the James and what is now the York River. Across the Chesapeake Bay, on the eastern shore of the estuary, there were already numerous farms.

At this stage of the colony's development there were few large landholders in residence—persons of stature and rank in England. These made good use of their places on the governor's council to increase their status and their holdings, but for the most part the Virginians of the early amd middle decades of the seventeenth century were farmers, lesser relations of leading English families, tradesmen, artisans—many of them enabled to own land for the first time and ambitious to gain the higher status that, back home, traditionally went along with ownership of landed estates. Not a few had come over as indentured servants, had worked out their indentureship, and had acquired farms of their own.

These men built small cottages for their homes and, as their prosperity increased, added to them or replaced them with larger farmhouses. Though they grew foodstuffs for their tables, they concentrated their efforts upon tobacco, not only because it was their most valuable export crop but because it was the medium of exchange—the currency, even—of a place without coinage or mint. In exchange for his tobacco the settler could get the manufactured goods he needed; letters of credit, notes made upon tobacco credits with London merchants, became almost the sole medium for financial transactions, and remained so for long decades to come.

The mortality rate for English people in the New World, however, continued for decades to be appallingly high. Only by heavy immigration had the Virginia Company been able to keep the population figures increasing, and under the crown the same conditions prevailed. When in the late 1640s the population figures began showing a notable increase, it was because for the first time the English in Virginia were surviving past a few years of their advent in the New World. As Edmund S. Morgan points out, no one is sure just why the earliest Virginians died off so rapidly, or why the death rate began dropping in the

1640s,[11] but the fact that Virginia expanded its population and its boundaries even as rapidly as it did during the first several decades of settlement is an indication of just how much the nonlanded Englishman of the seventeenth century was willing to risk in exchange for the chance to make a life for himself across the ocean.

When in 1634 the General Assembly divided the colony into eight counties and established for each a formal administrative and judicial system, there were some five thousand persons resident in Virginia. Each county was governed by a board of commissioners, later called justices of the peace, and each had a court, which met monthly. In each county a sheriff enforced the decisions of the court, and there were also coroners, constables, and clerks. Anyone brought into court could demand a jury trial and, if convicted, could appeal the decision to the general court, made up of the governor and his council. All offices were appointed; only the burgesses were elected by vote of the people.

Government in the colony was thus tied to possession of land—by 1670 only property owners retained the right to vote—and was already becoming decentralized. The hope of the original architects of Virginia that a series of flourishing villages would spring up throughout the colony, with manufactures and craftsmen, showed little sign of being realized. Virginia was an affair of farms, and as its boundaries expanded and its population grew, it merely reproduced the same rural ordering. There was comparatively little detailed supervision by the royal governor and his administration, and such towns as began developing were little more than places where the court could meet. The county governments quickly assumed a powerful role in Virginia life; local hegemony became a fixed feature of the society, with the elected burgesses chosen geographically to represent the wishes and speak to the needs of a citizenry living and working well away from the seat of the king's government.

Though King Charles I at first proved no more enthusiastic than his late father over the idea of an elected legislature in the

---

11. Edmund S. Morgan, *American Slavery, American Freedom: The Ordeal of Colonial Virginia* (New York: W. W. Norton, 1975), pp. 158–179.

colony, the General Assembly continued to meet from time to time, until in 1628 the king was constrained to authorize its coming together, even though there would be no formal legitimization of the right of its existence for another eleven years after that.

As the Virginians began to survive and prosper, they tended to become more assertive in their dealings with the various English officials sent to oversee their affairs. Since these functionaries considered themselves the agents of their king, they tended to view Virginia problems from the standpoint of what was best for the English economy. By no means did this always coincide with what the Virginians wanted, and there were occasions when royal governors were hard put to maintain their dignity and authority.

In 1642, however, there came to Virginia Sir William Berkeley, scholar, playwright, and member of a distinguished English family, who for much of the next thirty-five years would be quite popular and successful as governor. The colony he found when he arrived consisted of some 15,000 white people and 300 black slaves. It was expanding its borders northward to the Potomac, westward to the fall line, southward to the Dismal Swamp. The eight early counties were divided and then redivided; by 1643 there were fifteen in all, and during Berkeley's two tenures of office eleven more would be formed. The freeholders of each county chose their own burgesses, and each county was governed by a board of commissioners appointed by the governor and his council. The planters who held land did so as in effect freehold tenants of the king, to whom a quitrent was paid. Since the primary occasion for the awarding of land patents was in return for the planter having paid the cost of importing a laborer into the colony, this meant, as Wesley Frank Craven has noted, that the colony was assured of a steady supply of immigrants,[12] and that the planters who owned the land and brought the settlers in were not absentee capitalists but men who possessed a deep stake in, and a growing affection for, the soil of Virginia.

12. Craven, *The Southern Colonies*, pp. 176–177.

Tobacco was by long odds the principal crop. Though the royal authorities, including Berkeley, did their best to encourage diversification, it was difficult to get the Virginians to forego tobacco growing, especially now that the bronze-yellow, "sweet scented" leaf, which commanded the highest prices in England (and, 350 years later, still does), had been developed in some Virginia counties. The planter consigned his tobacco to an English merchant, who graded and sold the tobacco, deducted shipping and storing charges and his commission, and deposited what remained to the planter's account. Since the prices paid for the tobacco were set by the merchants in London who sold the tobacco, the planter was in a disadvantaged position. But as long as prices were high, the Virginians prospered.

Berkeley's early years as governor were years of much achievement. Taxes were made more equitable for smallholders, rules for land titles were improved, a poll tax was abolished, colonists were permitted to settle on lands which had been abandoned or never occupied, the election of burgesses was democratized, and a law was re-enacted to the effect that neither the governor nor his council might levy taxes or appropriate money without authorization by the General Assembly.

Berkeley also won the gratitude of Virginia for his decisive response to another major attack by the Indians. Once again Opecancanough, now an aged man but still of strong will and avenging heart, sought to drive the white men from the land that had once been his people's own. On April 18, 1644, the redmen struck suddenly at points all along the frontier, and though this time the attack did not penetrate into the interior of the colony, loss of life was severe, with more than five hundred men, women, and children killed. Berkeley at once mobilized his forces and drove the Indians back, killing many of them, burning their towns, and destroying their corn crops. Ultimately old Opecancanough was himself captured and taken to Jamestown. Blind, unable to walk, he was treated with much respect by Berkeley, who intended to send him to England, but one of the Virginia soldiers, outraged at the treatment being given the werowance who had caused the death of so many of his fellow settlers, shot him in the back.

As for the civil war which was under way back in England,

the governor of Virginia and most of his constituency were in full agreement. When Charles I marched his army northward out of London, Berkeley pledged his allegiance to his sovereign, and the Virginians were quick to express theirs as well. When word came of the execution of Charles I in 1649, Governor Berkeley denounced the deed and affirmed his continued loyalty to the House of Stuart, and the General Assembly, upon receipt of a notice of change of government, declared the proceedings against the king no less than traitorous. *Their* rightful head of state, the Virginians asserted, was the youth now in the Hague, the future Charles II.

To the colony now came numerous refugees from the king's side, including many whose families would become some of the colony's most distinguished, bearing such names as Lee, Carter, Washington, Randolph, Mason, Digges, Page, Molesworth, Skipwith, and others soon to be numbered among the First Families of Virginia. Some of the newcomers represented the Cavalier element that would become a central ingredient of the Virginia mythology—the day was to come when all Virginians, and all Southerners, for that matter, who counted for anything would be thought of—and would think of themselves—as lineal descendants of the Cavaliers who fought under Prince Rupert at Marston Moor and Naseby, in contradistinction to New Englanders, who were all of them supposedly descendants of the dour, crop-headed Parliamentary army.

Cromwell's government was too concerned at first with internal problems to notice what was going on overseas. Finally, in 1652, Parliament was ready for direct action against the recalcitrant colony, and commissioners were dispatched to Virginia, together with a fleet and a sizeable military force to reinforce their arguments. After a show at resistance, the assembly decided to capitulate; Berkeley disbanded his army, and articles of surrender were drawn up and signed.

The terms of the agreement were generous. The Virginians, in agreeing to renounce their allegiance to the deposed monarchy, were to retain the freedoms and privileges of English citizenship. The General Assembly was to be the governing body, with the burgesses in control. No taxes or duties could be levied without the assembly's consent. Land titles and headrights were secured. As for ex-Governor Berkeley and his council, their persons, past salaries, and lands were to be protected. Berkeley retired to his estate at Green Spring, where he stayed right on throughout the Commonwealth period. The bitter religious schism that helped bring about the Civil War and characterized the middle-seventeenth century in England had little or no counterpart in Virginia. Anglicans and dissenters managed to get along well enough. There was some persecution of Quakers, to be sure, but that was not unusual for the time; everybody persecuted Quakers.

In March of 1660, well before the monarchy was brought back to England, the assembly elected Sir William Berkeley as governor once again. When in September 1660 the news of the Restoration reached Virginia, there was widespread public celebration. The king for his part raised the colony, his oldest and most loyal, to the status of a dominion, and placed the seal of the Virginia Company upon his shield along with the arms of England, Scotland, and Ireland. Henceforth, he declared, Virginia was to be known as his Old Dominion.

The colony of which Sir William Berkeley took repossession in 1660, however, was in certain important respects very different from what it had been during his first term. By 1670 Berkeley estimated the population, no doubt a bit optimistically, at more than forty thousand, including six thousand indentured servants and—importantly—two thousand black slaves. In other words, while the total population had recorded an increase of something more than two and a half times its size over the course of thirty years, the number of black slaves in the colony, though proportionally still small, was almost seven times what it had been in 1642. Over the course of the decades a set of laws and customs had evolved to fix upon black Virginians the permanent status of slavery. In 1667 an act was passed that took care of one troublesome scruple: it was decreed "that the conferring of baptisme doth not alter the condition of the person as to his bondage or Freedome . . ." [13]

The immediate significance of the rise of slavery for late-seventeenth-century Virginia lay in what it would come to mean

13. Billings, ed., *The Old Dominion*, p. 172.

for the average Virginia farmer. There were fortunes to be made in raising tobacco. But to plant it required labor, and when the price of tobacco began dropping precipitously after England's Navigation Acts in the 1660s restricted the European market, only a large estate with a sizeable labor force could continue to produce at a profit. The smaller farmer, with his acres that he had cleared himself, was in a disadvantaged position. He could not purchase slaves for labor, for slaves were costly; the demand for them in the West Indian sugar plantations was intense, and their price came high. As for persons without any land of their own, by 1670 the suffrage, earlier given to all freemen, was restricted to freeholders and householders.

If the Virginians thought that their loyalty to the monarchy during the Civil War and Commonwealth period, or the fact that many of them had fought in the Civil War on the Stuart side, would earn them their king's gratitude when he regained the throne, they were very soon disabused. King, Parliament, and the financial entrepreneurs of Restoration London co-operated in a system designed to funnel the wealth of the colonies through the countinghouses of London, enhance the power of the British merchant marine, break the dependence of England upon other countries for raw materials and agricultural products, develop a market for its manufactures, and enable England, rather than the Dutch, to serve as the entrepôt through which the produce of the New World would reach Europe. For Virginians it meant that tobacco, their principal export crop, could be transported to Europe only in English or colonial ships, could be placed on sale only in England, and the price that London merchants were willing to pay them was what they would receive. The result was a glut that drove the price to levels at which only the larger plantations could make a profit. Governor Berkeley presented the Virginians' case in urgent terms; it was shameful, he wrote, "that forty thousand people should be impoverished to enrich little more than forty merchants, who being the only buyers of our Tobacco, give us what they please for it, and after it is here, sell it how they please. . . ." [14]

14. Wesley Frank Craven, *The Colonies in Transition, 1660–1713* (New York: Harper and Row, 1968), p. 39.

The king's lack of concern for the welfare of the Virginians, who had been so loyal to his father and himself, showed itself vividly in 1669. While still in exile, Charles II had granted to a group of his friends all the land between the Potomac and Rappahannock rivers—the entire Northern Neck—though of course there had been no way of enforcing the gift. But in 1669 he made a new grant, giving the proprietors control over local government, with final authority in the hands of the Jamestown government. Then in 1672 the king proposed to grant the rest of the colony to the Earl of Arlington and Lord Culpeper. The General Assembly of 1674 drew up a vigorous protest, declaring that the grant was a threat to Virginians' basic rights as Englishmen. Agents were dispatched to England to plead the colony's case, and they eventually succeeded in getting Arlington and Culpeper to renounce all claims except quitrents and escheats.

Misfortune dogged the colony. In 1674 a Dutch flotilla destroyed eleven ships of the tobacco fleet. A plague killed half the cattle in the colony. The shipping of numerous criminals from English prisons to the colony caused problems and made everyone uneasy. Tobacco prices remained low; large planters with their slave labor managed tolerably well, but the majority of those who farmed in Virginia experienced difficult times.

Troubles of this sort had the effect of intensifying the discontent of many Virginians with Governor Berkeley and his council. Taxes were oppressively high; the ruling group associated with Berkeley lost few opportunities to collect fees and perquisites, and those made to pay were resentful and discouraged. The once popular Berkeley would appear to have gotten out of touch with the concerns of important elements of the population. His patience with those he considered his inferiors deteriorated. He was, after all, an aging man now, in his late sixties. The economic and social changes in the colony itself had brought about a division between the group of planters with whom Berkeley associated himself, and other segments of the population.

What brought matters to a crisis in the middle 1670s was the colony's old nemesis, Indian trouble. In the thirty years since the onslaught of old Opecancanough in 1644, the Virginia tribes had been reduced in numbers to a point where they no longer constituted a threat to the existence of the colony. The frontier area of Virginia, however, was advancing westward, as new arrivals took up lands and old settlers extended their holdings. The settlers along the fall line, though they coexisted with the Indians, were not easy over the Indians' continued presence. The Indians' ways and theirs did not always fit well together, and moreover they coveted Indian lands. Trouble came on a Sunday in July 1675 when Thomas Mathews's plantation overseer in Stafford County was found lying mortally wounded. Before he died, he identified his attackers as Doeg Indians, a tribe just across the Potomac in Maryland. The incident was potentially inflammatory because of what it represented. From New England had been coming news of King Philip's War, complete with details of frightful torture, murder, and massacre. There was the rumor that all the Indians—northern and southern, "friendly" and unfriendly—were preparing a concerted attack on the English settlements. Added to the general economic and political uncertainty, all this made the Virginians along the borders extremely apprehensive.

The raid on the Mathews plantation resulted in a series of retaliatory attacks and counterattacks, culminating in a strike by Susquehanna Indians at plantations near the falls of the James River, where they killed an overseer on Nathaniel Bacon's land and three men on William Byrd's plantation.

In fear and alarm the frontier looked to Governor Berkeley to take action, as he had done so effectively in 1642. Berkeley called the council into session, and Sir Henry Chicheley was commissioned to lead a force against the Susquehannas. But when the Indians sent word to the governor that, having killed ten whites for each of their murdered chieftains, they were now ready to make peace, the governor countermanded Chicheley's marching orders. When the legislature convened, it formally declared war against the Indians, but adopted Berkeley's plan for building a series of ten forts along the border, with mounted troops patrolling between them. No Indians were to be attacked unless they attacked first, and no punitive force was to be sent out against them for now.

Before very long the frontier had reached a state of complete hysteria, and the settlers' wrath was vented against the governor and his council back in Jamestown. Berkeley and his councillors were not themselves menaced by the Indians, the settlers claimed, and did not wish an all-out frontier war that might disrupt their trading activities, so they were callously willing to leave the border areas exposed to murder and pillage.

Two years earlier, there had come to Virginia one Nathaniel Bacon, M.A., Cambridge. Governor Berkeley, who was related to young Bacon by marriage, had welcomed the twenty-six-year-old newcomer heartily and had him appointed to his council. The young aristocrat purchased a large tract of land at Curles' Neck in Henrico County and established himself there, close to the plantation and trading post of William Byrd.

In April of 1676 a body of Virginians assembled across the James River from Bacon's plantation, and when Bacon, Byrd, and another planter rowed across the river to investigate, they were greeted with shouts of "Bacon! A Bacon!" and the young planter was importuned to become their leader. This was no mere mob; as Wesley Frank Craven emphasizes, it included men of substance and position, and whether or not Bacon himself was aware of what would take place when he got there, Byrd doubtless was.[15] The young Bacon responded to the invitation with alacrity, and became their leader.

What they proposed to do, and soon did, was to inform the governor of their willingness to undertake an expedition against the Indians, entirely at their own expense. When Berkeley refused the offer, as must have been anticipated, Bacon and his force headed out into the wilderness after the Susquehannas, who were reported to have camped near the North Carolina frontier, close to a group of Occaneechee Indians living on an island in the Roanoke River. The Occaneechees apparently offered to attack the Susquehannas for the whites, and did so successfully. Afterward a quarrel ensued between the Occaneechees and Bacon's men, whereupon the whites attacked the Occaneechee village and wiped it out, along with most of its inhabitants.

15. Craven, *The Southern Colonies,* p. 380.

Meanwhile the governor, having proclaimed Bacon a rebel and traitor, had gathered a force of three hundred horsemen and had ridden to Charles City County to force Bacon's men to disperse. Finding them gone after the Indians, Berkeley could do nothing. After promising Mrs. Bacon that he intended to hang her husband, the alarmed governor rode back to Jamestown, while Bacon and his men soon returned in triumph to the plantations.

Upon arriving back in Jamestown Berkeley immediately ordered new elections for the burgesses, the first in fourteen years. If the burgesses then found him at fault, he said, he would join them in petitioning the king "to appoint a new Governor of Virginia and thereby to ease and discharge mee from the great care and trouble thereof in my old age. . . ." [16] He also wrote home to England asking to be replaced.

The subsequent events of Bacon's Rebellion have been chronicled many times, and need be only briefly summarized. Bacon was himself chosen as one of the new burgesses, and showed up for the General Assembly with some forty or fifty armed men. He was captured, made his submission to Berkeley and the assembly, and received a pardon and was reinstated to the council. Leaving Jamestown then, no doubt in fear of being arrested as soon as his supporting troops had gone, he returned with a large force, and directly challenged the governor to give him a commission as head of the colony's military forces. The old governor bravely stood his ground, opening his coat to expose his breast, and daring the rebels to shoot him down. Members of the assembly, however, fearful for their own lives, persuaded him to give Bacon his commission.

Bacon then left Jamestown to march against the Indians, but when he learned that Berkeley had crossed the York River into Gloucester County to raise troops against him, he turned back, and at Middle Plantation (the future town of Williamsburg) issued his Declaration of the People, to "let Truthe be bold and all the world know the real Foundations of pretended guilt." He cited the way in which those in control of the colony, like

16. Billings, ed., *The Old Dominion*, p. 270.

"spounges," had "suckt up the Publique Treasure and wither it hath not bin privately contrived away by unworthy Favourites and juggling Parasites whose tottering Fortunes have bin repaired and supported at the Publique chardg." Only the selfish and uninformed could call him and his supporters by "the aspersion of Traitor and Rebell," he concluded, and appealed to his king "as our Refuge and Sanctuary" for vindication of his conduct.[17]

As the countryside rose against the governor, Berkeley fled across the Chesapeake Bay to Accomac County, while Bacon raided the "friendly" Pamunkey Indians. Berkeley next returned to Jamestown, where he collected forces for an attack on Bacon's army. The attack was made in indifferent fashion, with the governor's forces clearly loth to risk their lives against Bacon. Berkeley then boarded a ship and went back to the Eastern Shore again, while Bacon and his forces entered Jamestown and burned it in anticipation of further attack.

What might have happened after that is difficult to conjecture. Word of the rebellion had reached England, and a royal commission headed by Colonel Herbert Jeffreys sailed for Virginia. Bacon is said to have talked of resisting, even if that meant full-fledged war against the crown. The hard campaigning had told on the young rebel, however, and while in Gloucester County, Nathaniel Bacon died and was secretly buried, no one knows where. The rebellion soon afterward collapsed, and Berkeley proceeded to bring many of its leaders to trial, confiscate their property, and hang them.

Finally Colonel Jeffreys, backed by a thousand troops, formally declared himself governor of Virginia. Berkeley was forced to accept his replacement; he sailed for England in May 1677, bitter and ill, and, when he arrived, sought to see his king and explain his side of the matter, but in vain. It is said that Charles II had remarked of him, "That old fool has hanged more men in that naked country than I did for the murder of my father," though there is no direct contemporary evidence for the attribution.

17. Billings, ed., *The Old Dominion*, pp. 278–279.

Nathaniel Bacon, as the novelist-historian John Esten Cooke wrote in 1883, "was the first American who declared, sword in hand, that he would die rather than submit to an invasion of his right. As such this young Virginia rebel of 1676 takes his place with the great American rebels of 1776, who followed in his footsteps." [18] This has been the popular view of Bacon; thus in 1916 the General Assembly of Virginia memorialized him with a plaque celebrating "A great Patriot Leader of the Virginia People who died while defending their rights." Recent historians, however, have severely modified that estimate, maintaining that it was not the oppressive rule of Governor Berkeley and his coterie that brought about the rebellion, but the desire of the whites for land and the inability of the government, whether colonial or national, to prevent encroachments upon Indian land despite sworn treaty agreements. "Bacon," wrote Wilcomb E. Washburn, "does not change with the hemispheres, from a spoiled son of a well-to-do English country squire to a dedicated democratic frontier hero. Nor does Governor Berkeley, after being the 'Darling of the People' for thirty-five years, suddenly reveal his true identity as their blackest oppressor." [19]

Such cautions are well taken. Yet whatever Bacon's private motives, it cannot be gainsaid that the General Assembly elected in 1676—Bacon's Assembly, it was called, since a majority of its members were supporters of Bacon—enacted a number of laws that significantly furthered popular sovereignty and representative government, and struck at the perpetuation of an oligarchy in positions of power. Much of the legislation by Bacon's Assembly was clearly class legislation designed to equalize opportunities, the response of a disadvantaged populace to ruthless economic victimization. What Berkeley's faction thought of it is evident from a letter that William Sherwood, at the time the governor's strong supporter, wrote home

---

18. Cooke, *Virginia,* p. 291.

19. Wilcomb E. Washburn, *The Governor and the Rebel: A History of Bacon's Rebellion in Virginia* (Chapel Hill: University of North Carolina Press, 1957), p. 166. For a contrasting view of Bacon see Thomas J. Wertenbaker, *Torchbearer of the Revolution: The Story of Bacon's Rebellion and Its Leader* (Princeton, N.J.: Princeton University Press, 1940).

to England. Sherwood complained that the "common people of this once hopefull country" constituted a greater danger than did the Indians, and that "Now tag rag and bobtail carry a high hand . . ." [20] That Nathaniel Bacon himself took little part in the deliberations and was interested primarily in fighting Indians does not obviate the fact that the forces unleashed by him and the cause he represented were implicitly destructive of entrenched privilege.

Perhaps the wisest, and certainly the most accomplished, commentary on the nature of Bacon's Rebellion by a contemporary observer is to be found in a document known as the Burwell Papers, written by one John Cotton, or perhaps by his wife, Ann, in 1676 and entitled "History of Bacon's and Ingram's Rebellion." The document consists of a sardonic, witty, rather cynical prose account of the rebellion, with Bacon hardly depicted as leader of a democratic revolt against oppression. It ends, however, with two poems, which the author says were "among many coppes of Verces made after Bacon's departure, calculated to the Lattitude of there affections who composed them. . . ." The two poems that follow are apparently by the same hand, and would appear to have been designed to conceal the author's true sympathies, since they take diametrically opposite views of Bacon and his motives. The best of the two, "Bacons Epitaph, made by his Man," begins:

> Death, why soe crewill! what, no other way
> To manifest they splleene, but thus to slay
> Our hopes of safety; liberty, our all
> Which, through thy tyranny, with him must fall
> To its late Caoss?

In slaying Bacon, Death has "more then thousand slaine / Whose lives and safetys did so much depend / On him . . ." Though Bacon has been branded a criminal, it was his foes' guilt that styled him thus:

> Onely this differance doth from truth proceed:
> They in the guilt, he in the name must bleed,

20. Morton, *Colonial Virginia* 1:258.

While none shall dare his Obseques to sing
In disarv'd measures, untill time shall bring
Truth Crown'd with freedom, and from danger free,
To sound his praises to posterity.[21]

The two poems are perhaps the most accomplished and, from a literary standpoint, quite possibly the best poetry composed in North America during the entire colonial period, perhaps with the exception of the work of Edward Taylor of New England.

More important for our purposes here, however, is the fact that even to the learned contemporary Virginian colonist who wrote the two poems, Nathaniel Bacon's motives and the meaning of his rebellion admitted of contradictory interpretations. It is hardly surprising, therefore, that future generations of historians would disagree about them, too. Yet the lines of the first poem, whether composed merely as a literary exercise or not, did contain an accurate prophecy: A time was to come when Virginians did indeed sound Bacon's praises to posterity.

21. "Bacon's Epitaph. Made by His Man," in Richard Beale Davis, C. Hugh Holman, and Louis D. Rubin, Jr., eds., *Southern Writing, 1585–1920* (New York: Odyssey Press, 1970), pp. 73–74.

2

The Plantation Era

*In which Virginians achieve the Age
of Gold.*

*T*HE collapse of Bacon's Rebellion did not end the economic and social turmoil that had helped bring it about. The widespread plundering, some of it with legal sanction, that had taken place during and after the rebellion only made matters worse. The hope in London was that Virginia could maintain sufficient domestic order to keep the tobacco coming and the resulting import duties and merchants' profits undisturbed. A royal governor, therefore, who could keep the Virginians peaceable was what was needed, and for the closing decades of the seventeenth century and the early decades of the eighteenth, a succession of governors was sent to do so.

Under the Stuart monarchs Charles II and James II, a steady effort was made to curtail the self-governing powers of Virginia's General Assembly, and after the Glorious Revolution of 1688 brought William and Mary to the English throne and substituted Parliament for king as the ultimate source of power, subsequent governors also had their difficulties. So long as tobacco prices remained low, there was bound to be discontent.

The cleavage within Virginia between the group of powerful planters who controlled the council, manipulated the laws to suit their purposes, and dominated the colony's public offices, and the smaller planters and farmers, many of whom had come over as indentured servants, reached its sharpest division in the years just after Bacon's Rebellion, and then began to diminish. Ultimately there developed a balance between the large planters and the less wealthy, and a *modus vivendi* with the royal government, which together with a rise in tobacco prices made possible a long quarter-century of reasonable prosperity, which was ever afterward looked back upon as the Golden Age of the plantation in Virginia.

Before that could happen, however, the Virginians went through a series of royal governors. Among these were Edmund Andros and Francis Nicholson, both of whom clashed with the council and assembly and ultimately met their match in the person of the Reverend James Blair, the bishop of London's Commissary for the Anglican Church in Virginia. A Scotsman, Blair had come to Virginia in 1685, and not long afterward won the hand of Sarah Harrison, the seventeen-year-old daughter of Benjamin Harrison II of Surry County. It was a shrewd marriage, for it allied the ambitious young clergyman with the powerful Harrison-Burwell-Ludwell planter faction, which for long maintained a virtual stranglehold on lucrative and important civil offices within the colony.

Blair was adept at playing the royal governor off against the British Board of Trade, and both these against the General Assembly. It was probably Blair's idea to revive the long abandoned plan for establishing a college in Virginia. The difficulty of persuading competent Anglican clergy to make the long ocean journey to Virginia, and the advantage of having the parishes controlled by their vestries, rather than by a bishop as in England, made it desirable to establish a college right on the scene to train its own resident ministers. Blair went to England, secured powerful aid for his plan, then returned to set up his college at Middle Plantation, eleven miles inland from Jamestown. When in 1698 the statehouse at Jamestown burned to the ground, Blair and Governor Nicholson maneuvered the House of Burgesses into moving the capital to Middle Plantation, which was renamed Williamsburg.

Blair was able to get Governor Andros ousted by convincing

the Board of Trade that Andros sought dictatorial powers and showed undue favoritism to a faction in the council. Nicholson ran afoul of Blair and his allies when he attempted to enforce quitrent collections and tighten up land acquisition requirements; for a time the governor was able to play the burgesses off against the council, but ultimately planter opposition, together with Nicholson's choleric temper, was enough to give Blair the opportunity to bring him down as well.

Colonel Alexander Spotswood, Blair's third and final victim, was a tougher foe, and survived as governor (actually lieutenant-governor, with the titular governor remaining in England) for twelve years, from 1710 through 1722. It was Spotswood who moved symbolically to open up the country beyond the Blue Ridge for settlement when in 1716 he led an expedition westward across the Blue Ridge Mountains into the Shenandoah Valley, where they camped alongside the Shenandoah River. Afterward he presented to each gentleman companion a small golden horseshoe, studded with valuable stones. Thus were created the Knights of the Golden Horseshoe, so often written about and romanticized. Spotswood also effected a peace treaty between the Iroquois Indians and the English seaboard colonies, and did much to lessen the menace of pirates operating off the coast by dispatching an expedition to capture and execute Edward Teach, the notorious Blackbeard.

Suppressing pirates and Indians was one thing; curbing the power of the closely interlocked faction of planter families that controlled the council and held many of the most influential offices was another and more difficult problem. The governor set out to reform the land-grant operations, but was foiled. He sought to standardize and regulate tobacco production procedures, and for a time seemed to be succeeding, only to have the London merchants intervene to get the system repealed. Then he attempted to break the council's power by insisting upon the right to appoint judges to the courts of oyer and terminer, customarily administered by the councillors, and to induct Anglican ministers and fill vacancies in parishes. By 1718 matters were at an impasse: the governor was at loggerheads with his council

and the burgesses, and Blair was out to get him, with the full
backing of council, burgesses, vestries, and others.

At that point Spotswood gave up. He compromised on the
right to appoint judges and accepted amendments that weakened
the controls on land titles. He joined up with the Virginians and
got in on the real estate business himself by securing an eighty-
five-thousand-acre domain in the Piedmont, where he set up an
iron foundry and brought Germans to work it. Powerful planters
such as Robert ("King") Carter aided him in getting title to
lands, now that he had decided to become one of them. It was
too late to stave off Blair's machinations back in London, and in
1722 Spotswood was removed from office by the Board of
Trade, but he stayed on in Virginia, returned later to England to
get himself married, then brought his family back to what was
now called Spotsylvania County, where he lived out his days as
a gentleman planter and as deputy postmaster general for the
American colonies.

The colony of Virginia had grown to include more than sev-
enty thousand persons, and by now the settlers were spreading
out into the Piedmont. In 1701 some five hundred French Huguenots, refugees from Catholic France, established a settlement
some miles west of the Falls of the James near present-day
Richmond, where the Manakin Indians had lived until evicted.
Many of Virginia's most distinguished families ultimately bore
such names as Flournoy, Latané, Maury, Fontaine, Michaux,
Moncure, Munford, and others that certify their descent from
the Huguenots.

During the years of Spotswood's governorship the importation of Negro slaves, which had already shown a gradual upturn, became the major source of labor. By 1715 there was almost one black for every three whites. Though large planters
such as King Carter owned them by the hundreds, their use was
by no means confined to large plantations only; owners of
smaller estates purchased them as well, and worked side by side
with slaves in the fields. The wider ownership of blacks served
to bring about a much closer identification of interests between
large and small planters, since the fact of slave proprietorship,

no matter of how many or how few blacks, became an emblem of status distancing the men who owned slaves from those who did not. Since the right to vote was restricted to freeholders, it is not surprising that during the early 1700s the House of Burgesses came more and more to be made up of members of a landed slave-owning class.

With the great increase in slaves, of course, came the danger of slave rebellion. Several incidents of plots increased the apprehension of white Virginians for their own safety; indeed, in the Tidewater counties the militia was maintained primarily as a safeguard against servile insurrection, now that the Indian danger was past.

Most slaves were decently treated—as slaves. They were too valuable an economic acquisition to be jeopardized by mishandling. Yet the planter's right of life and death over the slaves, unhindered by external restraints, could mean something terrible in a country in which, particularly in the early period of colonial history, blacks were regarded, in Thomas Jefferson Wertenbaker's words, ''as hardly human, mere savages that were no more deserving of consideration than oxen or horses.'' [1] In later years Virginians liked to claim that the colony had done its best to stop the increase in slaveholding, but had been prevented from doing so by the British government; Jefferson cited the indictment in the Declaration of Independence. The chances are, however, that the several attempts to restrict importation had less to do with the baneful effects of slavery than with economic conditions which called for measures against overproduction of tobacco.

In September 1727 Major William Gooch, forty-six years old and a retired soldier of distinction, arrived with his family in Williamsburg, and was installed in the governor's palace. With his accession began the Golden Age of the Virginia plantation society.

When Gooch commenced his twenty-two-year incumbency as lieutenant-governor of Virginia, there were well over a hundred

1. Thomas J. Wertenbaker, *The Planters of Colonial Virginia* (Princeton, N.J.: Princeton University Press, 1918), p. 129.

thousand inhabitants in the colony, of whom some one-fourth were slaves. Virginia had twenty-eight counties, including several which lay far beyond the old fall line of the rivers, which had for so long marked the limits of settlement. During the years that followed, population moved steadily out along the lines of the James, Rappahannock, and Roanoke rivers toward the mountains, and first Germans and then Scotch-Irish immigrants came flooding down through Pennsylvania and Maryland into the Shenandoah Valley, until by the end of Gooch's tenure there were forty-four counties, and the area of settlement was reaching out along the southwestern finger of the great Valley toward present-day Tennessee and Kentucky.

Life in the Tidewater society had long since emerged from frontier conditions. It was settled, orderly, and almost exclusively rural; the capital, Williamsburg, was only a village, and recurring attempts to create seaport towns had come to nothing. In the seventeenth century, Virginia had been a poor man's colony; a yeomanry had come to the New World and made a place for itself. But the wealth that could be amassed through tobacco cultivation now that prices had risen, and the greater efficiency of larger farm units under slave labor, had pretty much ended that. Big planters with estates thousands of acres in size became the models for smaller planters with more modest establishments. Only one planter in ten, perhaps, had an estate of more than a thousand acres, but his lesser neighbors with their smaller estates and few slaves tended to identify their interests with his. There was room at the top for the ambitious and hard-working smaller planter. Within the planter society upward and downward movement was constant. If the wealthiest planters tended to run the colony, a network of marriages and connections spread out to bring about a more or less homogeneous unit, a squirearchy rather than aristocracy, perhaps.

If it was an aristocracy, it was of middle-class origin, a bourgeois aristocracy. Its great families had all become great in the New World; they had not brought their status with them. King Carter of Corotoman, for example, the greatest grandee of his time, held every major office the colony could offer, even up to the acting governorship. When he died in 1732, he left his descendants more than three hundred thousand acres of land and more than a thousand slaves. For each of his sons and sons-in-law he created magnificent estates. Through his children's marriages he allied himself with most of the important Virginia families. But the first Carter to come to Virginia was a self-made man with some connection to a family of London wine merchants, and he arrived not as a planter but as a trader.

No family has been more prominent in Virginia life than the Randolphs, whose very name connotes the age of the planter aristocracy. Yet William Randolph came over as nephew to a merchant, studied law, was appointed a clerk of the assembly, then brought over indentures and secured the headright to five hundred acres of land. His marriage to Mary Isham, daughter of a planter, gave him social connections and property. One of their sons, John, was knighted by the king of England. All their children married into the Virginia planter families, and among their direct descendants were Thomas Jefferson, "Light Horse Harry" Lee, Robert E. Lee, John Randolph of Roanoke, Peyton Randolph, Edmund Randolph, John Marshall, and others.

The first Lee in Virginia, Richard, though probably descended from the nobility, came over as a merchant. His son, Richard Lee II, was a councillor, austere in bearing and, as Clifford Dowdey notes, almost alone among his peers in not using his position for profit—a family trait that was to reappear notably in one of his descendants.[2] He was a scholar, with a large and varied library. Among his sons was an acting governor, whose sons in turn were Richard Henry and Francis Lightfoot Lee. From another son of Richard Lee II came Light Horse Harry and Robert Edward Lee.

Finally, William Byrd II, planter, merchant, scientist, man of letters, perhaps the finest gentleman of his era, was the grandson of a London goldsmith. The first William Byrd had inherited numerous properties near the Falls of the James, and built up great wealth as Indian trader, land purchaser, importer of slaves and indentured servants, and merchandiser of goods

2. Clifford Dowdey, *The Virginia Dynasties: The Emergence of 'King Carter' and the Golden Age* (Boston: Little, Brown, 1969), p. 53.

from England. His son, educated in England, came home a man of distinction, with numerous important friends in British social, political, and intellectual life. At Westover on the James, he presided over his estates, bought and sold property, corresponded with social and scientific friends in England, accumulated a library of 3,600 titles, and left behind him 179,000 acres of land and numerous manuscripts such as his witty, urbane, amusingly descriptive chronicle, *A Secret History of the Dividing Line,* which when published in the nineteenth century, made him the colonial South's most important literary figure. Though his son squandered the family fortune, the line survived to flower again in the late nineteenth and twentieth centuries.

These men, then, and others, foremost among the First Families of Virginia in the Golden Age of the plantations, were all homemade aristocrats, men of status and power, and not remotely democratic. They were, with some exceptions, energetic and opportunistic businessmen, with an eye toward their own best advantage, willing and able to exploit labor and land to grow rich quickly. It never occurred to them that the colony was not to be governed in their interests. Yet they were men of probity, they felt strongly a sense of responsibility, and if their ideal was that of the English country gentleman, they believed in duties as well as in privileges. They valued learning—especially of a practical sort. They patronized the arts. Architecture was one of their strongest points; the great homes they built along the banks of the Tidewater rivers were monuments to their good taste. Their gardens were the admiration of visitors from afar.

They were indeed, as Louis B. Wright describes them, a "working gentry"; [3] they had to be, for their plantations were immensely complicated operations, and the supervision of hundreds of workers required constant attendance. Everything that was not imported from England had to be manufactured, for there were no factories in Virginia.

The Virginians were churchgoers; the leading planters not

3. Louis B. Wright, *The First Gentlemen of Virginia: Intellectual Qualities of the Early Colonial Ruling Class* (Charlottesville: University Press of Virginia, 1964), p. 58.

only served on and indeed all but controlled the vestries, but they built the churches. Their libraries all contained works of theology and numerous volumes of sermons. Theirs was an established church, but though Anglican in theology, it was distinctively local in its forms. Having come through the religious turmoil of the Commonwealth period with a minimum of internal friction, Virginians were inclined toward tolerance, and the English Act of Toleration only confirmed them in their attitudes. Until the Scotch-Irish began pouring into the Valley, there was little in the way of a dissenting church; dissenters after the 1600s, even Papists and Quakers, were allowed to go their own way, provided that they did not disturb the peace. The Virginians admitted diversity, for they were not threatened by it.

An odd society to have produced a republican, representative form of government, perhaps, yet that is what soon happened. As the basis of the planter society grew broader, during the 1730s, 1740s, and 1750s, the power and authority of the great planters diminished but did not disappear; their children were now leaders of a society of landowners large and small, increasingly made up of general farmers rather than tobacco planters, and the burgesses rather than the council became the locus of legislative power. To win election to the burgesses, however, the successful candidate must consult the freeholders; he must understand them and know how to win their approval. All evidence is that in proportion to total population the electorate of eighteenth-century Virginia was fully as large as that in any of the other colonies—larger than that in such colonies as Massachusetts. In Charles Sydnor's words, "democracy was strong enough to moderate autocratic tendencies in the gentry," [4] so that those men who were now named to office were acceptable both to the leaders and to the rank and file.

Thus the young men who entered political life in the middle eighteenth century had several constituencies to satisfy if they would rise to positions of prominence. It proved an excellent

---

4. Charles S. Sydnor, *Gentlemen Freeholders: Political Practices in Washington's Virginia* (Chapel Hill: University of North Carolina Press, 1952), p. 76.

training school for political leadership. When the time came for united action by all the colonies, the Virginians were ready.

If, of course, one was not of the freeholding constituency, the age was considerably less golden. The man without either property or wealth was coming more and more to find that his opportunities lay elsewhere. Slavery, as Thomas Jefferson Wertenbaker has asserted, "practically destroyed the Virginia yeomanry, the class of small farmers who used neither Negroes nor servants in the cultivation of their fields." [5] There were few schools available for their children; they were taxed and tithed, but could not vote unless they owned land; as tobacco growers they could not compete against slave labor; so many of them left, or else hung on in what was often an increasingly disadvantaged condition. Gooch and the assembly were concerned over the steady emigration of the nonslaveholding white population from Tidewater Virginia, and they understood its connection with the institution of slavery, to the extent of attempting once more in the late 1720s to put a prohibitive duty on the importation of blacks. The Board of Trade vetoed it; the slaves were purchased by shipowners on the African coast in exchange for British manufactures, the board explained, and such a tax by Virginia would in effect be a tax on the importation of British manufactures.

The landowning, slaveholding Virginians could have their Golden Age and get on well with their governor because under the ministry of Robert Walpole and of the duke of Newcastle, who was in charge of colonial affairs, the British government was interested in preserving peace and prosperity, and so long as the merchants in London could turn a tidy profit from tobacco and British manufactures could find a ready market in the colonies, there was no disposition to disturb arrangements overseas.

Governor Gooch favored a liberal policy of land grants; the awarding of large tracts in the west to wealthy planters, he said, meant that "the meaner sort of people" would be encouraged to move there in order to receive their protection. After 1730 it

5. Wertenbaker, *The Planters,* p. 160.

was necessary for a land speculator to settle only one family upon every thousand acres in order to receive title. The Tidewater gentry was swift to respond. Not only did the planters buy land to sell to settlers, but many went westward themselves and set up new estates in the Piedmont and along the mountain slopes. Randolphs, Beverleys, Bollings, Carters, Cockes, Pages, and others moved west. And there were opportunities, too, for those of the lesser gentry to make their mark. One such was Peter Jefferson, whose father had made a place for himself in the Tidewater. A strong, active man, cultivated and talented, he had married Jane Randolph, granddaughter of William Randolph, and so he had good connections. He and Joshua Fry later made a map of Virginia and Maryland that was for decades the authoritative charting of the western regions. Patenting acres west of the Falls of the James, he built a home, Shadwell, in Albemarle County, where his son Thomas would be born.

In Orange County, in the foothills, Ambrose Madison, who had married Frances Taylor, a daughter of one of Colonel Spotswood's companions on that earlier western expedition, had settled upon five thousand acres and was cultivating them with slaves. John Henry had established himself as clergyman, magistrate, and planter in Hanover County, north of Richmond, where his son Patrick was born. To the north, between the Potomac and Rappahannock rivers, on the vast area which James II had granted to Lord Culpeper and which was now claimed by Lord Fairfax, Augustin Washington secured ten thousand acres on the Potomac River. He was not of the leading planter families himself, but his son Lawrence married a cousin of Lord Fairfax, and later on, his other son, George, married Martha Dandridge, the widow of Daniel Parke Custis, and so allied himself with a family descended from the Byrds.

In 1726 Jacob Stover led a group of German and Swiss settlers into the Shenandoah Valley. The year after, Adam Miller (Müller) guided a group of his friends down from Pennsylvania, settling between the Massanutten Mountains and the Blue Ridge. Then in 1732 Joist Hite took a group of Alsatian settlers to a hundred-thousand-acre tract near the present city of Winchester, earlier granted to John Van Meter. The Germans made good settlers, attentive to the crops and careful of the soil.

That same year John Lewis led a group of Scotch-Irish settlers over the mountains and settled near the present-day town of Staunton on land patented by William Beverley. Soon a larger area was patented by a group of prominent Tidewater men, including Beverley; by 1736 Beverley had brought in so many Scotch-Irish families that the region began to be known as "Irish Tract." Down from Pennsylvania the Scotch-Irish came flooding along the Great Wagon Road. Carl Bridenbaugh's description of them is apt:

> Undisciplined, emotional, courageous, aggressive, pugnacious, fiercely intolerant, and hard-drinking, with a tendency to indolence, they nevertheless produced ambitious leaders with the virtues of the warrior and politician. As viewed by others, these were hard and unlovely qualities, effective in a new country withal.[6]

By the middle of the eighteenth century the Valley was filling up, and the Virginians were eyeing the country beyond the Alleghenies. In 1749 the Ohio Company was chartered. Two years later the Greenbrier Company was granted one hundred thousand acres along the Greenbrier River in present-day West Virginia, and James Patton and his partners received one hundred thousand acres along the Ohio and the New rivers. Settlers flooded into what are now the states of West Virginia, Kentucky, Tennessee, and Ohio, following in the wake of the surveyors. In moving to occupy the new lands the Virginians would be coming up squarely against not only the Indians but the French. There was likely to be trouble ahead.

There was still another important ethnic element in Virginia during this period: the Scotch. The Act of Union in 1707 made it possible for Scottish merchants to find their way to the colonies. Establishing shops where tobacco was sold and shipped, they placed agents throughout the colony. Thrifty, good busi-

---

6. Carl Bridenbaugh, *Myths and Realities: Societies of the Colonial South* (New York: Atheneum, 1963), p. 133.

nessmen, they soon took over a goodly portion of the tobacco export trade, and became very much a part of the Virginia scene.

Until the Scotch-Irish and the Scots came, the Established Church had encountered very little pressure from dissenters (Presbyterians, Congregationalists, and others who had left the Anglican communion). These new arrivals, however, wanted dissenting ministers sent from Pennsylvania. In the late 1730s, the religious revival and social phenomenon known as the Great Awakening was spreading through the American colonies. Under its influence Anglican church members in Hanover County, feeling that the established religion preached there was not the True Gospel, began absenting themselves from church and meeting separately. They were fined, but continued to dissent. The Reverend George Whitefield, a Methodist evangelist whose appearance in Massachusetts also created a great stir, arrived in Virginia and was permitted by the aged Commissary Blair to preach at Bruton Parish Church. Whitefield's emphasis upon the fires of Hell, repentance, and personal salvation filled a need on the part of thousands of religion-starved colonists.

Next the New-Light Presbyterians came, some of them riproaring evangelists whose fervent preaching sent congregations into displays of emotion. The New-Light Movement took on a much more respectable form, however, when the Reverend Samuel Davies, from Delaware, appeared before the General Court to ask for a license to preach. Thereafter Davies had a powerful influence in missionary work in Virginia, and when the French and Indian War broke out, he led in rallying the settlers to the defense of the colony. A man of great eloquence, he was an accomplished writer and poet as well.

On May 11, 1749, William Gooch gave a farewell address to the General Assembly, and in August he and his family boarded a merchant ship at Yorktown and sailed for home. The Virginia he left behind him had ceased to be a frontier society east of the mountains, and had become a settled community, with order, social gradation, a population tolerably secure in its institutions and arrangements. If England was still its model, and the ultimate source of its authority, it had evolved a style of its own, and had become accustomed to electing its own legislators to deal with its internal affairs. By the standards of the time its political constituency was reasonably broad; within its midst was no large body of disfranchised and disadvantaged persons capable of disrupting the workings of government. For those who were members, the Virginia community seemed able to offer genuine stability and domestic tranquility. Those who did not possess membership privileges—the slaves, the lower orders of landless whites—had little voice in affairs, no way of demanding a share in the benefits. They existed in order to serve the community, and to the eighteenth century's way of thinking this was as it should be. Thus the Virginians had arrived, for the first time in their history though not for the last, at a state of affairs in which all seemed ordered and tranquil and—to those whose opinions mattered—reasonably permanent. "Truth, Justice, Vertue, be pursu'd," wrote the poet John Markland:

> Arts flourish, Peace shall crown the Plains,
> Where GOOCH administers, AUGUSTUS reigns, [7]

It was left to the next generation to discover the precarious nature of that peace, and the less than Augustan merits of King George III.

7. For excerpts from John Markland, "Typographia: An Ode, on Printing," see Davis, et al. eds., *Southern Writing*, p. 246.

3

The Pre-War Era

In which the Virginians,
after driving off the French and Indians,
decide that they can do without
the British as well.

N a sense, William Gooch had been all too satisfactory a royal governor. Temperament and circumstance alike had placed him in a position whereby he had quarreled with few of the objectives of the Virginians and had worked to further their fortunes. But in the 1740s the magisterial Walpole ministry in England had given way to the less serene administration of the Pelhams, and a renewed spate of wars with the French and Spanish had begun to disrupt trade and cause unrest in British commercial circles, a situation that soon made itself felt in relations with the colonies.

At his first session of the assembly Robert Dinwiddie, who succeeded Gooch, had found it necessary to announce that King George II had vetoed ten acts passed by the assembly of 1748–1749 and, in addition, had pointedly confirmed a number of other acts. Since during the years of Gooch's reign the Virginians, as Richard Morton has said, "had come to regard their legislature as their final lawmaking authority in matters not involving commerce and the Empire,'' [1] the new developments were disturbing, for they indicated that in the eyes of the government of England, Virginians were not Englishmen living in the New World, but mere colonials without the right of self-determination. And if Gooch had allowed them to feel that it was their interests that mattered most to him, his successor swiftly showed that he viewed matters differently, for immediately following the adjournment of the assembly Dinwiddie announced that henceforth he would grant new land patents only upon payment to him of a pistole fee (a Spanish coin worth about $3.50).

So furious was the protest that Dinwiddie would have liked to keep the assembly prorogued indefinitely, but suddenly events along the frontier forced him to convene it. As the English settlements of the Ohio Company pushed beyond the mountains into the Ohio River territory, they began to encroach upon territory claimed by France by virtue of its exploration of the Mississippi River. When young Major George Washington came back from a scouting expedition to report that the French were at Fort Le Boeuf, not far from Lake Erie, and clearly planned to move southward, Dinwiddie was deeply alarmed. He asked the House of Burgesses to vote funds to prepare defenses, and the Virginians came across with £10,000—but with a provision that a committee of the house was to supervise expenditures. Washington took a small force to the mountains and was surrounded and forced to surrender. The trans-Ohio was now in much peril, but the burgesses showed little interest in defending the Ohio Company's prospects.

England soon decided to send regulars to drive out the French, and Major General Edward Braddock, with two regiments, arrived in Virginia in February 1755, and set out for the west. Unfortunately, it was Braddock who was routed; eight miles from his objective his army was ambushed, and his bro-

1. Richard L. Morton, *Colonial Virginia,* 2 vols. 2: *Westward Expansion and Prelude to Revolution, 1710–1763* (Chapel Hill: University of North Carolina Press, 1960), p. 603.

ken troops retreated to Fort Cumberland; their general, dead from a bullet wound through the lungs, was left in a grave on the Wilderness Road.

During the next several years the Virginia frontier was under constant attack from Indians. Families were massacred, outposts were raided, and refugees crowded back across the mountains. While Washington strove to protect a 350-mile frontier with several hundred troops, the assembly sought to raise money by new poll and land taxes. To add to the woe, there were crop failures and a severe drought.

Yet the tide was turning. William Pitt had become the king's first minister, and the strategic objective had changed from pushing the French back from the Ohio territory to driving them out of America. Regular troops were sent to America. The hard-pressed Virginia General Assembly finally got the colony on as much of a war footing as was possible, and Washington received additional troops and supplies, together with money to pay his Indian allies. Enlistments increased. The Reverend Samuel Davies, among others, was doing his best to rally the citizenry. In one sermon he made what turned out to be a notably accurate prophecy: "I may point out to the public that heroic youth, Col. Washington, whom I cannot but hope Providence has hitherto preserved in so signal a manner, for some important service." [2]

Dinwiddie's successor, Francis Fauquier, arrived in June of 1758. Fauquier was intelligent, witty, a scholar and musician as well as an efficient and tactful executive; in Richard Morton's words, he was "perhaps the most brilliant of all the royal governors of Virginia." [3] He was soon able to report that two Virginia regiments were ready to take the offensive once the royal troops arrived. The attack, however, was made through Pennsylvania; on the night of November 24, 1758, the French evacuated DuQuesne. A three-pronged British attack severed the French communications with the Lakes, ousted them from the Lake Champlain Valley, and ultimately brought about the

2. Morton, *Colonial Virginia,* 2:677–678.
3. Morton, *Colonial Virginia,* 2:714.

capture of Quebec. When Montreal was taken the following year, the French had been all but driven from North America, except for Louisiana, and the frontier was secure.

Once DuQuesne fell, Washington resigned his command and came back to marry Martha Custis and to sit in the burgesses, which faced a number of problems created by the war. The Board of Trade in London, unhappy with the paper money Virginia had printed during the war, was in no mood to tolerate much self-assertion on the part of a colonial legislature. Trouble came when, during the drought year of 1758, the burgesses enacted legislation known as the Two-Penny Act. In 1755, as a war measure, the tobacco allowance paid as salaries to ministers of the Established Church and other officials had been changed to an equivalent of two pence per pound. Since tobacco was selling at a high price, this represented a loss to the gentlemen of the cloth. In 1758 the burgesses did it again, and this time the clergy was less co-operative; a group of ministers secured from the king an edict pronouncing the 1758 act illegal. Thus the clergy was due back wages, and—more importantly—the British crown was disallowing an act of the Virginia assembly relating purely to internal Virginia affairs. The veto of the Two-Penny Act touched off a barrage of pamphlets and addresses.

There were other ramifications, too. Though the Anglican Church in Virginia had long since been acclimatized to the conditions of the colony, friction between the clergy and the assembly had continued. The situation had been all the more complicated by the growth, in Piedmont and western Virginia, of the Presbyterians and other dissenting sects, the members of which strongly resented having to pay tithes to support the clergy of an established church.

When, therefore, the Reverend James Maury of Louisa County sued for the difference between the two-pence-per-pound he had been paid as minister in 1758, and the actual amount that a pound of prime-grade tobacco leaf had brought on the market that year, and the case was heard at Hanover County courthouse, there was considerably more involved than one widely admired and well-regarded Anglican clergyman's claim to damages. After the plaintiff's case had been made, the attorney for the vestry arose and delivered himself of an oration that declared in impassioned tones that for the king to annul the Two-Penny Act was a violation of the original contract between king and people, and that a king who continued to do so, "from being the father of his people, degenerated into a tyrant, and forfeits all rights to his subjects' obedience." Ignoring murmurs of "Treason!" young Patrick Henry went on to describe the Anglican ministers as enemies of the state, who would if permitted "snatch from the hearth of their honest parishioner his last hoecake, from the widow and her orphan children their last milch cow! the last bed, nay, the last blanket from the lying-in woman!" It was the jury's duty, he said, to seize this opportunity to show the clergy of the Established Church that it could not with impunity violate the rights of the ultimate authority for all laws—the people of Virginia.[4]

Not only did Henry's oratory sway the jury so that a verdict of a token one-penny damages only was awarded to the Reverend James Maury, but Henry's impassioned outburst signalized the political coming-of-age of a new generation of Virginians no longer willing to remain obedient subjects of a king and a Parliament three thousand miles away across the ocean.

Thereafter matters grew swiftly worse. In late 1763 King George III proclaimed the trans-Allegheny region closed to further settlement, which caused some uneasiness. Since the economy of England was under duress as a result of the financial strain of the recent war, and taxation was already extremely burdensome, Parliament decided in 1765 to make the Americans bear some of the cost of maintaining a standing army in the colonies and of enforcing customs patrols, through a Stamp Tax, whereby all documents and papers in the colonies would have to produce revenue for the king.

When news of the enactment came, Patrick Henry, whose election to the burgesses may have been arranged by the western delegates for just such a purpose, proposed five resolutions proclaiming the unconstitutionality of the tax, the fifth of which declared that the General Assembly of Virginia possessed the

4. Morton, *Colonial Virginia,* 2:811.

"only and sole exclusive Right and Power to lay Taxes," and that any attempt to decree otherwise "has a manifest tendency to destroy British as well as American freedom." It was on this occasion that Henry made his famous statement to the effect that "Caesar had his Brutus, Charles the First, his Cromwell, and George III"—here he was interrupted with cries of "Treason! Treason!"—"George III may profit by their example. If this be treason, make the most of it!" Whether Henry actually added the last defiant statement is doubtful; one account is that instead he hastily backed down and assured the hearers of his loyalty.[5]

The Stamp Act unified Virginia. Opposition to it was well-nigh unanimous and had the effect of crystallizing sentiment against king and Parliament. The Virginians refused to buy the stamps. It was with much relief that Governor Fauquier was able to announce in June of 1766 that Parliament had repealed the Stamp Act. The Virginians exuberantly professed their approval and their undying loyalty to their king. Parliament, however, had expressly declared its full power and authority to make laws and statutes for the American colonies, and what this meant was discovered in 1767 when the Townshend Acts, imposing duties on numerous articles imported into America, were passed. The revenue was to be used to pay the salaries of royal officials in America. Among other effects this would effectively remove the salaries of the governor and other officials of the crown from the control of the General Assembly. The Virginians passed resolutions declaring that taxation without representation was unconstitutional, sent communications to the king and Parliament, and congratulated the Massachusetts house for its firm stand on the matter. When the new royal governor, Norborne Berkeley, baron de Botetourt, countered by dissolving the session, they retired to a tavern, agreed upon a program of nonimportation of English goods, and set up an association to enforce it. The other American colonies soon followed suit.

The boycott plan in actuality did relatively little harm to British manufactures, but the British merchants did not like it,

5. John Richard Alden, *The South in the Revolution, 1763–1789* (Baton Rouge: Louisiana State University Press, 1957), pp. 69–70.

and Frederick, Lord North, now chancellor of the exchequer, was able to convince Parliament that the excises had been a mistake—not because they were unconstitutional, but because they hurt British trade. So in 1770 the duties were withdrawn, with the exception of the tax on tea.

In the meantime Lord Botetourt, who was popular with the Virginians, had died and been succeeded by John Murray, earl of Dunmore, who was not. When in 1772 the British proposed to transport to England a group of Rhode Islanders who had attacked a British ship engaged in preventing smuggling, and to try them there, the Virginia House of Burgesses not only protested, but established a Committee of Correspondence to keep in close touch with the other colonies. The other colonies fell in with the idea, and the British government grew alarmed. Then, late in 1773, a group of New England Patriots dressed up in Indian garb and tossed 342 chests of East India tea into Boston Harbor.

No East India tea had been offered for sale in Virginia, but the Virginians, though at first somewhat disapproving of the high-handedness of their Massachusetts compatriots, quickly rallied to their support after Parliament decided to make a heinous example of Boston by sending in troops and closing the port to all commerce until the colonials apologized. Virginia dispatched 8,600 bushels of corn and wheat, a supply of flour, and money to the city, adopted resolutions of sympathy, and set aside June 7, 1774, as a day of fasting and prayer. Governor Dunmore thereupon dissolved the assembly, and the burgesses retired to the Raleigh Tavern, elected Peyton Randolph as presiding officer, and directed the Committee of Correspondence to organize a convention of all the American colonies. Again their lead was followed by the other colonies, and the first Continental Congress was set for Philadelphia in September 1774. To represent Virginia the assembly chose Randolph, Richard Henry Lee, George Washington, Edmund Pendleton, Patrick Henry, Richard Bland, and Benjamin Harrison. In Philadelphia, the Virginians joined with the Massachusetts delegates in working out a series of nonimportation agreements, after which they came home and saw to it that the agreements were not violated or sidestepped in Virginia.

Governor Dunmore was desperate about what to do to keep the Virginians in line. Even a frontier war, in which Colonel Andrew Lewis led a force of more than eight hundred riflemen from the Shenandoah Valley out to the confluence of the Ohio and Kanawha rivers and defeated a Shawnee force under Chief Cornstalk, driving the Indians across the Ohio and stabilizing the frontier, did not divert attention from the rising crisis. When a Virginia convention assembled in Richmond at St. John's Church in March 1775, affairs had reached a point at which some delegates, led by Patrick Henry, were urging that the colony be formally put in a posture of defense for hostilities that were sure to occur. It was upon this occasion that Henry gave his oration with its famous ending: "Gentlemen may cry peace, peace,—but there is no peace. The war is actually begun! The next gale that sweeps from the north will bring to our ears the clash of resounding arms! Our brethren are already in the field! Why stand we here idle? . . . Is life so dear, is peace so sweet, as to be purchased at the price of chains and slavery? Forbid it, Almighty God! I know not what course others may take; but as for me, give me liberty, or give me death." (If he did not actually say those exact words, he said something close to it.) [6]

Intemperate oratory and the temper of the times were perfectly matched; the Virginians voted to raise troops. Dunmore, at wit's end, ordered the powder from the magazine at Williamsburg removed aboard a warship; the militia, led by Henry, marched upon the capital; Dunmore paid £330 in exchange for the powder, and proclaimed Henry an outlaw.

Then news came from Massachusetts; a British force had battled the militia at Lexington and Concord, and retreated back

6. No one actually wrote down Henry's speech. The version recorded by William Wirt in *Sketches of the Life and Character of Patrick Henry* (Philadelphia: Thomas, Cowperthwait and Co., 1838), pp. 137–142, was compiled from interviews with some who heard it delivered, and is generally held to be close in language and spirit to the original.

to Boston, harassed by the Patriots en route. The Virginia delegation set out for the second Continental Congress in Philadelphia. There the Congress voted to make the military confrontation at Boston a colony-wide affair, and on June 15, 1775, George Washington was chosen to command the Continental Army. Back in Virginia Governor Dunmore fled aboard a man-of-war in the York River.

The colony was placed on a war footing, with Edmund Pendleton as chairman of a Committee of Safety. Detachments of British sailors began raiding plantations, and Dunmore occupied Norfolk. He also announced that any slave or indentured servant who would join his forces was henceforth a free man. The Virginians were outraged; this was fomenting a servile insurrection. (Before the Revolutionary War was done, Virginia planters were to end up losing more than 30,000 slaves, most of them captured as plunder.) An expedition was dispatched to Norfolk, and Dunmore and the British were driven back to their ships, numerous Tories going aboard with them.

On June 28, 1776, the Virginia revolutionary convention adopted a constitution, which contained George Mason's extensive Bill of Rights. Two weeks before, its delegates to the Continental Congress in Philadelphia had been instructed to urge the other colonies, in the words of Edmund Pendleton's resolution, "to declare the United Colonies free and independent states, absolved from all allegiance to, or dependence upon, the crown or Parliament of Great Britain." [7] Accordingly, Richard Henry Lee had so moved. Meanwhile, in Richmond Patrick Henry was chosen to be the Commonwealth of Virginia's first governor.

Thus ended the 169-year history of Virginia as an English colony; while the last royal governor was preparing to set sail from the Chesapeake Bay, a 33-year-old Virginian, Thomas Jefferson, was at work in Philadelphia drafting the Declaration of Independence, asserting that the thirteen United Colonies "are, and of Right ought to be Free and Independent States," and declaring that the signatories "mutually pledge to each other our

7. David John Mays, *Edmund Pendleton, 1721–1803: A Biography*, 2 vols. (Cambridge, Mass.: Harvard University Press, 1952), 2:109.

Lives, our Fortunes, and our Sacred Honor.'' What had once been a Stuart king's Old Dominion, loyal to the throne even while civil war raged at home, had now taken the lead in the resolve of the thirteen colonies "to dissolve the political bands" with the Mother Country, and "to assume among the powers of the earth, the separate and equal station to which the Laws of Nature and of Nature's God entitle them. . . ."

Of all the royal colonies Virginia had been the most closely tied to the old homeland. As Charles M. Andrews wrote, "No one of the other settlements can compare with it in the length of its membership in the British family, in the uniform and consistently forward flow of its political and economic life, and in the completeness with which it seemed to conform to the English expectation of what a colony should be. . . ." [8] Why, then, did Virginia enter into the Revolution, and not only that but take the lead in it, committing itself to resistance and then independence, with less dissent and less holding back than almost any of the other colonies?

If in other colonies the Revolution constituted what to many Britons seemed the revolt of "rag, taggle and bob" against authority, an affair of mobs, a struggle of have-nots against haves, this was not so in Virginia. The Revolution in Virginia was led by the gentry. Washington, Jefferson, Pendleton, the Lees, Peyton and Edmund Randolph, George Mason, Richard Bland, Archibald Cary, Robert Carter Nicholas, James Madison, John Page, Thomas Nelson, Benjamin Harrison, Jr.—these were not ambitious men on the make, rebels against the so-called Establishment. They *were* the Establishment.

True, in the 1750s and 1760s the balance of political power had been shifting from the Tidewater to the Piedmont, and the old tobacco-growing gentry had fallen upon difficult economic times. The scandal over the John Robinson estate, in which the much-revered longtime speaker of the House and treasurer of the colony was revealed to have loaned more than £100,000 from the Virginia treasury to his planter friends before his death

---

8. Charles M. Andrews, *Our Earliest Colonial Settlements: Their Diversities of Origin and Later Characteristics* (Ithaca, N.Y.: Cornell University Press, 1959), p. 27.

in 1766, was revelatory of what had happened. Realizing that many of his friends, including some of the leading figures in the Tidewater aristocracy, faced bankruptcy and ruin, Robinson had loaned supposedly retired paper money to them.[9] The truth is that the shift in power from Tidewater to Piedmont meant little change in colonial Virginia politics. The burgesses continued to be dominated by the gentry of Virginia, elected by a constituency of freeholders, and there was no significant change in leadership in the years leading up to 1776. And that leadership, in the 1760s and 1770s, was the spearhead of the American movement toward independence from Great Britain.

Economics was certainly involved; Virginia tobacco planters were in heavy debt to British merchants, and the Tidewater plantations were foundering under the load. The removal of the Navigation acts, which required that all tobacco be shipped to England in British or American vessels and sold there, was certainly a temptation. Yet a number of the planters who were most debt-ridden in the 1760s and 1770s were among those who least favored the Revolution, and some of them remained Loyalists to the end. Conversely, most of the leaders in the independence movement were *not* themselves importantly in debt to British merchants. So any such easy economic explanation of the matter is difficult to maintain.

British attempts to keep the settlement of English America east of the Alleghenies caused great resentment. Yet it is doubtful that this of itself was a major factor in impelling Virginians to break with the crown, for the simple reason that well before the break with England the western lands were already being opened; settlers were thronging across the mountains into Kentucky and Tennessee in complete disdain of royal policy. As John Richard Alden points out, royal policy for the west was an irritant; it was not a determining factor.[10]

If we want to get at the factors that led to independence, we might well examine the specific set of grievances that Thomas Jefferson set forth in the Declaration, written to acquaint "the

9. The Robinson scandal is explicitly detailed in Mays, *Edmund Pendleton.*
10. Alden, *The South in the Revolution,* p. 139.

opinions of mankind'' with the causes that impelled the colonies to the separation. The Declaration was designed, of course, to justify what was already a fact: first armed resistance, then declared rebellion. The "facts" that were "submitted to a candid world" in the Declaration consisted of two kinds generally: those which set forth acts that led up to resistance and rebellion, and those which protested the acts of king and Parliament to suppress incipient and actual rebellion. These latter grievances, however just, cannot be considered as having caused the resistance that led up to the Declaration; they are the results of the break.

It is the other grievances, those which catalog the growing division, that are significant. What Jefferson does is catalog the various ways whereby the crown frustrated self-government in the colonies. He cites the royal veto power, the suspension clause whereby colonial legislative acts were held up until approved in England, dissolution of legislatures, indefinite proroguing, blocking of immigration, refusal to permit the colonies to set up an adequate judicial system, establishment of numerous royal customs officials and other officers responsible to the crown rather than to the colonial legislatures, and other offenses. What these all add up to is the refusal of the British government to allow the overseas colonies to govern themselves; and that, it seems clear, is the ultimate "cause" of the American Revolution. For the obvious fact is that by the 1740s and 1750s, colonies such as Virginia were ready, willing, and able to govern themselves. The Virginians had, during the long years under Governor William Gooch, grown to maturity as a self-governing society and had evolved a workable, successful representative assembly. It was not the insistence of the royal government that the Virginians tax themselves to pay what Parliament considered their share of the costs of that war and the maintenance of the regular army on the frontier that began the ultimate trouble, so much as the attempt of the Pelham ministry, following the fall of Walpole, to bring the colonies under much greater control than had been exercised for many decades.

The French and Indian War only acted to postpone the developing crisis; its results, however, served to intensify the schism.

Not only had the menace of the French been removed, diminishing thereby the need of royal military and naval protection, but it created a severe financial deficit in England, necessitating heavy taxation, and thus prompted Parliament to look to the colonies for additional revenue. The Virginians sensed, too, that the general tightening of royal control in the colonies from 1748 onward was a result of British unease at the growing size and potential strength of the overseas possessions in America. Each additional act designed by the royal government to raise revenue and assert control fed the resentment.

The American Revolution came about because by the 1750s almost all the thirteen colonies, and Virginia perhaps most of all, were strong, prosperous, increasingly self-sustaining political and social units, grown accustomed to governing themselves and ever more insistent upon doing so. Virginia, with its population of 550,000, was ready for self-government, had, in fact, all but enjoyed just that in the 1730s and 1740s, and was not willing finally to accept royal government that did not offer it what in effect was the status of a self-governing dominion.

The Virginians of 1776 had reached political maturity. The shift in power from the Tidewater to the Piedmont was being effected in an orderly, responsible manner, and there was every reason to expect that as the western areas opened up, the result would be to strengthen rather than challenge representative government in the colony. When, therefore, the movement for independence developed, western Virginia did not view it as an eastern matter; indeed, in January of 1775, the freeholders of Botetourt County, westernmost of the new counties, met in Fincastle and passed a set of resolutions commending the Virginia delegates to the Continental Congress for their "steady and patriotic conduct, in support of American liberty," and pledged their willingness to "stand prepared for every contingency." [11]

What Virginia had to offer Americans, therefore, as they moved toward their independence, was not only a matchless set

11. Robert Douthat Stoner, *A Seed-Bed of the Republic: A Study of the Pioneers in the Upper (Southern) Valley of Virginia* (Roanoke: Roanoke Historical Society, 1962), pp. 98–99.

of able, vigorous leaders, but—by the standards of the time—a thoroughgoing commitment to representative government. The very fact that of all the colonies, Virginia was closest to England in outlook and temper meant that it was most prepared to demand liberty. In Daniel Boorstin's words, "An unpredictable alchemy transformed the ways of the English manor-house into the habits of a New World republic. Squire Westerns and Horace Walpoles underwent an Atlantic sea-change which made them into Edmund Pendletons, Thomas Jeffersons, and George Washingtons. What made them American was not what they sought but what they accomplished." [12] Well might an anxious John Adams of Massachusetts have written home, as he did, upon the occasion of the arrival of the Virginia delegates to the first Continental Congress to express his satisfaction with his new colleagues: "These gentlemen from Virginia appear to be the most spirited and consistent of any." [13]

12. Daniel J. Boorstin, *The Americans: The Colonial Experience* (New York: Vintage Books, 1958), p. 98.
13. Alf J. Mapp, Jr., *The Virginia Experiment. The Old Dominion's Role in the Making of America, 1607–1781* (LaSalle, Ill.: Open Court, 1974), p. 360.

4

The Revolutionary Era

*In which the Virginians
win the Revolutionary War and then get the nation
off to a sound beginning.*

FROM the time that the earl of Dunmore and his fleet
sailed away from Virginia in May of 1776 until another
British squadron showed up in Hampton Roads in 1779,
the territory of Virginia was out of the combat zone in the Revolutionary War. Not so its people. When its leading citizen,
George Washington, took over command of the Patriot forces
before Boston, Virginia regiments were at his side, and
throughout the bitter four-year term of retreat, battles lost and
battles won, war-weariness and extreme privation that followed
as the Continental Army somehow managed to stay intact and
maintain pressure upon the British enemy, thousands of Virginians remained in the fight.

The Virginians produced a host of distinguished soldiers,
including Daniel Morgan, who led his riflemen down from the
mountains to fight for independence; Colonel Light Horse Harry
Lee, peerless leader of cavalry; Colonel William Campbell,
militia leader of Washington County; Brigadier General Peter
Muhlenberg of Woodstock, who put aside his Lutheran clergyman's garb to fight for his country; and George Rogers Clark,

who raised a force of riflemen and took it down the Ohio River to surprise the British garrison at Kaskaskia, fought a bitter winter's campaign to entrap another force at Vincennes, and, in effect, secured much of the entire northwest for Virginia and the Americans.

The men that these commanders led served with far less individual glory but no less fidelity. Indeed, Virginia's troops so thronged to the cause that later on, when the British invaded the state while Washington's army was deployed in the north, it was all but defenseless against attack. Only the militia remained, and its performance was, as with most militia forces during the Revolution, usually less than glorious.

George Washington had little use for militia. From his headquarters in the north he kept urging the Virginia authorities to push the enlistment of more regular troops, and to keep his ragged, ill-equipped army supplied with food and clothes. But though Governors Patrick Henry and Thomas Jefferson and Speaker Benjamin Harrison of the Virginia Assembly tried their best to sustain him, it was difficult going. Normal outlets for Virginia crops were now all but closed off; there were severe shortages of almost everything. The price of goods skyrocketed. To meet the costs of government the Virginia authorities printed paper notes, and to back them—and to raise the state's contribution to the Continental treasury as well—taxes were increased over and again. But it was one thing to levy taxes, and another to collect from farmers who had little enough to spare as it was. Inflation was rampant; the value of paper notes plummeted. By the time Jefferson succeeded to the governorship in 1779, the Virginia state treasury was practically empty.

Yet during the years from 1776 to 1779, life went on. It is difficult for a modern reader to visualize the extent to which, because of the slowness of communications, the rarity of roads, and infrequency of travel, the rural areas were out of touch with the war. Planters and politicians might talk of freedom from tyranny and of pledging one's life, fortune, and sacred honor to the cause of liberty; but for the most part the farmer went about his business, tried to earn enough to pay his taxes, and the war to the north seldom entered his life. Not until British troops actually invaded the state in 1779 did he feel the direct impact of the war for independence.

Devoted politicians that they were, of course, the Virginians had made the most of the opportunity, well ahead of the formal Declaration of Independence in 1776, to begin setting up a state government. Even before they had adopted a new state constitution, and months before the Declaration of Independence, they had already enacted George Mason's Bill of Rights, with its ringing declaration that "all power is vested in, and consequently derived from, the People," and its assertion of the right of trial by jury, the illegality of general warrants of arrest, the importance of freedom of the press, the subordination of military to civil power, and the right of all men "to the free exercise of religion, according to the dictates of conscience. . . ." Mason's Bill of Rights influenced the Declaration of Independence and became the basis of the first ten amendments to the Constitution of the United States.

One of Jefferson's first moves in the new assembly was to introduce a bill abolishing entails. By breaking up the system whereby ownership of land could be entailed across the generations, he was striking a blow at the perpetuation of an aristocracy of wealth and power. Edmund Pendleton—"the ablest man in debate I have ever met with," Jefferson termed him [1]—fought to block and then to cripple the bill, but it became law. Next it devolved upon Jefferson, Pendleton, and George Wythe to undertake a thorough revision and modification of the laws of Virginia. The result, though never adopted as a whole, was drawn upon from time to time by the legislators.

Not long after Jefferson became governor, his Statute for Religious Freedom was brought to the floor of the House of Delegates. It proposed, simply, that no man should be compelled to support or to attend a church, or suffer any disability or restraint because of his religious opinions, and that all men "shall be free to profess, and by argument to maintain, their

---

1. Thomas Jefferson, "Memoir," in Thomas Jefferson Randolph, ed., *Memoir, Correspondence, and Miscellanies from the Papers of Thomas Jefferson,* 4 vols. (Charlottesville, Va.: F. Carr and Co., 1829), 1:30.

opinions in matters of religion,'' without their civil capacities being in any way affected.

In moving to establish complete freedom of religion, Jefferson and Madison were in a position to capitalize upon the loss of prestige that the Anglican clergy had suffered by virtue of the fact that a number of its ministers had supported the Tory cause. By 1778 it is probable that a majority of the population of Virginia were no longer Anglican in faith.

Not all dissenters, however, agreed on the theory of disestablishment as such; some proposed multiple establishments, whereby all Virginians would continue to be compelled to support churches, with the choice of churches to be left open. This was hardly what Jefferson had in mind. He and Madison were able to secure repeal of the English laws that made a criminal offense of dissenting opinions or failure to attend the Anglican church, and to discontinue enforced contributions to the Established Church by dissenters. As a temporary war measure it was also agreed that compulsory support of the Established Church by its own members would be suspended.

Jefferson soon had more immediate concerns, however. After three years during which the war was being fought far from Virginia's borders, the state was now to become the target of British military strategy. As a safeguard against attack from the sea the capital was moved from Williamsburg to Richmond in April 1780—in the process the continued demands of the western areas were met for a state capital more accessible to its elected legislators. In October the British struck at Portsmouth. Meanwhile General Gates, preparing to oppose Lord Cornwallis's northward thrust from South Carolina, begged for militia, and finally some fifteen hundred men were sent, but many were without usable arms, ammunition, or provisions. When Gates's army was subsequently all but destroyed at Camden, S.C., Jefferson tried to ready Virginia for the expected invasion, but to little avail. There was also an uprising of Tories in the New River country to the west, threatening the critically needed lead supply. It was suppressed by militia under William Campbell, and the summary treatment given Tory leaders by Judge Charles Lynch has been said to have inspired the term "Lynch law."

On December 30, 1780, a British fleet hove into sight at Hampton Roads, bearing Benedict Arnold, until his recent desertion one of Washington's most trusted commanders and now a brigadier general in the British army, with a force of more than one thousand British troops. Arnold sailed straight up the James River to Westover, disembarked his force, and marched unopposed to Richmond, which he entered on January 5 and proceeded to devastate. Finally the militia, which Jefferson was now exerting himself to the utmost to assemble, began gathering under Baron Von Steuben and Thomas Nelson; Arnold retreated to the fleet at Westover, plundering as he went, and sailed downstream to Portsmouth.

Washington sent a force southward under the Marquis de Lafayette, and Jefferson attempted to concentrate what militia was available. But to the south, Cornwallis was moving up into North Carolina, with Nathaniel Greene, who had relieved Gates in command, retreating before him. Greene led Cornwallis further and further away from the British base of supplies on a fine chase all through Piedmont North Carolina up to the Virginia line. Finally Greene thought himself sufficiently reinforced to make a stand, whereupon he gave battle at Guilford Court House. Though the British retained possession of the field after the fighting, the Americans inflicted heavy casualties while suffering considerably fewer.

At this point the British army might wisely have moved back to South Carolina and protected the gains won earlier there and in Georgia; instead, Cornwallis chose to strike toward Virginia and effect a junction with Arnold's force, now reinforced and commanded by Major General William Phillips. This left Virginia in considerable danger, since Greene had taken his army southward to clear out the Carolinas, but it also put Cornwallis in a potentially perilous position. For if the French naval fleet should appear in Chesapeake Bay and cut off his escape route, and the Americans could concentrate enough troops, he would be in a precarious situation indeed.

Cornwallis, for a long while, did not realize his danger, however, and before he did, he gave the Virginia General Assembly a scare. Jefferson, frustrated at his inability to get the militia to

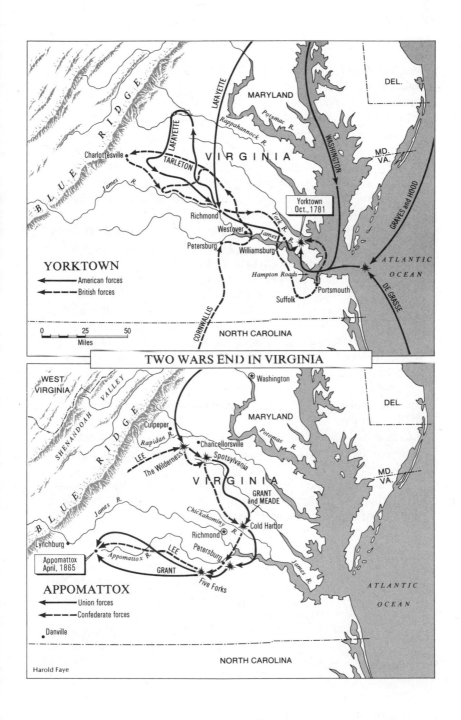

TWO WARS END IN VIRGINIA

YORKTOWN

⟵ American forces
⟵--- British forces

MARYLAND

DEL.

Potomac R.

Rappahannock R.

VIRGINIA

MD.
VA.

LAFAYETTE

BLUE RIDGE

Charlottesville

TARLETON

James R.

WASHINGTON

GRAVES and HOOD

Richmond

Westover

James R.

York R.

Yorktown
Oct., 1781

Petersburg

Williamsburg

ATLANTIC
OCEAN

Hampton Roads

DE GRASSE

Suffolk

Portsmouth

CORNWALLIS

0   25   50
Miles

NORTH CAROLINA

APPOMATTOX

⟵ Union forces
⟵--- Confederate forces

Danville

WEST
VIRGINIA

⊛ Washington

DEL.

SHENANDOAH VALLEY

BLUE RIDGE

Culpeper

Rapidan R.

LEE

The Wilderness

MARYLAND

Potomac R.

Chancellorsville

Spotsylvania

VIRGINIA

MD.
VA.

GRANT
and MEADE

James R.

Chickahominy R.

Cold Harbor

Lynchburg

Appomattox
April, 1865

Appomattox R.

LEE

Richmond ⊛

Petersburg

GRANT

Five Forks

James R.

ATLANTIC
OCEAN

NORTH CAROLINA

Harold Faye

assemble and, once having assembled, to stay in place and fight, resigned as governor on June 1, 1780, at the end of his second term. The assembly had moved to Charlottesville for the time being, and Cornwallis dispatched Colonel Banastre Tarleton and his troop on a surprise raid, hoping to capture all its members. Had it not been for one Captain Jack Jouett, who rode through the night to give the alarm, the plan might have succeeded, and Jefferson, Patrick Henry, Thomas Nelson, Jr., and other noted Virginia leaders might have been captured. Even as it was, Tarleton managed to bag seven legislators.

As for the Virginia General Assembly, such members as had managed to avoid capture reconvened at Staunton, beyond the Blue Ridge, discussed whether a dictator was needed and decided against it, then elected Thomas Nelson, Jr., governor. Having done very little to protect the state from what had happened, and looking for a scapegoat, the assemblymen also resolved that at the next session of the assembly an inquiry be made into Jefferson's conduct as governor. Patrick Henry (who would probably have liked to be the dictator) would seem to have been behind the movement to discredit Jefferson. Furious, Jefferson got himself re-elected to the assembly, demanded that specific charges be drawn up, and issued a devastating rebuttal. In the climate of good will following Cornwallis's surrender, the assembly voted both to clear Jefferson and to declare its high opinion of Jefferson's ability, rectitude, and integrity as chief magistrate.

All this, however, came after George Washington had pulled off perhaps his most outstanding military feat as commanding general of the Continental armies. Early in July he received word that the French fleet of Admiral DeGrasse, with several thousand French soldiers from the West Indies, would arrive in the Chesapeake Bay in late August. He therefore left only enough troops to keep the main British army contained in New York City and moved his army of ragged Continentals and well-dressed French swiftly southward.

Had Cornwallis decided to break out of the Virginia peninsula before Washington's army got there, it is doubtful that Lafayette could have prevented it, but Cornwallis now chose to wait. Thus Washington was able to converge upon the peninsula and, with some ten thousand Continentals and militia and eight thousand French troops, to encircle Cornwallis's position at Yorktown, while the French fleet, patrolling the mouth of the York River, prevented the British from escaping by sea.

On October 19, 1781, Cornwallis, all escape cut off and under artillery fire from all sides, accepted terms of surrender and marched his British regulars and Hessians out of the entrenchments. An entire British army had surrendered.

Great Britain had had enough. The might of England was manifestly unable to subdue the rebellious American colonies, and though two more years would elapse before the Treaty of Paris was signed, the independence of the new nation was secured. British forces in New York and Charleston prepared for evacuation. On December 4, 1783, George Washington bade farewell to his officers at Fraunces Tavern in New York, and on Christmas eve the Squire of Mount Vernon rode up to his door in Virginia, in time to spend Christmas at home. In Douglas Freeman's summation, "He was a patriot of conscious integrity and unassailable conduct who had given himself completely to the revolutionary cause and desired for himself the satisfaction of having done his utmost and of having won the approval of those whose esteem he put above every other reward." [2]

Thomas Jefferson, meanwhile, sick of public life, had written a book, the *Notes on the State of Virginia,* prepared in response to a query from the French government forwarded to him while he was still governor. Once free of public responsibility, and having seen to it that his name was cleared, he plunged with delight into its preparation, and produced what William Peden properly calls "one of America's first permanent literary and intellectual landmarks." [3]

Probably the most famous sections are those on the injustice of slavery and on the virtues of the yeoman farmer. He had al-

2. Douglas Southall Freeman, *George Washington, A Biography,* vol. 5, *Victory with the Help of France* (New York: Charles Scribner's Sons, 1952), p. 500.

3. William Peden, "Introduction" to Thomas Jefferson, *Notes on the State of Virginia* (Chapel Hill: University of North Carolina Press, 1955), p. xxv.

ready described what he considered the permanent mental and social inferiority of the Negro; but slavery was another matter. "The whole commerce between master and slave," he wrote, "is a perpetual exercise of the most boisterous passions, the most unremitting despotism on the one part, and degrading submissions on the other." Only when slavery was removed from Virginia could there be liberty. "Indeed I tremble for my country when I reflect that God is just; that his justice cannot sleep forever: that considering numbers, nature and natural means only, a revolution of the wheel of fortune, an exchange of situation, is among possible events: that it may become probable by supernatural interference! The Almighty has no attribute which can take side with us in such a contest. . . ." [4]

Later generations have found it difficult to understand how Jefferson and others could be so thoroughly opposed to slavery, and fearful of its moral and social evil, and yet own slaves themselves. The essential point to remember, however, is that a belief in the evil of slavery did not necessarily imply a belief in the equality of blacks. Jefferson and others could not envision hundreds of thousands of freed blacks living peacefully in a white man's commonwealth; the only solution they could imagine was transportation back to Africa. With his entire agricultural establishment and his already precarious finances dependent upon slave labor, and with children and later grandchildren to provide for, Jefferson could only see the presence of slavery as a vast evil that he could not himself effectively redress by any gesture of his own.

Were men such as Jefferson and Madison hypocrites? Their political enemies claimed they were, and nowadays there are numerous commentators who have scored the limitations of their antislavery stance. Such historical hindsight is always impressive. Much more to the point, I think, is Edmund S. Morgan's hypothesis that the society of eighteenth-century Virginia produced its Jeffersons, Madisons, Masons, and so many opponents of slavery and advocates of human liberty *because* of the existence of slavery as a foundation of the planter

4. Jefferson, *Notes on the State of Virginia*, pp. 162–163.

society.[5] The rise of Negro slavery in the 1710s and 1720s, he reasons, removed from the Virginia scene most of the dynamite of class struggle that had earlier threatened its stability, and created a community of economic and social interest between large planters and smaller planters. This consensus was based upon the relegation of the working force to the status of slavery, made possible because the slaves were blacks and hence to the men of that time they constituted no threat to the ideals of republican freedom. Thus the Virginians led the American colonies to liberty because they did not feel themselves threatened by the terrors of unlimited democracy represented by the mob. It is an intriguing theory. In any event, perhaps the best way to evaluate the positions of Jefferson, Mason, Madison, and other Virginians concerning slavery is to think of it this way. There were doubtless hundreds, even thousands of planters in Virginia and the other southern states in their time who owned slaves and whose fortunes depended upon slave labor. What is remarkable is not that Thomas Jefferson was a Virginia slaveholder, but that a Virginia slaveholder could hold Thomas Jefferson's view on slavery.

The Virginians did not wait until the Revolutionary War was settled to begin moving into the territory beyond the Alleghenies. The backcountry, including present-day West Virginia, had already been filling up. Most of these people arrived by way of Virginia, and the majority of them were, or had been, Virginians. By virtue both of royal charters and of George Rogers Clark's brilliant conquest of the Northwest, Virginia laid claim to the trans-Ohio territory, and as governor, Jefferson had set up a land office and laid out districts. The Virginians realized, of course, that it would be impossible for a single state to govern so vast a territory, and that to retain possession would result in Virginia dwarfing almost all the other states. Finally, in 1781, to further the cause of union, Virginia offered to cede the entire trans-Ohio territory to the new nation, with the proviso that all deeds given by Indians—i.e., those purchased by speculators— must be declared void. Here Thomas Jefferson was the moving

5. Morgan's views are developed in Morgan, *American Slavery*, pp. 376–386.

force. Jefferson was not worried about the western country being controlled by unruly and lawless squatters, as many, including George Washington, feared. He felt that such settlers should indeed possess the land, and that as soon as enough people were settled, new states, to the number of ten, should be established. Give the land to those who would live on it, he urged, and not to land speculators to sell to those who would occupy it. Jefferson's proviso barring slavery was defeated, but in 1784 the ordinance was passed, only to be overturned several years later when the Northwest Ordinance of 1787 was enacted, setting up territorial governments that were considerably larger, making it much more difficult for the new territories to become states, and much easier for land speculators to profit from the transaction. Though disappointed, Jefferson was partly consoled by the fact that the prohibition against slavery was reinstated.

During the course of the war, nineteen new Virginia counties had been formed, including three in what is now Kentucky. The Kentuckians soon wanted separate statehood, and Virginia was not averse to the idea, provided that the new state assumed its share of the war debt; but though in the 1780s the General Assembly four times passed enabling acts, it was not until 1792 that Congress voted to make Kentucky the fifteenth state of the Union.

Virginia entered the post-Revolutionary era with a huge wartime tax debt—printing of paper notes to supply the armies and keep its government functioning had left its coffers empty and its obligations massive. The Virginians, however, went to work to raise the money even before the war officially ended, and within a few years' time the debt was reduced to more manageable proportions.

There was, even so, much difficulty in collecting revenues, particularly in the western counties. Sheriffs were empowered to foreclose on property, but popular resentment often forced them to hold off. Frequently persons owing taxes simply pulled up stakes and fled to the areas beyond the mountains. Since taxes were customarily payable either in coin—which was extremely scarce—or in tobacco, the western counties, which did not grow tobacco, were especially hard hit. The General Assembly, however, was made up primarily of planters, who felt considerable sympathy with the smaller farmers, so it voted to permit payment in hemp and flour, and at one point even suspended all tax collections for six months. The result was that, primarily because there was no large merchant and industrial faction within the Old Dominion, the Virginians generally seemed to avoid the hardship, sectional rancor, and outright resort to violence that marked the post-Revolutionary history of states such as Massachusetts, where the mercantile-creditor group held a firm grip on the state government.

Virginia had been fairly rough on Tory sympathizers during the middle years of the war. Once the war was over, however, the General Assembly decreed that all loyalists who had left during the fighting might come back to live, provided they had not actually borne arms against the Patriot cause. Not all the citizenry was so hospitable; there are some instances in the Norfolk area of unpopular returning Tories being greeted with tar and feathers. On the matter of prewar debts owed to English merchants, however, the state was not very obliging. It took the signing of the U.S. Constitution and a ruling by the Supreme Court of the United States before the British merchants finally collected what was owed them.

The losses that Virginia planters suffered during the war from slaves carried away by the British or seeking freedom behind British lines were considerable; it has been estimated at some 30,000 slaves. Not all slaves who took part in the Revolution served on the British side, however; many were active in the Patriot cause. Most served as orderlies and laborers, but blacks were used to good effect, too, as spies. Many slaves served in the army in place of their owners, on the agreement that after the war they would be freed. Unfortunately, not all masters honored these promises, and in 1783 the General Assembly had to pass legislation enforcing such agreements.

After Jefferson departed for France in 1784 to join Benjamin Franklin and John Adams in conducting negotiations on treaties with the various European countries, it was left to his friend James Madison to carry out the several legislative projects they had proposed. Small of stature and with a low voice, Madison was no great public speaker (nor was Jefferson, for that matter), but his incisive, logical mind more than made up for the absence of histrionics. In 1785 Madison and George Mason finally secured passage of the Statute for Religious Liberty, with Jefferson's ringing assertion that "truth is great and will prevail if left to herself; that she is the proper and sufficient antagonist to error, and has nothing to fear from the conflict unless by human interposition disarmed of her natural weapons, free argument and debate. . . ."

Another Jeffersonian measure failed of enactment. Jefferson had proposed a Bill for the More General Diffusion of Knowledge, which would set up a public school system for Virginia. All children were to be given three years of elementary education in reading, writing, and computation. After that, those parents who wished might send their children on for more education as they pleased; the state, however, would select from the children of the poor those who were most able and provide them with a curriculum of more advanced education. In turn, from those given such training, a select number of especially able youths would be given three years of college education at William and Mary. Madison introduced the measure in 1786, but it got nowhere; not until ten years later was a proposal for a limited number of state scholarships passed by the assembly. Like the other southern states, Virginia lagged behind in public education, and though there were numerous academies and "old field" schools, it would be decades before any kind of systematic school program was developed.

As the flood of immigration into the western areas increased, that part of the state became underrepresented in the assembly, and the Tidewater overrepresented. But during this period at least, the west-east cleavage was perhaps mildest in Virginia, for the Virginians were prompt to look after the interests of the westerners. The question of the right of the United States to navigation of the Mississippi had been sidetracked at the Treaty of Ghent. But when in 1784 Spain announced that the mouth of the Mississippi was thenceforth closed to American commerce, the west was outraged, and there was considerable talk of resort to arms and even of separation from the United States in order to force a showdown.

When the Jay-Gardoqui Treaty was proposed to the Congress in 1786, calling for the United States to "forbear" the right of navigation for a period of 25 or 30 years, the transmontane areas were indignant, and the Virginians, with their strong western interests, led the protest. There was bitter debate in Congress, and the treaty was approved, with the five southern states voting against it and seven northern states in favor. Since a two-thirds majority of the states was necessary for approval of a treaty by Congress, Jay's treaty languished, and negotiations were broken off.

Virginia's position during the middle and late 1780s, by comparison with that of most of the other states, was enviable. The Old Dominion was the largest and most populous of the thirteen states. One out of every five inhabitants of the country was a Virginian, and this does not include those living in what would someday become the state of Kentucky, where already there were as many inhabitants as in the state of New Hampshire. The state's war debt was for the most part either retired or on the way to retirement. Revenues were adequate, despite periods of economic stress during which tax collections were temporarily suspended by the assembly. In Merrill Jensen's words, "Virginia shaped tax policy with an eye to the capacities of the taxpayers, and yet at the same time it managed to collect handsome revenues and to pay off a large part of the state debt." [6] The tobacco trade with England had been pretty much restored, and now there was also direct access to the European market. Not only that, but many planters were converting from tobacco to wheat, corn, and hemp, for which a ready market existed. Something of a merchant marine was even being developed, though most of the export produce still moved under New England or British flags.

Why, then, did the Virginians take the lead in the movement

---

6. Merrill Jensen, *The New Nation: A History of the United States During the Confederation, 1781–1789* (New York: Vintage Books, 1950), p. 312.

to replace the Articles of Confederation with a Constitution that would make the American Union a much more unified nation? There were, of course, various issues on which Virginia stood to gain by creation cf a more powerful central government. For one thing, the financial disarray of certain of the other colonies, and the proliferation of paper currency, might have long-range effects on Virginia's own relatively sound finances. For another, the inability of the Confederation to maintain and finance the kind of military force needed to keep the western areas protected involved Virginia's own interests beyond the mountains. Furthermore, the Kentuckians were clamoring for statehood, and talked of making arrangements with Spain and Britain if denied such status, and the weak Congress under the Articles of Confederation could and would do nothing to bring about statehood. There was also the difficulty of working out boundary and commercial disputes with other states, when there was no final authority.

Yet at the same time, there were issues on which Virginia was very likely to suffer in the event of a stronger national arrangement. If, for example, the new nation were to assume the debts of the various states, as many advocated, Virginia, which had largely paid its own indebtedness, would be in the position of having now, through its taxes, to make good part of the other states' debts as well. If customs revenues were to be collected by the national government instead of by the state, then Virginia would lose an important source of its state revenue. The loss would surely have to be made up in increased property taxation, which was not a very felicitous prospect. If a protective import tariff were set up to encourage native manufacturing, as the Middle Atlantic states wished, the Virginians might well find themselves being made to pay much of the cost of sponsoring such manufactures, without any compensatory gain. Finally, pressure from the commercial and shipping interests of the northern states for American navigation acts as retaliation against trade exclusion by European powers might result in Virginia's flourishing export trade being made to suffer in order to benefit the economy of other states.

To understand why Virginians took the lead in developing a

strong central government out of the loosely tied Confederation, therefore—why a political "conservative" such as Edmund Pendleton and a "liberal" such as James Madison could unite in their advocacy of the Constitution—no simple explanation involving immediate and private advantages to Virginia will suffice, since it would be as easy to argue the other way around, and say that a powerful, flourishing state such as Virginia had relatively little need of such an arrangement. A better way to think of it is to consider that, as the most populous and powerful of the American states, Virginia approached the matter of a government for America out of a long heritage of domestic self-government, and a society that had for at least a half-century been pretty much a stable, going concern, offering, to its freeholders at least, the blessings of a reasonably ordered, workable government. It was the anarchy, the potentiality for disorder and social chaos, that disturbed them about arrangements under the Confederation. What Virginia wanted was *order*. The Virginians were deeply social beings; they believed in an orderly society. The Confederation, with its loose central government and its system of one-vote-per-state, regardless of size or wealth, could neither enforce order among the states nor achieve representative government.

The leading Virginians thought in national terms, and they expected that in an American union, Virginia would be the leading state. They assumed that Virginia would head the American Union, as indeed in a measure it did for the first several decades of its existence. A large and powerful state such as Virginia would have comparatively little to fear from a union in which government was representative. Sectionalism, they felt, would be likely to work against rather than in favor of the interests of Virginia; the slavery issue had not yet presented itself in compelling terms and changed that assumption. If one reads, for example, Jefferson's correspondence to Madison, Washington, and others, written from Paris during the years when the Constitution was coming into being, one is quick to note that it is seldom the particular interests of the state of Virginia that he worries about; he assumes that Virginia's best interests as a state will be identical with those of the other states, and that to the extent that they might not be, they would not be affected by the central government but would remain the province of the state government alone. What he is much more concerned about is the protection of the individual citizen against tyranny, and such reservations about the proposed Constitution as he expresses to Madison have almost entirely to do with that.

Thus it was that in 1785 a meeting of Virginia and Maryland commissioners, assembled to draw up an agreement on the use of the Potomac River and the Chesapeake Bay, decided to expand their deliberations to other affected states the next year, and at Virginia's insistence the meeting was enlarged to include all thirteen states. The resulting Annapolis Convention was attended by representatives of only five states, but one of them was Alexander Hamilton of New York, who like Madison had long been urging a stronger constitutional union. With Hamilton and Madison providing the impetus, the Annapolis Convention unanimously recommended that in May of 1787, a convention of all the states assemble in Philadelphia to consider not merely trade agreements, but "such further provisions as shall appear to them necessary to render the Constitution of the Federal government adequate to the exigencies of the Union. . . ." [7]

Twelve states sent delegates to the Constitutional Convention. Virginia had appointed hers first of all the states, and they comprised a brilliant group indeed: George Washington, Governor Edmund Randolph, James Madison, George Mason, John Blair, George Wythe, and James McClurg. Missing were Jefferson, who was away in France; Edmund Pendleton, recently crippled and thus unable to make the trip; and Patrick Henry. The last-named had sensed that the idea of a stronger union would not be popular among many Virginians. He "smelt a rat," he declared. Later he would spearhead the opposition to ratification.

The story of the Constitutional Convention is so well known that only a brief summation is necessary here. [8] Washington was

---

7. Alden, *The South in the Revolution*, pp. 378–379.

8. For an excellent discussion of Virginia's role in the Constitutional Convention, see Helen Hill Miller, *George Mason: Gentleman Revolutionary* (Chapel Hill: University of North Carolina Press, 1975), pp. 229–268.

unanimously chosen to preside, and Edmund Randolph proposed a resolution that "a *national* government ought to be established, consisting of a supreme Legislative, Executive and Judiciary." He then presented Virginia's plan, which proposed a legislature with a lower house chosen by the people of the states and an upper house elected by the lower house; a National Executive who would be chosen by the legislature; and a National Judiciary, also chosen by the legislature. Together with the executive and members of the legislature, the judiciary would be part of a Council of Revision which would have the power to review acts of the legislature. The legislative branch would have the power to "legislate in all cases to which the separate states are incompetent" and to veto laws passed by individual states which contravened the articles of Union.

After some weeks of debate, the smaller states, led by New Jersey, introduced another plan. It would continue the one-house Congress of the present Confederation, with each state having a similar vote, provide for a plural Federal Executive elected by the Congress and a Judiciary to be appointed by the Congress, and would extend the powers of the present Congress to permit raising revenue from import duties, stamp taxes and postage, regulating of interstate and foreign commerce, and federal collection of taxes within any state that failed to pay its share of the requisitions upon the states.

Finally, Connecticut introduced a compromise between the Virginia and New Jersey schemes whereby, though election to the lower house would be proportional according to population, the upper house would be elected by the state legislatures and would consist of two senators from each state.

There were other issues to be ironed out. How were the slaves to be counted in reckoning proportional representation? The taxation formula that the Congress used under the Articles of Confederation had been three to five—a slave was counted as three-fifths of a free man. Ultimately that formula was adopted. Madison wanted a two-thirds vote of the Senate for confirmation of federal judges, but was defeated; for confirmation of treaties, however, the two-thirds majority was retained—the Southerners had not forgotten the Jay-Gardoqui vote.

Perhaps the most vicious fight came over the slave trade.

Virginia had long since outlawed it for herself. Madison and George Mason led in demanding that it be banned outright. Georgia and South Carolina wanted it kept untouched. The New England states, in particular Connecticut, supported the lower South. The Constitutional Convention at this point showed distinct signs of breaking up, but ultimately a compromise was reached. Importation of slaves was to be allowed for thirteen years—later extended to twenty years, until 1808. The Virginians were indignant; Edmund Randolph said he would prefer to drop the whole Constitution than to have it include a slave-trade proviso, while Mason said he would ''chop off his right hand'' rather than sign the document as it existed.[9] Randolph later changed his mind, but George Mason neither signed the Constitution nor supported its ratification.

Thirty-nine of the fifty-five delegates to the Constitutional Convention signed the document, though none was completely satisfied with it. Ratification by nine of the thirteen states was now necessary, and acceptance was by no means a foregone conclusion. By the time that the Virginia Constitutional Assembly got ready, eight states had already ratified, but in Adrienne Koch's words, ''if the Constitution had been condemned by the state that had initiated the call for a Convention . . . that had pioneered its cause and that enjoyed an inevitable prominence for its great size, wealth, and illustrious past, the Constitution would have collapsed as a live plan, no matter how many states ratified. . . .''[10] In most of the other state conventions, the new Constitution had been approved either perfunctorily or with little rational debate and strictly by a show of legislative strength. Not in Virginia. Both sides wished the benefits and disabilities to be fully debated. Washington, Jefferson, and Richard Henry Lee were almost the only leading Virginians not taking part. The proratification forces looked to the delegates

9. Catherine Drinker Bowen, *Miracle at Philadelphia: The Story of the Constitutional Convention, May to September, 1787* (Boston: Atlantic Little, Brown, 1966), p. 230.
10. Adrienne Koch, *Madison's 'Advice to My Country'* (Princeton, N.J.: Princeton University Press, 1966), pp. 86–87.

from the Tidewater and Northern Virginia for their greatest strength; the opponents' strength lay in the Southside and the Piedmont. The Valley was divided. Fourteen of the delegates came all the way from the Kentucky territory; their vote might well swing the outcome.

There is little doubt that a majority of Virginians were not in favor of ratification, and the more so because Patrick Henry had been furiously assailing them with arguments against it. Yet in the matter of delegates, the pro-Constitution forces were believed to have a slight numerical advantage, and this not because the selection process had been (by eighteenth-century standards) undemocratic, but because—and this should go far toward explaining the faith of such men as Jefferson and Madison in representative government—in choosing their representatives the Virginians in large part were determined, as David John Mays points out, to have their wisest and most trusted leaders present, regardless of how they were known (or not known) to stand on the issue of adoption or rejection.[11]

From June 2 through June 25, 1788, the Virginians debated the merits of the Constitution. In Catherine Drinker Bowen's words, "this was to be the ablest of all the ratification conventions and the best prepared, a gathering studded with stars, with names and faces known throughout the state and beyond—well-speaking gentlemen on both sides, well-dressed, wellborn." [12] Visitors from afar crowded into the little village of Richmond, which was now the state capital, to watch the proceedings. Here were the Virginians at their best, engaged in their favorite pursuit—politics, and debating large issues openly and eloquently, with the future of their state and nation at stake. They did not have to sidestep the central issues, to equivocate or dissemble so as to defend with reason what was basically unreasonable, as a later generation of Virginians would be forced to do. The Virginians of 1788 were not on the political, economic, or moral defensive; they could speak their minds, and they did.

Perhaps the best brief account of the ratification debates is

---

11. Mays, *Edmund Pendleton*, 2:223.
12. Bowen, *Miracle at Philadelphia*, pp. 294–295.

that in David Mays's biography of Edmund Pendleton.[13] Here it will suffice only to say that the proratification forces succeeded in getting the new Constitution debated clause by clause, as Madison had hoped, thus weakening the effect of Patrick Henry's soaring oratory against the whole idea. The advocates of the Constitution were also far better organized, while Henry and George Mason, the leaders of the anti forces, often worked to cross purposes and to different ends.

Ultimately, the proratification forces prevailed. Agreeing fully that a bill of rights would need to be joined to the Constitution in the form of amendments after it was enacted, they called for ratification. The final vote in favor was 89–79. On June 26, Pendleton, as president of the convention, signed the document. The day following, the members drew up a set of amendments, added a proviso that the people of Virginia would retain the right to withdraw their ratification "whenever the powers granted unto (the Union) should be perverted to their injury or oppression," and voted to adjourn. New York ratified soon afterwards, with Alexander Hamilton performing a herculean job of changing the opinions of the anti-Constitution majority, a task much more difficult than the job Madison, Pendleton, and their supporters had with Henry, Mason, and their Virginia opponents, since, as Burton J. Hendrick wrote, "the Virginia statesmen were sincere, seeking the best interests of the country, while Hamilton's antagonist was George Clinton and his political machine, working against the new government because it would rob them of power." [14]

On April 16, 1789, George Washington departed from Mount Vernon for New York, to be inaugurated as the first President of the United States. His countrymen had elected him unanimously to head the new nation. Of his six cabinet posts, two were to be filled by Virginians—Edmund Randolph as attorney general, Thomas Jefferson as Secretary of State. He would have liked Edmund Pendleton to be a justice of the Supreme Court, but

---

13. See Mays, *Edmund Pendleton*, 2:217–272.

14. Burton J. Hendrick, *Bulwark of the Republic: A Biography of the Constitution* (Boston: Little, Brown, 1937), p. 98.

Pendleton's health would not permit. Virginia's first two senators were Richard Henry Lee and William Grayson—James Madison was defeated for the Senate and had to participate as a member of the House of Representatives, for Patrick Henry and his allies had schemed successfully to repay the "Father of the Constitution" for the defeat he had administered to them at the ratification convention. No matter; the ship of state had been properly launched, with a Virginian at the helm.

5

The National Era

*In which the Virginians furnish
the nation with its first president,
become impatient with the politics of his successor,
and elect another Virginian in his place.*

N the Virginia Constitutional Convention of 1788, fourteen delegates had represented the counties that now comprise the state of Kentucky, and of these, eleven had voted against ratification. It was not until February of 1791 that the Congress voted to admit Kentucky into the Union; the northeastern states finally consented to allow it, following the admission of Vermont. Kentucky thereafter became a strong ally of Virginia in national councils, and set about establishing an economic and social system strongly modeled upon Virginia, though with more emphasis upon democratic political arrangements.

Many Virginians realized the importance of the Old Dominion's having strong economic and political ties with the west. George Washington, for example, felt that not only the state's but the new nation's future prosperity depended upon such ties. Of the westerners, he wrote, "Smooth the road and make easy the way for them, and see what an influx of articles will be poured upon us; how amazingly our exports will be increased by them, and how amply we shall be compensated for any trouble and expense we may encounter to effect it." [1]

The new capital of Virginia, Richmond, was now graced with an impressive state capitol, designed by Thomas Jefferson himself, and set atop a hill overlooking the low wooden buildings of the otherwise unpretentious town of less than 5,000 inhabitants. Richmond was growing, however; the capital city was already becoming a center for transshipment of goods, and flour mills and tobacco factories began to make an appearance. Richmond had a bank, a mutual fire company, and several newspapers. Its leading citizen was a tall, ungainly, highly sociable young lawyer, John Marshall, a veteran of the Revolution and an advocate of a strong central government. Political sentiment in Richmond was likewise predominantly Federalist, as befitted a community in which Scots-born merchants played a predominant role and whose interests were strongly commercial and financial.

Norfolk, at the mouth of Chesapeake Bay, had made a swift recovery from the destruction of the war years. It was now the largest town in Virginia, with some seven thousand inhabitants. Its docks and warehouses received for shipment abroad produce from Richmond and the interior, and it was also an important port of call for the growing coastwide trade between the seaboard states. Across the Elizabeth River the town of Portsmouth also participated in the burgeoning opportunities for foreign trade. As might be expected, the Norfolk area, like Richmond, was predominantly Federalist in sympathies.

The party lines that were soon to make the late 1790s a period of vicious rivalry between Hamiltonian Federalists and Jeffersonian Republicans did not develop until several years after the first Congress of the United States met in New York under the new Constitution. Bitter disputes there were from the start, but initially these were along state lines. When in December 1790, however, the Secretary of the Treasury proposed to establish a Bank of the United States, mingling the private and public financial sectors, and the measure was enacted by the Congress in spite of opposition from Virginia and other southern delegates,

1. Dabney, *Virginia: The New Dominion,* p. 177.

Jefferson urged President Washington not to sign the measure into law. For the federal government to take a single step "beyond the boundaries thus especially drawn around the powers of Congress," he wrote, "is to take possession of a boundless field of power, no longer susceptible of any definition." [2] Attorney General Edmund Randolph also advised Washington that the Bank plan was unconstitutional. Washington, however, decided on Hamilton's side and signed the bill.

The battle lines now were shaping up, with the two Virginians, Jefferson and Madison, leading one side and the New Yorker, Hamilton, the other, but with another Virginian, Washington, increasingly leaning toward Hamilton's concept of a strong national government. The old division of Federalist and anti-Federalist, with reference to advocacy of the ratification of the Constitution, was giving way to a new alignment, whereby Hamilton headed a Federalist faction which favored close relations with England, a fiscal policy designed to encourage financial investment, and an interpretation of the provisions of the Constitution that permitted the national government the broadest possible fiscal and governmental role. The Jeffersonian Republicans, by contrast, sought closer ties with France and were hostile to England; supported a fiscal policy that did not favor the financial interests and investments of the cities; and restricted the federal government's role to what was explicitly stated in the Constitution only, with all other powers residing in state and local governments.

The revolution in France, and the subsequent war of England and the other European powers against the revolutionary French government, exacerbated tensions. Congress passed a neutrality act, forbidding Americans to take part in the war and denying to both sides the use of American soil. Because of the help that France had given during the American Revolution, public sentiment was strongly in favor of France. In Richmond a French military victory was celebrated in Capitol Square with three barrels of gunpowder. When the French government dispatched

2. Nathan Schachner, *Thomas Jefferson: A Biography*, 2 vols. (New York: Appleton-Century-Crofts, 1951), 1:420.

Edmond Genet as its ambassador, he was greeted with enthusiastic demonstrations from the time he arrived in Charleston onward. Intoxicated by his reception, however, Citizen Genet overplayed his hand, openly flouting the provisions of the neutrality statute and appealing to the people over the President's head. Realizing that the ultimate result was sure to discredit the Republicans, Jefferson wrote to the American minister in France, Gouverneur Morris, instructing him to maneuver for the Frenchman's recall.

In 1794 the English fleet began seizing American ships trading in the French West Indies, and war seemed likely. Jefferson had resigned from the State Department and had been succeeded by another Virginian, Edmund Randolph, who was even more strongly pro-French. When President Washington decided to send a special commissioner to England to negotiate a treaty that would resolve questions of disputed boundaries, debts, and West Indian trade, and named Chief Justice John Jay to the post, there was outrage in Virginia. Jefferson wrote to James Monroe that "a more degrading measure could not have been proposed. . . ." [3] The Democratic Society of Wythe County accused Washington of acting as a virtual despot; the government had "uniformly *crouched* to Britain," the society said; "Blush, Americans, for the conduct of your government!" [4] (Had it been known that Alexander Hamilton had privately tipped off the British ambassador that the United States did not really intend to push matters to a conclusion, the society would have been even more outraged.) As it was, when news of the Jay Treaty arrived home and the Senate ratified it, the Virginians and most other Americans thought they had been betrayed by the concessions to British demands. The General Assembly passed resolutions condemning the treaty. Norfolk celebrated Bastille Day, July 14, instead of the Fourth of July.

In 1797 George Washington retired from the Presidency after his second term, having the previous autumn published his Fare-

---

3. Schachner, *Thomas Jefferson*, 2:565.
4. Nathan Schachner, *The Founding Fathers* (New York: G. P. Putnam's Sons, 1954), p. 323.

well Address, written by Hamilton, in which he urged Americans to avoid permanent alliance with foreign powers and cautioned against the baneful development of party politics. John Adams was elected to succeed him. Had it not been for the presence of the Squire of Mount Vernon in the office of the President during the new nation's first eight years, it might not have survived. But George Washington, who had won the war for independence and had shown himself to place his country's welfare above all else, provided all Americans, whatever their sectional or economic allegiances, with a symbol of integrity and disinterested patriotism that proved superior to the potentialities for division and chaos. It was Thomas Jefferson whose estimate was most appropriate: "Perhaps the strongest feature in his character was prudence, never acting until every circumstance, every consideration, was maturely weighed; refraining when he saw a doubt, but, when once decided, going through with his purpose whatever obstacles opposed. His integrity was most pure, his justice the most inflexible I have ever known, no motives or interest or consanguinity, of friendship or hatred, being able to bias his decision. He was indeed, in every sense of the words, a wise, a good and a great man. . . ." [5]

America's public opinion, which had favored France over England at the time of the Jay Treaty, had soon veered in the opposite direction when in 1796 three American envoys sent to France to negotiate a treaty were asked to pay a bribe to the government in Paris in return for French friendship. The United States was swept by a wave of resentment. Congress revoked treaties with France. A navy department was created, and an army of 10,000 men organized, with Washington as nominal commander and Hamilton as his second in command. American warships began capturing and sinking French warships in an undeclared naval war.

The Jeffersonian Republicans were deeply embarrassed, and the embarrassment changed to outrage when in 1798 the Federalist-dominated Congress enacted laws empowering the President to deport "such aliens as he shall judge dangerous

5. Randolph, ed., *Papers of Thomas Jefferson*, 4:235–236.

to the peace and safety of the United States'' and to imprison and
fine anyone who ''shall write, print, utter, or publish, or shall
cause or procure to be written, printed, uttered, or published
any false, scandalous, and malicious writing or writings'' against
the government, the Congress or the President. Even Alexander
Hamilton felt the measures went much too far, while John Marshall, staunch Federalist though he was, publicly condemned the
legislation. Three of the nine Virginia congressmen, however,
voted for the laws, and George Washington, having suffered
virulent abuse by anti-Federalist editors during his tenure as
President, was all for the legislation, declaring that opposition
was intended only ''to torture, and to disturb the public
mind. . . .'' [6]

The vice-president of the United States, Thomas Jefferson,
thought differently. Together with James Madison, James
Monroe, the aged Edmund Pendleton, John Taylor of Caroline,
William Branch Giles, and other Virginia Republicans, he
began mapping out a strategy to defeat the laws and to turn
them into a Republican weapon in the presidential election of
1800. Jefferson penned a series of resolutions, which declared
that the states had granted the federal government certain specific powers through the compact of a Constitution, reserving all
others to themselves, and that ''whenever the general government assumes undelegated powers, it acts are unauthoritative,
void, and of no force.'' The resolves denounced the Alien and
Sedition acts in detail, called for the states to set up committees
of correspondence such as had existed before the Revolution,
and declared that the states had the natural right ''to nullify of
their own authority all assumptions of power by others within
their limits.'' The authorship of the resolutions was kept a secret. James Madison, meanwhile, worked up a set of similar
resolutions, which John Taylor introduced in the Virginia House
of Delegates; Madison's were milder in tone, so far as prescrib-
ing state action went, and he also persuaded Jefferson to tone

6. John Alexander Carroll and Mary Wells Ashworth, *George Washington*, vol. 7,
First in Peace, March 1794–December 1799 (New York: Charles Scribner's Sons,
1957), p. 539.

down his proposal that the states should unite to put down illegal authority on the part of the national government. As it happened, however, John Breckenridge removed the section proposing nullification from the Kentucky Resolves, while John Taylor strengthened the wording of Madison's draft for Virginia by inserting the words "null" and "void."

It was President John Adams who managed to defuse the crisis. Against the violent objections of Hamilton and other Federalists who wanted war and military glory, Adams determined to avoid conflict with France, and appointed an envoy extraordinary to work out a settlement. The Federalists were dismayed; the Republicans were overjoyed. Only a few Federalists, including John Marshall of Virginia, approved of the President's resolute courage. His party was divided, at odds, and for the moment more angry at their titular leader than at the Jeffersonians.

The tide was now turning in favor of the Jeffersonian Republicans, and it was helped along by Federalist excesses. The Sedition Law in particular was employed with such brazen disregard for free speech that people were revolted. As the election of 1800 neared, Virginia, as Noble E. Cunningham, Jr., wrote, was "the bulwark of [Jeffersonian] Republicanism. The Virginia delegation in Congress had always formed the backbone of the party in Congress, and Virginia had supplied the ablest leaders of the party. To Virginia leaders, Republicans throughout the nation looked for direction." [7] The campaign was hard fought and incredibly bitter. Jefferson was viciously attacked; in particular the clergy of the northeast assailed the author of the Virginia Statute for Religious Freedom as an infidel and atheist who would destroy religion and morality in the United States. In New York Aaron Burr, the Republican nominee for vice-president, was able to outgeneral Hamilton and deliver that state's votes to the Jeffersonian ticket. Virginia went solidly for Jefferson. Finally, on December 2, 1800, the legislature of South Carolina decided in favor of all eight of the

7. Noble E. Cunningham, Jr., *The Jeffersonian Republicans: The Formation of Party Organization, 1789–1801* (Chapel Hill: University of North Carolina Press, 1957), p. 149.

Jeffersonian Republican electors, and Thomas Jefferson of Virginia was elected as the third President of the United States.

Or was he? For the electoral college arrangements at that time made no distinction between votes for president and vice-president, and Jefferson and Burr each had 73 votes. The Federalists controlled a majority of states' votes in the House, which would make the choice, and could thus determine which of their opponents was to be President. Alexander Hamilton, who detested Burr even more than he detested Jefferson, fought to have the Federalists select Jefferson. A Maryland congressman warned that if the will of the electorate was thwarted by the Federalists, Virginia would "instantly proclaim herself out of the Union." [8] This was unlikely, but Governor James Monroe of Virginia announced that he intended to keep the General Assembly in constant session and to install a chain of expresses between the new national capitol at Washington and Richmond to get word on any Federalist action. Jefferson remained calm. Ultimately on February 17, 1801, on the thirty-sixth ballot, the Federalist ranks broke; and Jefferson's election was validated.

Political campaigning was not the only concern of Virginians that year of 1800. At the end of August word came from Richmond that sent cold chills throughout the state and, indeed, all regions of the nation with slave populations. On the morning of Saturday, August 30, two slaves reported to their owner, Mosby Sheppard, that a slave insurrection was being planned for that night; all whites in the neighborhood were to be killed and Richmond seized. Sheppard alerted Governor James Monroe, who called out militia to guard the city, the penitentiary, the arsenal, and to patrol roads leading into town. The patrols noted one odd circumstance: instead of the blacks flocking into town as was their custom on Saturdays, every black seen on the road was heading away from the city.

That afternoon a tremendous thunderstorm broke over the area, swelling most of the streams and creeks until they were impassable. It was apparently this circumstance that made it impossible for many hundreds of slaves to gather as planned,

8. Schachner, *Thomas Jefferson,* 2:654.

collect the crude spears, pikes, bayonets, and a few muskets which had been made and concealed for them, and march upon Richmond.

Arrests were made, hundreds of blacks rounded up and questioned, and the full story began to emerge. Under the leadership of Gabriel, a huge young slave belonging to Thomas Prosser of Henrico County, more than a thousand blacks in the area were going to strike for their freedom.

Some fifty active conspirators were taken by police. Ultimately Gabriel himself was captured aboard a boat in Norfolk. Some forty blacks were eventually executed. Many others who had been arrested were later freed. Governor Monroe sought and obtained legislative authority to deport and sell slaves convicted of complicity in the revolt.

In 1802 Thomas Jefferson proposed that in the future slaves suspected of conspiracy be deported to Africa. In words that echoed his remarks in *Notes on the State of Virginia,* he wrote "They are not felons, or common malefactors, but persons guilty of what the Safety of Society, under actual circumstances, obliges us to treat as a crime, but which their feelings may represent in a far different shape. They are such as will be a valuable acquisition to the settlement already existing there. . . ." [9] For as David Mays has remarked, "Gabriel had dared to fight for freedom with the very words of 'death or liberty,' consciously or otherwise reversing the cry of Patrick Henry. But Henry's oratory was not meant for slaves." [10]

No free black man had been implicated in Gabriel's conspiracy, but there followed a host of laws aimed at restricting that class, whose continuing presence in the state obviously constituted an implicit refutation of the very premises on which slavery was based. Freed blacks remained an important part of the Virginia scene, however; in 1810 approximately one in ten blacks in the state was a free man.

In Congress President Jefferson enjoyed a firm Republican

---

9. Jefferson to Rufus King, July 13, 1802. Quoted in Fawn M. Brodie, *Thomas Jefferson: An Intimate History* (New York: Bantam Books, 1975), p. 456.

10. Mays, *Edmund Pendleton,* 2:329.

majority. Virginia gave him solid support: of its nineteen representatives, only one was a Federalist. The Virginia congressional delegation was headed by the brilliant, erratic John Randolph of Roanoke, who was named chairman of the House
Ways and Means Committee, and by William Branch Giles, an
enthusiastic Jeffersonian Republican who later was elevated to
the Senate.

Another Virginian proved to be Jefferson's most formidable
obstacle. John Marshall had been named Chief Justice in January 1801, and in the waning weeks of Adams's administration
he and Adams had taken advantage of the Judiciary Act of 1801
to appoint a substantial number of Federalists as judges and justices of the peace. These had been confirmed by the Federalist
Senate, but many had not yet taken oaths of office, and their
commissions awaited signature when Jefferson took over. The
new President declined to honor what he considered those
"midnight appointments." One of the thwarted appointees sued
to compel delivery of his commission. In 1802, in the famous
decision of *Marbury* v. *Madison,* Marshall used the opportunity
to assert the power of the Supreme Court to rule on the constitutionality of acts of Congress. The province and duty of the
Court, he declared, was to determine what the law is, and to
decide that "a law repugnant to the Constitution is void, and
that courts, as well as other departments, are bound by that instrument."

Though such doctrine was anathema to the strict constructionists among the Virginians, early in Jefferson's administration they faced a situation in which the welfare and future prospects of the United States depended upon the President's
willingness to set aside his scruples and use his executive powers decisively and without regard for niceties of constitutionality. In 1803 Napoleon Bonaparte offered to sell the entire
Louisiana Territory to the United States for a price of about fifteen million dollars. But nowhere did the Constitution specifi-
cally authorize the national government to acquire new territory,
and good Virginia strict constructionists such as Jefferson believed in a scrupulous adherence to the literal language of the
Constitution.

Jefferson decided to go ahead anyway. John Randolph, as chairman of the House Ways and Means Committee, backed him. It was unconstitutional, but immediate action was needed before Napoleon changed his mind. A few Federalists in the Senate raised objections, but consent was given at once, and the House, under Randolph's leadership, voted the money for the purchase, and Louisiana belonged to the United States. Virginia strict constructionists had acted to secure for their country a domain stretching from the Gulf of Mexico to the Great Lakes, and from the Mississippi River to the Rocky Mountains and beyond—nobody was quite sure just where the boundaries were.

Even before Napoleon's offer to sell, Jefferson had secured a secret appropriation from Congress to fit out an expedition to explore all the way to the Pacific and to gather geographical data and information about Indian trade prospects. To head it, he selected his private secretary, Meriwether Lewis, a Virginia neighbor with experience in Indian fighting. Lewis asked another Virginian, William Clark, younger brother of George Rogers Clark and also an experienced frontiersman, to join him; and with four dozen men they set out from St. Louis in the spring of 1804. Eventually they scaled the Rocky Mountains, followed the Columbia River to the Pacific Ocean, and returned to St. Louis in September of 1806.

Jefferson's re-election in 1804 was a foregone conclusion. This time, however, there was a new vice-president—George Clinton of New York. Aaron Burr had been dropped by his party and then defeated for renomination in New York as well. After his duel with Alexander Hamilton at Weehawken in April 1804 resulted in Hamilton's death, Burr became a fugitive from justice. Eventually he became involved with the double-dealing General James Wilkinson in a vague but apparently quite serious conspiracy to detach the western areas of the United States from the Union and, possibly with British protection, to set up a separate confederacy. Betrayed by Wilkinson, however, Burr was ultimately arrested near Pensacola, Florida, and brought to Richmond for trial before the U. S. Circuit Court.

The trial was held in the state capitol in June 1807, and it soon developed into a confrontation between President Jefferson and Chief Justice Marshall, who presided. Ultimately Marshall came up with a complicated ruling establishing a definition of treason that virtually destroyed most of the prosecution's case, and the jury brought in a verdict that Burr had not been "proved to be guilty under this indictment by any evidence submitted to us." [11]

By the end of Jefferson's second term, the consensus that had marked his administration was crumbling. The leadership of Virginia in the national councils was resented in the northeast: "May the dominion of Virginia be limited by the Constitution," went one of the toasts at a Federalist dinner in Boston in 1804, "or at least by the Delaware." [12] In Virginia itself, the erratic John Randolph was leading what was beginning to take shape as a movement of discontented Republicans who, while they held no brief whatever for northern mercantile and shipping interests, were impatient with what they saw as a growing tendency of the Jefferson administration to advance the role and power of the national government at the expense of the states.

The Jeffersonians, with the base of their power in the south and the west, favored policies which would draw the two sections more closely together. When it was proposed, however, to build a road from Cumberland, Maryland, to Wheeling, Virginia, which would have opened up the trans-Ohio and western Virginia to easy access to the Chesapeake Bay community, only one of twelve Virginia congressmen voted for the bill providing for the survey. Tidewater Virginia in particular, fearing that the development of the western areas would endanger its still-dominant position within the state, wanted the west left alone to develop as it could, without help from the national administration.

It was relationships with the European powers that proved most vexing during Jefferson's second term. Britain, fighting for its life against Napoleon, sought to prevent American vessels from trading with the French West Indies and began inter-

11. Dabney, *Virginia*, p. 199.

12. Thomas P. Abernethy, *The South in the New Nation, 1789–1819* (Baton Rouge: Louisiana State University Press, 1961), pp. 307–308.

cepting such ships on the high seas, confiscating their cargoes and impressing British-born crewmen into service in the Royal Navy. Jefferson's considered response to the situation, and to the British order in council prohibiting American ships from trading with any port hostile to England, was to call for an embargo on all American foreign trade. Norfolk and Portsmouth were hard hit; trade came to a standstill. Shipping interests in the northeastern states were scathing in their denunciations of Jefferson and his party; there was considerable talk of nullification. After fourteen months Jefferson and the Congress agreed upon an end to the embargo. William Branch Giles introduced a bill in the Senate calling for repeal except for trade with England and France, which was passed by the Senate and the House, and the outgoing President signed the repealer three days before retiring from office.

In Virginia a vigorous attempt was led by John Randolph to block the succession of Secretary of State James Madison to the Presidency, in favor of James Monroe. Though Monroe received substantial support in the Tidewater, Madison won the state's entire electoral vote; the Father of the Constitution was handily elected to succeed the author of the Declaration of Independence as fourth President of the United States of America.

6

The End of an Era

In which the Virginians furnish two more presidents,
and meanwhile go into a decline.

T was with undisguised pleasure that Jefferson departed from Washington a week after Madison's inauguration, bound for his beloved Albemarle County home. Though deeply in debt and facing an uncertain and precarious financial future, he was content to be at Monticello. He stayed there for the rest of his life. Dissidents like John Randolph might call him "Saint Thomas of Cantingbury," and Federalists damn him for "a coward, a calumniator, a plagiarist, a tame, spiritless animal" (to quote the editor of the *New England Palladium*),[1] but no living American possessed more of the confidence, respect, and love of the vast majority of Americans than did he. Long after his death, his name would continue to possess political lure. To be a Jeffersonian in politics was close to a requisite for future generations of Virginia politicians. Conservatives would invoke his name as justification for decentralized government and states' rights, strict interpretation of the Constitution, a minimum of government interference in business, and the general proposition that that government governs best which gov-

1. Quoted in Brodie, *An Intimate History,* p. 500.

erns least. Liberals would note his championship of human
rights, his unswerving devotion to free speech and a free press,
his hatred of entrenched economic and social privilege and injustice, and his faith in a democratic society. As Guy Friddell
expressed it recently in an imaginary "Letter to Jefferson,"
"There is much conjecture on how you would stand on issues of
civil rights and the imbalance between the State and the Federal
government. (You would be astonished at the power accumulated in the central government, and your old adversary,
Alexander Hamilton, would be aghast at the social uses in
which it is employed.)" [2]

Jefferson's chosen successor as President, James Madison,
found that the embargo on exports, even in its modified form,
was no guarantee of peace. The pressure for a declaration of
war against England grew. The Virginia General Assembly memorialized Congress in favor of a declaration of war, though
Federalist areas in the Shenandoah Valley were strongly opposed, as was the *Tertium Quid* States' Rights element in the
Tidewater, led by John Randolph, who warned that war and invasion might bring slave rebellion. "The night-bell never tolls
for fire in Richmond," he declared, "that the mother does not
hug the infant more closely to her bosom. I have been a witness
to scenes of alarm in the capital of Virginia." [3] It was a
Virginia-born congressman from Kentucky, Henry Clay, who
together with John C. Calhoun of South Carolina led the prowar
movement. Born in Hanover County in 1777 in an area known
as The Slashes, Clay had been a protégé of George Wythe in
Richmond and studied law with Attorney General Robert
Brooke of Virginia before moving to Kentucky shortly after it
became a state. As speaker of the House of Representatives he
now championed the invasion of Canada and a peace dictated
from Quebec.

Things did not, however, go well. The conquest of Canada,
which even Thomas Jefferson thought would be a mere matter

2. Guy Friddell, *We Began at Jamestown* . . . (Richmond: Dietz Press, 1968),
p. 110.
3. Abernethy, *South in the New Nation,* p. 406.

of marching, failed, and though William Henry Harrison won a victory that secured the frontier against the Indians, and Winfield Scott, another Virginian, won military laurels at Chippewa and Lundy's Lane, the war soon became a matter of defending American soil rather than annexing that belonging to Britain. In 1813 a British fleet under Admiral Sir George Cockburn showed up in Chesapeake Bay. In June the British staged an amphibious assault on Craney Island, just off Willoughby Spit at the entrance to Hampton Roads, but were driven off with considerable loss. The attackers then turned their attentions to the town of Hampton, across the Roadstead, and having dispatched the small defending force, proceeded to burn, loot, kill, and even rape, in the best Continental military fashion.

The following year, after defeating a stubborn but undisciplined militia force at Bladensburg, Maryland, a British army marched into Washington, where it burned the public buildings. Fearing an invasion of Virginia, Governor Barbour called for militia, and so many thousands responded that there were not facilities to shelter them. The invaders turned northward instead, and were decisively repulsed at Baltimore, while another invasion from Canada was halted at the Battle of Plattsburg, New York. By this time the British were willing to discuss peace, and a treaty was signed at Ghent on Christmas Eve of 1814.

It was the Norfolk area that suffered most acutely from the War of 1812. The British blockade severely cut into its commerce, and when in 1813 the American government enacted a total embargo of all shipping, its carrying trade was almost completely stagnated. Richmond underwent considerably less hardship from the war catastrophe. The shutting off of imports from England gave a boost to the city's manufactures, and its role as a commercial center for the upper Southeast was enhanced.

Why, one wonders, did Richmond not develop into the major manufacturing and transportation center that it might well have been? And why did Norfolk not become a great port city that could keep pace with Baltimore, Philadelphia, New York, and Boston? The state had abundant coal and iron deposits. It pos-

sessed river systems into the interior. In Hampton Roads it had
the largest and most accessible deepwater seaport on the eastern
seaboard. Furthermore, its ties with the transmontane regions of
the upper South and the Midwest were of long standing. Kentucky, Tennessee, Ohio, Illinois, Indiana—these states had been
opened up for settlement by Virginians, and their population
was heavily Virginian in origin. Virginia was already manufacturing a large supply of the nation's homespun cotton goods.
Why did New England, and not Virginia, become the great tex-
tile-producing area for the nation?

Virginia had always been an agricultural commonwealth, but
then so had the remainder of the seaboard states. The leadership
of Virginia, however, had been and continued to be the
planters. Washington, Pendleton, Mason, Jefferson, Madison,
Monroe—all these were landed gentry. The great Virginia
statesmen of the nation's beginning years were practical men,
sensible politicians, and no dogmatists. While in positions of
power, therefore, they realized that if their beloved Old Dominion was to grow and flourish, and to continue its leadership of
the Union, it could not stand still, but must change with the
times. (Afterwards, in retirement, they sometimes tended to
become more doctrinaire.) Their convictions, though deeply
held, did not make them rigid in their reliance upon precedent
and tradition. "I like the dreams of the future better than the
history of the past," Jefferson wrote to John Adams.[4]

Yet so far as flexibility, adaptability, receptivity to new ideas,
and willingness to change were concerned, by the late 1810s the
day of Jefferson and Madison in Virginia was done. The only
way that Virginia could have maintained its growth and its role
was to accept the need to keep up and enhance its economic and
political ties with the emerging west, and to buttress the Jeffersonian dream of a republic of farmers with the commerce and
manufacture necessary to maintain it and keep it healthy and
thriving. There was talk to that effect in the nationalistic excitement just after the War of 1812. "Must the productions of our

4. Lester J. Cappon ed., *The Adams-Jefferson Letters,* 2 vols. (Chapel Hill: University of North Carolina Press, 1959), 2:485.

soil be continually subject to obstructions on the way to market?'' asked Thomas Ritchie in the *Richmond Enquirer*. ''Must our want of internal communication forever remain the laughingstock of strangers and the reproach of our citizens? Where are the public *schools* which we have erected, the *colleges* which Virginia has endowed? Let us seize this precious moment and devote it to *Internal Improvement*. Now is the time for Virginia to extend her character and preserve her influence in the union.'' [5]

It was not to be. While Washington, Jefferson, Madison, and their generation were giving direction to the new nation, back at home their own native state had been changing its economic and social posture. The long descent into agricultural stagnation, the symptoms of which were already evident in the 1760s and 1770s, had had its effect. Tobacco prices remained more or less at their same low level from the early 1790s onward. With so much of their capital bound up in land and slaves, the Virginia planters were tied to an increasingly unprofitable and inefficient system.

Even more debilitating than the economic effects of the system was the accompanying social and political desuetude. From being the single most vital, creative, innovative force in the new nation's councils, Virginia now seemed to be drifting into a stagnation of mind and spirit. The direction of the political destiny of Virginia, once so bold and imaginative, had become narrow and constrained. For Jefferson and Madison in the 1790s, strict construction of the U.S. Constitution had been a means for preventing the financial establishment of the eastern seaboard from using the central government to thwart the needs and aspirations of the rural American majority. Now strict construction came to mean something entirely different: a way of preserving the ruling planter faction's control over state government and of blocking the prospects and aspirations of the non-slaveholding majority in western Virginia.

Had Virginia's representatives in Congress given support to the plan to develop a canal connecting the Potomac River with

5. Abernethy, *South in the New Nation*, pp. 424–425.

the Ohio at Wheeling, in western Virginia, the Hampton Roads
area would have been a major ocean terminus for the trade of
the Midwest, with Alexandria an important transfer point. But
that would have required federal funds, and Richmond would
have lost ground to Alexandria and Norfolk, so Virginia instead
backed the James and Kanawha Canal, without funds to develop
it properly, and the opportunity was lost forever. Later, when
the railroads came along in the late 1820s and 1830s, merchants
in Baltimore quickly pushed the Baltimore and Ohio Railroad
westward to tap the trade of the Midwest. Virginia not only did
not follow suit, but sought to keep the B&O even from crossing
Virginia territory.

In education the picture was as unpromising and as unimagi-
native. When Jefferson had led the fight to break up the domination of the old aristocracy by the abolition of primogeniture, he
had proposed an ambitious system of public education, culminating at the college level. Education was fundamental to his
hopes and his aims for his state and his country: no republic
could hold onto its freedom, he declared repeatedly, without an
educated citizenry. Not until 1810, however, was a fund for
schools—known as the Literary Fund—set up to educate the
children of the poor; the notion of public schools for all was out
of the question. As late as 1850, Virginia's system of public education combined had the smallest proportion of whites in
school of any nonfrontier state in the Union.

The one glory of Virginia education during this period, and
the capstone of Thomas Jefferson's career, was the new state
university at Charlottesville. Jefferson drew up plans for the
proposed buildings; he staked out the grounds himself, made a
survey, and designed a two-story building fronting a range of
pavilions, drawing upon classical models but simplified to his
own taste. He drew up administrative rules and a course of instruction. To provide a faculty he searched in America and
abroad for the most qualified scholars. His path was not easy,
for members of the clergy, in particular the Presbyterians, attacked him at every stage, fearing that the "godless, atheis-
tical" Jefferson would create a university dedicated to the destruction of religion in Virginia. Finally, in March of 1825, Mr.

Jefferson's university began its work, with an elective curriculum revolutionary for its time.

So Thomas Jefferson had his university, but at a cruel cost. Much of the money for it came out of the Literary Fund, which had been set up for the public education of the poor. For its colleges, Virginia had money; for public schools, no money was forthcoming. A writer on education in 1825 put his finger on the underlying problem when he declared that too many Virginians "considered the education of the poor as of no importance. The slaves they looked upon as the persons who are to perform the chief part of the labor necessary in society, and their masters as the persons who are to be our politicians, our lawyers, our physicians, and our merchants, but the poor are a supernumerary class, of little use in society, and deserving of but little attention." [6]

With agricultural depression, little or no effort by the state to create or encourage internal improvements that would make farming more profitable in the west, a government dominated by a planter oligarchy and denying the suffrage to half its potential voters, and almost no opportunity for public education except in certain of the cities, the Virginia of the post-Jeffersonian years was hardly a place of opportunity for the farmer without land or slaves, and the result was a steady exodus of population from the state. Virginia lost great numbers of citizens, and her population rank dropped steadily—in 1810 there were twenty-three congressmen from Virginia, but by 1860 the state was allotted only ten seats. By the year 1850, no fewer than 388,000 former citizens of Virginia (as well as hundreds of thousands who were black and therefore not citizens) were living in other states, and as Virginius Dabney says, they included thousands of her "ablest and most adventurous sons and daughters." [7]

By no means all of them were the sons and daughters of the landless poor. Even for a young man of good family and education, there was a paucity of opportunity in a generally static eco-

6. J. L. Blair Buck, *The Development of Public Schools in Virginia, 1607–1952* (Richmond: State Board of Education, 1952), p. 35.

7. Dabney, *Virginia*, p. 275.

nomic situation, and such a young man was apt to move west-ward in hopes of better prospects. One such was Joseph Glover Baldwin, who in his *Flush Times of Alabama and Mississippi* chronicled with much humor the vicissitudes the Virginians encountered in the newly opened territories of Alabama and Mississippi. Another such was John Marshall Clemens, also educated as a lawyer, who left the family homestead near Bedford, Virginia, for Kentucky, Tennessee, and finally Missouri, where in 1835 his son Samuel Langhorne Clemens was born. To have come from Virginia stock was a mark of distinction in the Deep South and the West. "In Missouri," wrote Mark Twain about the Judge Driscoll of *Pudd'nhead Wilson,* a figure very much like his own father, "a recognized superiority attached to any person who hailed from Old Virginia; and this superiority was exalted to supremacy when a person of such nativity could also prove descent from the First Families of that great commonwealth. . . ." [8]

The business panic of 1819 hit the declining economy of Virginia with great severity, and thereafter the state was caught in a prolonged depression. As the revenue from agriculture declined, and rural and urban properties were mortgaged and sold, the one most valuable asset of many a Virginia planter was his black slaves. In the Deep South, as the cotton culture spread, labor was needed badly. The result was that in the decade of the 1830s alone, the state of Virginia exported 118,000 slaves, for millions of dollars. The spectacle of the Old Dominion, the commonwealth which had given the nation its Declaration of Independence, its Constitution, and four of its first five presidents, having now fallen so low as to depend upon the slave trade for its financial survival was a source of much distress to many Virginians. Thus Thomas Jefferson Randolph, grandson of the third President, declared to the General Assembly in 1832 that "it is a practice, and an increasing practice in parts of Virginia, to rear slaves for the market. How can an honorable mind, a patriot, and a lover of his country, bear to see this ancient domin-

8. Mark Twain, *The Tragedy of Pudd'nhead Wilson and the Comedy Those Extraordinary Twins* (Hartford, Conn.: American Publishing Co., 1894), p. 156.

ion, rendered illustrious by the noble devotion and patriotism of her sons in the cause of liberty, converted into one grand menagerie where men are to be reared for market like oxen for the shambles?'' [9]

The end of Virginia's national leadership was signalized in 1825 when James Monroe was succeeded as President of the United States by John Quincy Adams. For the first time in two dozen years a Virginian would not occupy the White House, and, more importantly, the candidate that Virginia had backed, William H. Crawford of Georgia, a native of the Old Dominion, had been defeated, and in large part by the votes of states which had hitherto followed Virginia's leadership. In Charles S. Sydnor's summation, ''Virginia was in no position to regain its lost power. Its political leadership during the campaign had been inept and conservative; the spirit of revolt had entered its former satellites, making them unwilling longer to 'continue to drag along in the trail of Virginia'; and the new democratic movement found its strength and leaders south and west of the Old Dominion.'' [10]

On July 4, 1826, Thomas Jefferson died. His last years had been passed under grave financial crisis, but he had managed to maintain possession of his beloved Monticello. He had maintained his longtime friendship with James Madison, and though there had been a rift between him and Monroe, it was patched over, and now that all three of the triumvirate had come back to live in Piedmont Virginia, occasionally the citizens of Charlottesville were treated to the sight of three ex-Presidents of the United States seated together at a tavern discussing the problems of the nation.

Jefferson's onetime fast friendship with John Adams had been resumed, and the two old men commenced what both had long wished: a lengthy exchange of correspondence, lasting for the remainder of their lives. As George Dangerfield says, ''The

9. Joseph Clarke Robert, *The Road from Monticello: A Study of the Virginia Slavery Debate of 1832* (Durham, N.C.: Duke University Press, 1941), p. 97.

10. Charles S. Sydnor, *The Development of Southern Sectionalism, 1819–1848* (Baton Rouge: Louisiana State University Press, 1948), p. 175.

magic of this correspondence lies in the fact that it is almost the only occasion upon which the early American dream of unique republican virtue, uniquely residing in the United States of America, becomes reality. Here it is—with all its wisdom, its toleration, its amplitude, its fresh and astringent individualism—an actual and palpable event." [11]

It had been many years now since Jefferson's spirit had prevailed in Virginia. The leading public figures—John Randolph, Judge Spencer Roane, John Taylor of Caroline, James Barbour, Benjamin Watkins Leigh, Abel Parker Upshur, John Tyler— were men of conservative principles and essentially defensive minds. Like their predecessors they too were strict constructionists of the Constitution, but in their hands the assertion of state supremacy was directed at ends very different from those of Jefferson and Madison. For the central government to encroach upon state prerogatives was dangerous now, not because it might threaten the liberties of the people, but because it might endanger property rights, especially those in human property.

The precipitous decline in Virginia leadership and in the Old Dominion's place in the nation was clear for all to see, and was freely remarked by its politicians. Abel Parker Upshur, the Eastern Shore conservative who emerged in the 1820s as a powerful political force, asked the question, "Why should Virginia, hitherto distinguished alike for the soundness of her views and the greatness of her talents, sink to the second or third rank in the [American] Confederacy?" [12] But the answers he and his contemporaries gave—moral degeneracy, the tariff, the decline of true patriotism, the rising emphasis upon mere moneymaking— were, like Randolph's lament above, versions of the *Ubi sunt* requiem for simpler and nobler times that is always voiced at such a juncture. They blamed the pernicious effects of the protective tariff, which discriminated against the Virginia agriculturalist in favor of the northeastern manufacturer, which was

11. George Dangerfield, *The Era of Good Feelings* (New York: Harcourt, Brace, 1952), p. 383.
12. Claude H. Hall, *Abel Parker Upshur: Conservative Virginian, 1790–1844* (Madison: State Historical Society of Wisconsin, 1964), p. 32.

true, but not the point: for the true issue was why Virginia had not developed its commercial and political ties to the west as Washington and Jefferson had wanted, and thus bound its fate in with the future rather than the past, had allowed its interests to remain static and thus to become so narrow and constricted that change of any sort threatened its increasingly precarious economic stability.

It is easy to look at the political leaders of post-Jeffersonian and pre-Civil War Virginia and to remark the relative narrowness, the lack of stature, the failure of nerve that characterize them in comparison with their great predecessors. But these men were victims of a situation, by no means principally of their own making, that militated against precisely the imaginativeness, disinterested national patriotism, and boldness of conception that they are charged with generally failing to exhibit. It had not been necessary for an earlier generation of Virginians to measure every policy and every strategy against the yardstick of its possibly deleterious effect upon a slave economy. But in their time and place, the later leaders were bound in ways that the Jeffersonians had not been; and more and more they were forced onto the defensive, and their moves and tactics had to be in the nature of a response to the initiatives of others. What Virginia had been, it no longer was; and so what Virginians could once be was no longer possible.

It was the constitutional convention of 1829–1830 that demonstrated the extent to which Virginia conservatives were engaged in a holding action. Western Virginia had been expanding rapidly in the 1820s. Reformers pressed for abolition of the Council of State, representation by white population totals only, extension of suffrage to leaseholders as well as property holders and to all heads of families who paid state taxes, voting by ballot rather than viva voce, legislative reapportionment every twenty years, a governor and other state officials chosen by popular election, elected judges, and reform of the county-court system. The debate was long and often heated. It was, in Claude H. Hall's estimate, ''a struggle between aristocracy and democracy, between those who believed that the best government could be provided by an intelligent, propertied oligarchy and those who professed faith in the principle that popular rule meant justice and equality, not anarchy.'' [13]

The outcome was a revised constitution with only moderate reforms. Nothing really important was changed. The east had won, and remained in power in Virginia.

Meanwhile, life went on. If the Old Dominion was not thriving, if east of the mountains a decline had set in, it was a very gentle, even genteel decline, and in the short if perhaps not the long run, still comfortable enough. The Virginia of the first half of the nineteenth century remained vastly rural; its cities and towns were small and served as trading centers for a life that from the sea to the mountains was centered in agriculture. Virginians lived on farms and plantations. There were few really large estates, many small ones—average acreage for a farm in 1850 was 340. By far the most typical Virginia farmer owned no slaves at all; he worked in the fields with his family.

It was a somewhat remote, self-sufficient life. Roads were few and very poor. Mails were infrequent and slow; it took a while for the news to penetrate into the countryside. Visitors were welcome—hospitality was a byword for the state; and there was much visiting around among the planter families. The courthouse was the center of life in each county; there supplies were purchased, business was transacted, politics was argued. The Virginia gentleman was intensely, if often affably, political; politics was his avocation, and he took it seriously, subscribed to his favorite newspaper, which reflected his own views—Thomas Ritchie's *Enquirer,* voice of the Democracy, or John Hampden Pleasants's *Whig,* in the area centered on Richmond. Churchgoing was an important activity—the Episcopal and Presbyterian churches remained for the most part the affiliations of the gentry, though the Methodists had made considerable advances, and the Baptists flourished as well. In the Valley there were numerous Lutherans, and also many Mennonites.

Status was important; in a society with a property qualification for voting, family and connections mattered. There was still, in antebellum Virginia, something of the old assumption

13. Hall, *Abel Parker Upshur,* p. 32.

that lucrative public offices and seats in the legislature were the perquisite of the gentry, who, however, had to win and retain the confidence of the voter. But the gentry was a numerous clan, and providing one were of "good family," one might be of widely varying economic status.

For politics the Virginian cared intensely; for the belles-lettres and the fine arts, not so very much. The lady of the house read novels, to be sure, but the gentleman generally concentrated upon the public press. Hunting and fishing were far more to his liking and, in Northern Virginia especially, the breeding and racing of horses. In the summertime, the gentry traveled to the mountain springs: the Warm, the Hot, the White Sulphur, the Salt Sulphur, the Red Sulphur, the Sweet Chalybeate, others—it was fashionable to make the rounds seriatim, taking the waters for their supposed medicinal benefits, and also escaping the fetid lowland heat during yellow-fever season. One began the circuit at the White, since in Percival Renier's description, "Nature herself had arranged the springs in order for their best action on the human system, and it was Nature's inscrutable purpose that the bowels of the ailing should have the White Sulphur purge first of all." [14]

Yet, for all the fashionable vacationing in the mountains, this must be said for the Virginians, or for a good many of them: they did not go in for ostentation or show. They did not flaunt their money (few had much to flaunt). And they did not reckon things by the dollar or the gross, for if they had wealth, or had once had it in the family, they had learned over the generations to value other and more comfortable things.

In Renier's words, "the Virginian liked to think of himself as a plain and homespun-appearing gentleman with a noble pedigree, which naturally put him above airs and snobbery and fine clothes and turnouts." [15] Not only was he unspoiled, but he made a point of looking, dressing, and acting the part, even to the conscious use of country ways of speech. Or as George W.

14. Percival Reniers, *The Springs of Virginia: Life, Love, and Death at the Waters, 1775–1900* (Chapel Hill: University of North Carolina Press, 1941), p. 28.
15. Reniers, *Springs of Virginia*, p. 143.

Bagby wrote of himself in personification of the old-time rural Virginian, "It will be a sad day for us when there is any regularity about anything in Virginia. . . . I don't want to live among no sich people. I want to go whar I kin build my house catty-cornered, lop-sided, slantingdicular, bottom-upward, any way I please, and have no correct idea about nothing, 'cept politics." [16] At the same time, the Virginian maintained his dignity and his formality of demeanor. There was "in the depths of the Virginia character," wrote Bagby, ". . . a stratum of grave thought and feeling that not seldom sank to sadness and even gloom." [17]

Oddly enough, it is this period of plantation Virginia life—the years of the 1810s and thereafter—and not the Golden Age of planter hegemony of the decades before, that many of those who have written best and most memorably about Virginia life have seemed to find most appealing. The days of the decline, not those of Virginia's ascendency, have exercised a powerful attraction upon the literary imagination both of Virginians and others, who have seemed to find in the somewhat shabby grandeur, the run-down nobility of a not too demanding life on the land, the proper image for a life of well-ordered and moderate gentility that could serve as pastoral counterpoint to the money-making and progress of an industrializing American nation. In perhaps the most memorable of the antebellum plantation novels, *Swallow Barn* (1832), by John Pendleton Kennedy, a Marylander of Virginia family connections, there is a wry, ironic, rather wistful sense of gentle decline and fall to the Tidewater scene. *Swallow Barn* is not so much a celebration of plantation glory as a nostalgic look backward at a style of American experience that was already outmoded.

As for the other white Virginians, the plain people, they made up the bulk of the population, and if generally unchronicled by novelists before and after the Civil War, peopled the

16. George W. Bagby, "My Uncle Flatback's Plantation," in *The Old Virginia Gentleman and Other Sketches*, edited by Thomas Nelson Page (New York: Charles Scribner's Sons, 1911), p. 79.

17. Bagby, "The Old Virginia Gentleman," p. 30.

farms, towns, and villages, and managed to earn a decent if not elegant living. They grew crops of corn, sweet potatoes, cow-peas, peanuts, vegetables; they raised hogs and cattle. They went to church regularly, voted, and in general there was no major cleavage between them and their more opulent neighbors who owned slaves. In the towns and cities they made up the ar-tisans and craftsmen and storekeepers and clerks. They were "of good people"—which was and is a very different thing from being "of good family"—and for want of a better term, historians have tended to refer to them as "yeomen farmers," though few of them would have known what the adjective meant. In the Great Valley and beyond, of course, they were much in the majority, and large estates and slave-owning were very much the exception. The proportion of black to white in the upper Valley was one to five. From Pennsylvania and Mary-land down to Martinsburg, and thence southward through Win-chester, Harrisonburg, Staunton, Lexington, Buchanan, to the turn westward at Salem, ran the Great Philadelphia Wagon Road, the Valley Pike, a heavily traveled artery, macadamized very early for better transit. Along this road the Virginians of the Valley lived and generally flourished. Germans and Scotch-Irish believed in schools, and so the Valley frequently memori-alized the General Assembly to do something about the wretched state of public education.

Throughout the Alleghenys and the Blue Ridge there were also mountaineers, living a primitive life remote from towns, roads, and schools. In colonial times they had built their cabins and settled in along the ravines and branches far up in the hills, and they stuck to their old ways. For all their poverty, these had the virtues, at least, of independence; but there were also, in Tidewater and Piedmont, some thousands of white Virginians whose poverty was abject and status degraded, and who lived as the riffraff, an existence both squalid and miserable. These "clay-eaters," who would later be known as Poor Whites, were at the bottom of the social stratification, and came in for little in the way of the well-known benefits of Virginia life.

After the financial panic of 1819 and the resulting depression, the cities of Virginia slowly regained their corporate health and

growth; it was not that they did not share in the process of urbanization that was getting under way in early-nineteenth-
century America, but merely that in proportion to other cities,
their growth was slower. Richmond, for example, experienced
a sixty-five-percent increase in population between 1820 and
1840, but fell from twelfth to twentieth in the rank of American
cities. Alexandria, on the Potomac, lost out in the commercial
competition. Norfolk suffered because of economic jealousy on
the part of the fall-line cities, and failed to become the great
ocean port it might have been. Much of its trade was with eastern North Carolina. Norfolk and Portsmouth, however, were
less indifferent to the needs of public education than much of
the state; by the 1850s a thriving public school system was in
operation. "I reckon," wrote a county school commissioner,
"it may be regarded as the banner district of the State." [18] The
low-lying terrain of the area, and its proximity to swampy areas,
however, made it especially vulnerable to outbreaks of yellow
fever; there was a series of outbreaks during the antebellum
years.

Richmond was less vulnerable to yellow fever, but it had its
proper share of other diseases. During all this time, however,
Richmond was steadily growing in population: 16,060 in 1830,
and in 1860, on the eve of the Civil War, 37,968. The city's
factories and warehouses were doing a good business; Richmond was becoming a banking, milling, and mercantile center.
The Scots merchants who had thronged to the city in the late colonial period were now among Richmond's more influential citizens, and their trading houses did a widespread business. Richmond's pace was enhanced during the winter months when
planter families from the nearby countryside came in to occupy
their townhouses and share in the city's social and cultural life.

Richmond had even become something of a cultural center.
While William Wirt lived there, he was the reigning literary
light, with his *Letters of the British Spy* (1803) and other essays
and the biography of Patrick Henry (1817) in which that patriot's famed oratory was recreated or else created for the first

18. Buck, *Public Schools in Virginia*, p. 60.

time. There were various gentlemen around town who liked to dabble in verse or to compose essays. The principal literary achievement of the city, of course, was the founding, by Thomas Willis White in 1834, of a monthly magazine, *The Southern Literary Messenger*. Its lasting importance lies in the work it published by the young former resident of Richmond, Edgar Allan Poe, and the brief tenure of Poe, from August 1835 until January 1837 as assistant editor and editor, during which period he wrote a series of sometimes brilliant, sometimes wrongheaded, often caustic reviews of new books, which gave the magazine an immediate and startling national reputation. The more Poe slashed away at bad books, the more the *Messenger* attracted attention, but the proprietor, who wanted something more gentlemanly and mannered, grew increasingly embarrassed and impatient, and this, along with Poe's drinking habits, brought about a severance of the relationship. Thereafter the *Messenger* lapsed into a mediocrity that continued for most of its subsequent history.

There were, in the Virginia of the period, some writers of considerable talent. The poet-physician William Alexander Carruthers, a native of Lexington, did much to glamourize the colonial past with his novels *The Cavaliers of Virginia* (1835) and *The Knights of the Golden Horse-Shoe* (1845). The former described Bacon's Rebellion, the latter, the journey of Governor Spotswood and his retinue of gentlemen into the Shenandoah Valley in 1716. A better craftsman than Carruthers was John Esten Cooke, of Winchester, who before the Civil War published much fiction, of which the most memorable is *The Virginia Comedians* (1854), set in Williamsburg in the years before the Revolution. Cooke's older brother, Philip Pendleton Cooke, born in Martinsburg, was a poet of considerable gifts, who practiced law and was once advised by a Virginia friend of his not to "waste time on a damned thing like poetry; you might make yourself, with your sense and judgment, a useful man in settling neighborhood disputes and difficulties." [19]

19. Jay B. Hubbell, *The South in American Literature, 1607–1900* (Durham, N.C.: Duke University Press, 1954), p. 504.

Another writer of interesting though uneven talent was George Tucker, a native of Bermuda and kinsman of various Virginia literary Tuckers including the poet Nathaniel and the essayist-poet St. George. George lived in Richmond, Pittsylvania County, Lynchburg, and Charlottesville, and his novel of 1824, *The Valley of Shenandoah,* though careless and derivative in form, portrayed Virginia agricultural and social problems— including the depiction of a slave auction—with a realism that was not to reappear in the state's literature until the advent of Ellen Glasgow. Still another literary Tucker, Nathaniel Beverley, half-brother of John Randolph, is best remembered for his spirited defense of slavery, particularly *The Partisan Leader* (1836), which depicted a future civil war between North and South; the prediction as to the actual outcome was not so good, for in Tucker's novel the South won. It was Tucker who, while a judge in Missouri, reportedly urged the exclusion of all Yankees, proposing that every newcomer ferried across the Mississippi should be required to pronounce the word *cow;* those who said *keow* were to be turned away.

The one really important literary figure to come out of Virginia in all the nineteenth century, however, was Poe. So little do his poems, tales, and critical writings have to do with the Virginia scene that some have tended not to consider him a Virginia, or a Southern, writer at all. But Poe's art and his aesthetic came deeply out of his time and place. His insistence upon literary form—sound, rhythm, rhyme—rather than ideas in poetry, his extravagant imagery, even his morbidity of subject are characteristic of the literature that other and lesser Southern talents of his day were writing. In C. Hugh Holman's words, he was "the employer of surrealistic landscape and remote times and places to portray a world of the tortured inner soul, a kind of symbolic imagery of the inner self." [20] It is not surprising that, growing up in a society which for certain very obvious reasons was not drawn toward any kind of searching scrutiny of its social institutions and its underlying social and moral prem-

20. C. Hugh Holman, "Edgar Allan Poe," in Davis, et al., eds., *Southern Writing,* p. 533.

ises, a major imagination such as Poe's should have been directed toward the exploration of the tortured inner soul, amid remote times and places. But it is not difficult to see, in a story such as "The Fall of the House of Usher" or a poem like "The Raven," an ultimate relevance to a society caught in a decline of both estate and spirit.

7

The Antebellum Era

*In which are recounted the dire consequences
of the "peculiar institution."*

$\mathcal{T}$HE uneasiness of the Jeffersonian Virginians over the continued existence of slavery in the state we have already noted. The massive presence of the slaves, however, proved superior to all attempts to legislate or emancipate the problem out of existence. White Virginians may have disapproved of slavery on both moral and economic grounds, and deplored its continuing presence, but what they could not do was conceive of blacks in such numbers living alongside the whites in any relationship other than slavery. For like almost all other white Americans, white Virginians considered black men biologically and socially inferior. The only possible solution they could envision was to get the slaves moved elsewhere—to the west, some suggested, or back to Africa. The latter seemed the more promising alternative, and colonization societies soon materialized. There were, however, some real difficulties. For one thing, the sheer physical task of transporting what were now several million blacks to Africa was almost insuperable. Another difficulty was that few of the blacks themselves showed much enthusiasm for returning to Africa; they were Americans, most of them of generations standing, and what they wanted was to be free Americans, not Africans. The most important barrier by far, however, was the fact that the slaves were valuable investments, particularly after the development of ginning made the mass cultivation of cotton profitable in the lower South. Property in slaves constituted one-half of the taxable wealth of Tidewater Virginia, and in a declining economy that was an important investment.

Though from at least the time of the Constitutional Convention the issue of slavery had played a role in national politics, it was not until the Missouri Controversy of 1819 that it loomed up as a dangerously divisive issue. For if Missouri was admitted as a slave state, not only would the slave-state representation be increased in Congress, but the entire trans-Mississippi area might also be settled by slave owners, and the political and economic impact upon the nonslaveholding region of the northeast would be incalculable. In February 1819, therefore, Representative James Tallmadge, Jr., of New York introduced an amendment to prohibit further introduction of slaves into Missouri and to provide for gradual emancipation of those already there.

The political meaning was obvious. The manufacturing northeast now had an issue which could join all the free states against the South. It could ultimately unite those whose opposition to slavery was based on an abhorrence of human servitude, and those who opposed it because of economic competition. The inhabitants of the new states in the Midwest, many of them Virginians and descendants of Virginians who had fled the Old Dominion in search of greater economic opportunity, resenting the political, economic, and social hold of the planter aristocracy, were anything but pro-Negro in their sentiments, but they feared the domination of slaveholding interests, and the specter of having to compete for an agricultural living against the plantation system.

Though the Missouri issue was compromised, and for the time being the immediate issue was laid to rest, there were thoughtful Virginians in the 1820s who realized very well what the implications of the controversy had been. The colonization movement received new impetus. In western Virginia Joseph Doddridge, an Episcopal minister, published a book in 1824 condemning slavery and racial prejudice alike. "We debase them to the condition of brutes," he wrote of the slaves," and then use that debasement as an argument for perpetuating their slavery." [1] Conservatives, for their part, moved ever closer to the strict construction of the United States Constitution; as John Randolph declared in voting against an internal-improvements bill, the same power that gave the federal government the right to build a road would give it the right to emancipate the slaves.

Events beginning on the night of Sunday, August 22, 1831, were to shock Virginians out of their complacency about slavery in their midst, and were to have long-lasting repercussions throughout the South. News began trickling into Richmond and Norfolk the following day of an insurrection of slaves in Southampton County, in Southside Virginia near the North Carolina line. Several days elapsed before the complete story was put together. Led by Nat Turner, a slave preacher belonging to Joseph Travis, a band of some sixty blacks, mostly slaves but including several freemen, had murdered Travis, his wife, and their infant child, then moved through the countryside, slaughtering all whites as they went. For forty-eight hours they attacked homes and plantations, and fifty-eight whites, for the most part women and children, were killed. Upon meeting armed resistance their ranks began to crumble, and soon they were dispersed and most of those remaining were killed or captured. Turner himself hid out for several months before some slaves revealed his hiding place. In the immediate aftermath of the rebellion, groups of whites moved throughout the Southampton area, slaughtering blacks.

The news of the Turner insurrection spread throughout the South, and there was considerable panic, rumors and reports of similar conspiracies, and a general tightening of the laws regulating the conduct of slaves. Turner's ability to read and write and the fact that he was a preacher were singled out as reasons why education of blacks should be made illegal and black

1. This was doubtless Joseph Doddridge, *Joseph Doddridge's Notes on the Settlement and Indian Wars, of the Western Part of Virginia and Pennsylvania from the year 1763 until the year 1783 inclusive. Together with a View, of the State of Society and Manners of the First Settlers of the Western Country* (Wellsburgh, Va., 1824). Quoted in Carl N. Degler, *The Other South: Southern Dissenters in the Nineteenth Century* (New York: Harper and Row, 1974), p. 20.

preachers severely restrained. Governor Floyd of Virginia was convinced that the insurrection was part of a concerted plan for revolt throughout the state, with black preachers as leaders, and that abolitionist propaganda was responsible.

Floyd, a States-Rights Democrat from Montgomery County in western Virginia, immediately proposed to the General Assembly stricter laws regulating slavery and the removal of free blacks from the state, but in his diary he wrote that despite the reluctance of eastern Virginia to discuss the problem, "I will not rest until slavery is abolished in Virginia." [2] He was joined in his resolve by a number of members of the House of Delegates, most of them from the west, and in the last days of December 1831 and through January 1832, the House of Delegates engaged in a full-scale debate over the slavery issue. As never before, and as would not again take place in the future, the basic question of the right or wrong of slavery was openly argued. The fact that Nat Turner had testified that he had not personally been mistreated, and that his own master was a kind man, was what particularly concerned many Virginians. For if it was not mistreatment of slaves but the very fact of slavery itself that would trigger slave revolts, then slavery must be either removed once and for all, or accepted for what it was and regulatory laws rigidly enforced. James McDowell, Jr., expressed the matter openly: what made Virginians fearful of rebellion "was the suspicion eternally attached to the slave himself, the suspicion that a Nat Turner might be in every family, that the same bloody deed could be acted over at any time in any place, that the materials for it were spread through the land and always ready for a like explosion." [3]

The debate was widely reported in the newspapers of the day. It came finally to nothing, however. By a vote of 73 to 58, William Preston's general amendment to the effect that the legislature should take some action for the abolition of slavery

2. "The Diary of Governor John Floyd," in Henry Irving Tragle, ed., *The Southampton Slave Revolt of 1831: A Compilation of Source Material* (New York: Vintage Books, 1973), p. 262.
3. Degler, *The Other South,* p. 26.

was defeated. The failure of the assembly to act, in Virginius Dabney's summation, "was tragic in its consequences. For if Virginia had managed to produce an effective program for the ultimate achievement of this objective, the impact on the other slave states could have been far-reaching. As it was, the liberals became so disheartened that the conservatives took over." [4]

In the years that followed, a defense of slavery as a "positive good" began to be developed. Since the Virginians, like other Southerners, were stuck with the massive presence of the "peculiar institution," the effort was now made to justify it on positive rather than on negative terms—to make a virtue of a necessity. Thus in 1832 Professor Thomas Roderick Dew of William and Mary advanced his defense of slavery on the grounds that true equality in white society depended upon the existence of an inferior race. George Fitzhugh of Port Royal, in *Sociology for the South* (1854) and *Cannibals All!* (1857) declared that free capitalistic society was a failure, resulting inevitably in the pauperization of the weak; only in slavery was the problem of unemployment and resultant evils solved, since only in slavery did the wealthy formally accept the social responsibility of caring for the weak, the aged, the infirm. Edmund Ruffin of Hanover County, whose experiments in the use of calcareous marl were to revitalize Virginia's agriculture in the 1850s, borrowed Fitzhugh's argument that slavery was the only feasible alternative to wage slavery for the poor, and asserted that it was the most efficient system of labor, since it made maximum use of the laborer's time while also seeing efficiently to his wants and needs. A Baptist minister, the Reverend Thornton Stringfellow of Culpeper County, utilized the Old and New Testaments to justify slavery by Biblical account.

To what extent did the white Virginians and other Southerners actually believe in these elaborate justifications of slavery as a "positive good"? There is no doubt that they found such arguments attractive. Yet it is unlikely that many of them actually believed in the "positive good" of slavery; it might be a

4. Dabney, *Virginia*, p. 228.

necessity, might even be, as they told themselves, beneficial to the slaves at that stage of their progress toward civilization, but it is unlikely that the victims of the "peculiar institution" were widely thought to be existing in a state of ideal social bliss. Rather, the Virginians accepted it as a fact—for the foreseeable future at least. They believed in the innate inferiority of the black man, and they could not, in the antebellum years, bring themselves to envision his continued existence within Virginia in any condition other than that of bondage.

As for the slaves themselves, what they thought about it is for the most part not recorded, but one is sure that they considered being owned by other men neither a positive nor a negative advantage. Most black Virginians might not have known slavery at its worst, as in the rice fields of the Carolinas and the cotton fields of the Deep South—but there was the constant threat that they, or their children, might be sold into the Deep South variety of slavery. There were kind masters and unkind masters, and since both whites and blacks were human beings, they usually managed to reach some kind of day-by-day equilibrium. The existence of runaways, repressive slave laws, slave patrols, the Gabriel and the Nat Turner insurrections, and other and lesser plots and attempts at plots, however, all testify eloquently to the attitude of black Virginians toward being owned as property.

Once the immediate concerns of the Missouri Controversy were compromised, the slavery issue receded from the forefront of the public consciousness for almost twenty years. The issues of the 1820s and the 1830s were phrased in different terms, and required different alliances. The rise of Andrew Jackson and the Democratic party meant a struggle between the agricultural region and the manufacturing east, between the party intent upon limiting the power of the business community—through use of strict construction and states' rights—and the party anxious to use the power of the central government to further national and commercial aims, and committed to an expanded, loose construction of the Constitution which would permit that. But there were also States-Rights, strict-constructionist Whigs, allied to that party because of its antileveling, proproperty-rights attitude, and Jacksonians who cared little for strict construction but much for reform and equality.

The so-called Tariff of Abominations of 1828, which precipitated the Nullification crisis during the years 1828 to 1832, was the first big test of the Jacksonian alliance. For all its gradual loss of leadership in the nation, Virginia remained strongly unionist in sentiment. At the same time, however, South Carolina's Nullification Act was strikingly like Jefferson's and Madison's Virginia and Kentucky Resolutions of the Alien and Sedition laws era, and designed with the same goal in mind: to assert the ultimate sovereignty of the state over the national government. Thus when President Jackson mobilized the armed forces, and a Force Bill to insure South Carolina's compliance with the laws was enacted by Congress, with John Tyler casting the only vote against it in the Senate, the Virginia General Assembly enacted a compromise resolution urging both reduction of the tariff and postponement of the Nullification ordinance by South Carolina. A majority of Virginians stood behind the President in his insistence that South Carolina could not nullify laws of the Union, but at the same time they didn't like the idea of forcing compliance by the bayonet. Ultimately matters were worked out by Henry Clay, who came up with a compromise plan for a reduction of the protective tariff over a period of ten years, down to acceptable levels.

In 1841 the Old Dominion suddenly found itself with a President in the White House again. In the celebrated presidential election of 1840, the Whigs had ridden to victory by virtue of the famous "Log Cabin and Hard Cider" campaign, in which, capitalizing on Jacksonian-style election tactics and a financial slump, the party of property and business performed the impressive feat of convincing a majority of voters that William Henry Harrison and John Tyler were plain folk, men of the people, in contradistinction to the effete, aristocratic Martin Van Buren. Harrison, victor of Tippecanoe, a member of a Virginia family of almost two centuries' standing, who was born in the family mansion of Berkeley on the James River, whose father was a signer of the Declaration of Independence, and who lived in an

VIRGINIA

A photographer's essay by Junebug Clark

Photographs in sequence

impressive home in southern Ohio, was supposedly the inhabitant of a log cabin! John Tyler, whose father had been governor of Virginia and who lived in the handsome Tyler home, Greenway, in Charles City County, was also included in the formula.

Henry Clay had assumed that, with Harrison in the White House as figurehead, he could largely direct Whig policy. When Harrison succumbed to pneumonia within a month after his inauguration and Tyler succeeded him in office, the senator from Kentucky promptly began to operate under the same assumption. John Tyler, however, was very much a man of principle, and except for his distrustful attitude toward Jacksonian democracy and the rise of the common man, very few of his principles were unionist Whig. He vetoed national-bank bills, tariff bills, bills to distribute surplus revenue to the states, internal-improvement bills. The Whigs were enraged; they met and formally read him out of the party. Virginia Whigs of the John Marshall, protective-tariff variety, such as John Minor Botts of Richmond, were equally upset.

What Tyler and his friends were doing, of course, was gravitating back toward the Democratic party and John C. Calhoun—but on their own terms. The South Carolinian had already reestablished his credentials with the Southern Jacksonians, and now the planter leadership he represented was seeking to make that party the vehicle for the protection and enhancement of their interests. Tyler, Navy Secretary Abel Parker Upshur, and the others hoped to create a national party of what they considered the center, neither Jacksonian—i.e., small-d democratic—nor protectionist and promanufacturing. This, they thought, would not only unite the South behind them but also win over much Democratic support in the Midwest, because the western Jacksonians, though antislavery, were for Manifest Destiny and for a republic stretching from ocean to ocean. When Daniel Webster finally resigned as Secretary of State, Upshur eventually took over that cabinet post. What Tyler and Upshur determined to do was to press for the annexation of Texas as a slave state, even if war with Mexico was the result.

But on February 28, 1844, Tyler, Upshur, the new Navy Secretary Thomas Walker Gilmer, Senator Thomas Benton, other

congressmen, the Washington diplomatic corps, and other nota-
bles including 76-year-old Dolley Madison, went on a cruise
down the Potomac River aboard the U.S.S. *Princeton*. The
warship was Upshur's pride and joy, the fruits of his naval
reorganization. Late that afternoon the guns were to be fired as a
demonstration. As the guests gathered around, the breech of a
ten-inch gun exploded; Upshur, Gilmer, and six others were
killed instantly.

To replace the Virginian Upshur in the cabinet, Tyler selected
a South Carolinian, John C. Calhoun—supposedly because Tyler's friend Congressman Henry A. Wise of Accomack committed him to doing so without his knowledge, though this is problematical. Attention now was focused upon the Republic of
Texas, whose president, the Virginia-born Sam Houston, having several times sought incorporation into the United States in
vain, was now busy forcing the hand of the United States by
flirting with England and France. Fearful that Texas might be
lost, Tyler and Calhoun maneuvered to persuade Texas to apply
for American statehood once again, and in April 1844 a treaty
of annexation was introduced into the Senate. Had Upshur, who
was a cautious man, still been in charge, the measure might
have gone through. But Calhoun, in his letter of explanation to
the British, was not content with stating the territorial importance of Texas to the United States; he also went ahead to
defend the move in terms of the expansion of slavery, including
a statement of the moral rightness of slavery itself. Thus the annexation of Texas was made into a Southern, slave-state project.

The result not only caused the treaty to be defeated in the
Senate, but it split the Democratic party into proslavery and antislavery wings. Where even Andrew Jackson had held back on
Texas for fear of agitating the slavery issue, Calhoun, Tyler,
and the States-Rights planter-politicians now moved resolutely
into the fray, intent upon forcing a showdown. Democrats were
forced to take sides. The only Virginians who entertained
doubts as to the wisdom of pushing ahead with Texas seemed to
be old-line Whigs, and by no means most of them. At the Democratic convention in Baltimore, support for Van Buren melted
away. After Thomas Ritchie, Jr., and the Virginians persuaded

the delegates to enact a two-thirds rule, so that Van Buren's simple majority would not be sufficient, a deadlock resulted between him and General Lewis Cass of Michigan, who had come out for annexation, and soon a dark-horse expansionist candidate, James Knox Polk of Tennessee, emerged as winner.

Polk won the election over Clay, though not by a large margin, with an expansionist platform that included the annexation of Texas; even before he was inaugurated, the Democrats in Congress were able to get sufficient help from Southern Whigs to push through the acquisition of Texas by means of a joint resolution of both houses. Thus Texas, after a brief further show of reluctance, became part of the United States, and Tyler went home to his new Charles City County mansion at Sherwood Forest. John Tyler had added to the domain of the United States an immense territory, by far the largest since a previous Virginia President's Louisiana Purchase. But he had done so at a cost that he, Upshur, Calhoun, and his other planter friends were willing to pay: the reopening of the slave controversy.

Within a year the United States was at war with Mexico, and the considerable opposition to the war was based on the charge that it was only a proslavery imperialistic venture designed to create more slave states. It was to defend against this implication that Democratic Congressman David Wilmot of Pennsylvania introduced a bill providing that slavery should be excluded from any territory acquired from Mexico. Whereupon, after a thirty-year respite, the United States was once again plunged into a sectional crisis such as that involving Missouri in 1819–1820. Party ranks broke; northern and western Democrats voted with northern and western Whigs, while southern Whigs were forced into alliance with southern Democrats. Though the proviso passed the House, it failed in the Senate.

As for the war itself, that went smoothly enough. General Zachary Taylor, a native of Virginia, commanded the army that moved across the Rio Grande and into northern Mexico, while General Winfield Scott, another Virginian, landed an army at Tampico, assaulted the fortress of Chapultepec, and moved 260 miles into the interior to capture the Mexican capital. In the armies of Scott and Taylor served at least 130 Virginia officers, among them many who would later figure prominently in Civil War battle accounts.

The Whigs had decided that Zachary Taylor, though a slaveholder, was their best hope for the 1848 election. Enough northern Democrats split off to form a Free Soil party under Martin Van Buren to cost the Democrats New York's electoral votes, and the Whig nominee won. Virginia itself remained in the Democratic column, though by a narrow margin.

Those Virginians and other Southerners who supported Taylor, however, soon discovered that while "Old Rough and Ready" might have been born in Orange County and was a slaveholder in Tennessee, he was no worshiper of the "peculiar institution." Taylor showed himself quite willing to have California and New Mexico enter the Union as free states, and to Southern talk of secession he responded by stating his intention to suppress any such action, if necessary at the head of an army. As the congressional furor mounted, with the House going for days without being able to settle upon a speaker, the Virginia General Assembly did what always came naturally to it at such times and passed resolutions affirming the state's steadfast determination not to yield to violation of its rights under the Constitution. What the Virginians—like almost everyone else—really wanted, however, was a compromise.

Henry Clay now came out of retirement in Kentucky to re-enter the Senate and propose a settlement, as he had several times done before in the nation's times of crisis. President Taylor himself was of no mind to yield. But then, on July 9, 1850, Taylor died, and Millard Fillmore became President. Fillmore was in favor of the compromise, so by mid-September Congress had enacted and he had signed five laws, which provided for admission of California as a free state, organization of New Mexico and Utah as territories, a ten-million-dollar payment to Texas in exchange for New Mexico, abolition of the slave trade (but not slavery) in the District of Columbia, and a new and toughened Fugitive Slave Law, drafted by Senator James M. Mason of Virginia. Virginians, like almost everyone else, were relieved. In March 1851 the General Assembly voted overwhelmingly its approval. For a brief time the old political party loyalties seemed to reassert themselves over and above the sectional ties.

After decades of economic decline, Virginia was now entering a period of considerable prosperity. In part this was due to the scientific and propagandistic activities of agricultural experimentalists such as Edmund Ruffin, who had shown that the exhausted tobacco lands could be revitalized by the use of marl. Much attention was paid to the dissemination of information about scientific practices in agriculture. Crop diversification, livestock raising, deep plowing, and rotation of fields were introduced. Land values went up as farm prices rose. Better agricultural machinery was being used, too, though the chief beneficiary of Virginia's talent in this respect was the Midwest, where Cyrus McCormick of Steele's Tavern had moved following development of his mechanical reaper in 1831.

There was also considerable industrial development in Virginia during the 1850s. In Richmond the Tredegar Iron Works, using slave labor, was now manufacturing all manner of iron and steel implements and machinery, including railroad locomotives. After a belated start, an extensive network of railroads was being developed with state aid, though the east-west line that should have linked the port of Norfolk to the trans-Allegheny was still blocked by the fall-line ports. There were cotton and tobacco factories in Petersburg, Danville, and Lynchburg. Industrial output and the value of farmland both rose steadily.

The 1850s witnessed important and long-needed political and electoral reform in Virginia. The limited concessions made to the western areas in 1829 had long since ceased to provide adequate representation even for the Valley counties, and by 1850 the pressure for more equitable districting could no longer be resisted. At the constitutional convention of 1850–1851, the level of debate may have been, as Virginius Dabney says, "decidedly inferior—an indication of the drastic decline in the quality of Virginia's political leadership," [5] but this time property qualifications for voting were eliminated, free white manhood

5. Dabney, *Virginia*, p. 222.

suffrage finally established, voting wards set up in the larger cities, the governorship and other important state offices opened to popular election instead of being chosen by the General Assembly, the governor's council eliminated, and ownership of property no longer made a requisite for officeholding. The west was given a much larger share of the seats in the House of Delegates, though in the Senate the east still ruled. Public viva-voce voting, however, was retained, which meant that there was still ample opportunity for those in positions of power and authority in county government to see to it that the rank and file voted the right way.

The educational situation was also considerably improved, though not until Reconstruction times would the state have a full-fledged public school system. In 1841, following a full-scale indictment of public education in Virginia by Professor George E. Dabney of Washington College, the General Assembly took up the problem, and education conventions were held in Clarksburg, Lexington, and Richmond. Some reform was made, but the General Assembly declined to provide for overall state revenues, a board of education, or a superintendent. By 1855, however, ten counties and four cities had public school systems.

It was the Kansas-Nebraska Act of 1854, providing for "squatter sovereignty" in the territories beyond Missouri, that set the slavery controversy going full tilt once again. For the time being, Virginians generally stayed out of the fight. "We had enough, and too much, excitement during the Compromise Controversy of 1850," the *Richmond Enquirer* declared.[6] But as the fight developed, and the warring factions in Kansas took to shooting at each other, this changed. In place of the old Whig party in the South there was a new element, the Know-Nothing, or American party, campaigning on a platform of secrecy and resistance to foreigners, in particular to Catholics. In 1855 the Americans had made a run at the governorship of Virginia, but Henry A. Wise had defeated them decisively, ridiculing the

6. Avery O. Craven, *The Growth of Southern Nationalism, 1848–1861* (Baton Rouge: Louisiana State University Press, 1953), p. 196.

alleged foreign menace and branding the Know-Nothing concept as alien to the essence of American democracy and freedom of opinion. Wise also proclaimed them antislavery, which was an even more effective accusation.

In 1856 the Americans nominated Millard Fillmore for President, while the Democrats settled upon James Buchanan. There was, however, another party on the scene, and one that alarmed thoughtful Virginians. It called itself the Republican party, and its prime issue and principle of unification was opposition to the spread of slavery. Meeting in Philadelphia, it nominated John Charles Frémont, Southern-born but a foe of slavery. The American party now split, with the northern elements endorsing Frémont. For the first time Virginia and the South were now confronted by an avowedly and completely sectional party, drawn from the Midwest and the northeast, with no Southern ties.

The campaign that followed was of almost unparalleled bitterness. If the Black Republicans, as the Southerners termed them, were to win, Governor Wise warned, the Southern states would be forced to secede from the Union. If it came to war, Virginia could "arm and equip 50,000 men the next morning, ready for revolution." [7] Buchanan and the Democrats won, however, sweeping all the Southern states except Maryland, and capturing Pennsylvania, Indiana, New Jersey, Illinois, and California as well. Even Richmond, hitherto always lopsidedly Whig, almost went Democratic this time, giving the American candidate a majority of only 284 votes. The sectional issue, in short, was driving the old Virginia Whigs into the Democratic camp.

The Democratic victory brought no respite. Within three days of Buchanan's inauguration came the Dred Scott Decision, in which the U.S. Supreme Court ruled that since a slave was without rights under the Constitution, neither Congress nor a territorial legislature had the right to interfere with a master carrying his slave property into the territories. Virginians, gratified with the decision, soon became appalled at the Republican willingness to denounce and defy the Supreme Court.

7. Craven, *Southern Nationalism*, p. 244.

The national confusion was reflected in Virginia politics, which were in a wild tangle, with Democrats fighting among themselves. With the dominant party split between Buchanan and Stephen A. Douglas, the old Whigs began to hope they might form a Union party that could win the Presidency in 1860. Meanwhile the state balloted for governor in 1859, and a moderate Democrat from the west, John Letcher of Lexington, won out over the ardent proslaveryite William L. Goggin, with western votes transcending party lines. To win, Letcher had been forced to make clear his support of slavery, but he also stressed his devotion to the Union and denounced talk of secession by Goggin, R. M. T. Hunter, Roger Pryor, and others. Virginia was clearly still very much pro-Union.

The events of Sunday night, October 16, 1859, changed everything. An old man named John Brown led a little band of sixteen whites and five free blacks into the town of Harpers Ferry, in Jefferson County, Virginia. There he took possession of the U.S. arsenal. Meanwhile a detachment of his men went out into the countryside to round up slaves and to capture Colonel Lewis Washington, an aide to Governor Wise and a relative of the first President. Old Ossawatamie Brown, as he was called from the "Bloody Kansas" days, had brought a thousand pikes with him to Virginia, as well as more than a hundred Sharps rifles and other weapons for arming the slaves. His avowed plan had been to touch off a full-scale slave revolt. In the fighting on the next day, the insurgents killed several townsfolk, including a free black who worked as porter for the B&O, and the mayor of Harpers Ferry. By this time militia was swarming into the town, and in Washington a detachment of Marines was ordered to the scene. Early Tuesday morning, after Brown had refused a demand for surrender, the Marines stormed the arsenal engine house, captured Brown and his men, and freed the hostages.

Governor Wise had Brown brought to trial, and he was sentenced to die by hanging for treason, conspiring with slaves to commit treason, and first-degree murder. On December 2, 1859, Brown was led to his execution at Charles Town. As his body spun in the air, Colonel J. T. L. Preston of the VMI Cadet Corps called out, "So perish all such enemies of Virginia! All such enemies of the Union! All such foes of the human race!" [8]

The effect of the John Brown raid on Virginia and the South was incalculable. As the Virginians saw it, here a fanatic had come down into their state with the avowed intention of fomenting a servile insurrection, which, if successful, would have resulted almost certainly in a massacre of whites such as had occurred in Santo Domingo and during the Nat Turner insurrection. When Brown was captured and executed, leading spokesmen for the North had not only criticized that execution, but had, though still affecting to deprecate Brown's tactics, expressed great admiration for his motives. His raid had been financed by prominent New Englanders. Ministers of the gospel in the State of Massachusetts had declared publicly that by Brown's deed the word "treason" had been "made holy in the American language," and had blessed "the sacred, and the radiant 'treason' of John Brown." [9]

It was against this backdrop that the political parties moved to nominate their candidates for the presidency in 1860. Meeting in Charleston, South Carolina, the Democrats were split into a group that wanted Stephen A. Douglas of Illinois and a Southern wing that would have none of him. After the Southerners (including only a single Virginia delegate) walked out, the convention was reconvened in Baltimore. There Douglas was nominated, while the Deep South dissidents nominated John C. Breckenridge of Kentucky. The Republicans chose for their candidate an Illinois lawyer and onetime Whig congressman, Abraham Lincoln. A conservative, anti-Democratic group, mostly from the South and made up principally of onetime Whigs including Alexander H. H. Stuart, Wyndham Robertson, and other Virginians, organized the Constitutional Union party, with John Bell of Tennessee as its candidate, and a platform consisting of one plank only: preservation of the Union.

Throughout the hot summer and early autumn of 1860 the po-

8. Robert Penn Warren, *John Brown: The Making of a Martyr* (New York: Payson and Clarke, 1929), p. 439.

9. C. Vann Woodward, "John Brown's Private War," *The Burden of Southern History* (Baton Rouge: Louisiana State University Press, 1960), p. 58.

litical battles raged. Douglas struggled valiantly to hold the Democratic party together as the only alternative to Republican victory. Five thousand persons heard him plead earnestly for Squatter Sovereignty when he spoke from the portico of the city hall at Norfolk. He wanted the support of no man, he told his audience, who did not desire the Union preserved.

Bell and the Union party carried Virginia by a narrow margin, with Breckenridge second and Douglas third. Bell also carried Kentucky and Tennessee. But Abraham Lincoln was victorious in every one of the free states. Though his popular vote was far less than a majority, he was clearly and legally elected President. Six weeks later, on December 20, 1860, South Carolina seceded from the Union. In swift succession, Mississippi, Alabama, Florida, Georgia, Louisiana, and Texas followed.

The question now was, what would the upper South do? Above all, what would Virginia, the Mother of Presidents, do? As Avery Craven points out, "a new nation without Virginia would lack a genuine Southern quality . . . She was, after all, the founder and keeper of 'the Southern traditions.' " [10]

What Virginia did was to work with border-state moderates for a compromise that would keep the border states at least in the Union, and disarm the rabid secessionist leadership in the Deep South. The Virginia legislature called a peace conference in Washington, with ex-President John Tyler heading the delegation. Both the U.S. House of Representatives and the Senate established committees to work toward a settlement of the crisis.

Virginia was against secession. A referendum for a convention to consider secession was passed, but of 142 delegates, only 30 secessionists were chosen. Meanwhile the seceding states had met in Montgomery, Alabama, drawn up a constitution very much like the U.S. Constitution, and chosen Jefferson Davis of Mississippi and Alexander H. Stephens of Georgia as president and vice-president of the Confederate States of

10. Craven, *Southern Nationalism*, p. 384.

America. Virginia sent no delegates, though fire-eating Roger Pryor of Petersburg was very much a part of the proceedings. South Carolina garrisoned a semicircle of coastal artillery fortifications with guns trained upon Fort Sumter at the mouth of Charleston harbor, where the American flag still flew, and demanded the evacuation of the fort. President Buchanan refused to comply.

Compromise failed in the winter and early spring of 1860–1861 for numerous reasons. The Deep-South states would not send delegates to the peace conference. Many of the Northern states, though reluctantly sending delegates, instructed them to make no compromise whatever on slavery in the territories. Northern Republicans underestimated the intensity of disunion sentiment in the Deep South, and the repugnance of Virginia and the upper South both to coercion and the threat to slavery. The proslavery, secessionist forces treated the North with contempt and failed to discern the powerful spirit of Union sentiment in the west. All efforts by Virginians and others at compromise were thwarted by those who were determined, union or disunion, to hold to their advanced positions.

Virginians who were officers in the United States Army and Navy faced a bleak decision. As Colonel Robert E. Lee wrote from his station in Texas, "If a disruption takes place, I shall go back in sorrow to my people and share the misery of my native state, and save in her defence there will be one soldier less in the world than now. I wish for no other flag than the 'Star spangled banner' and no other air than 'Hail Columbia.' " [11]

On March 4 Abraham Lincoln was inaugurated. Lincoln sought to consult the Virginians; to Representative John B. Baldwin of Staunton he would seem to have proposed more or less a trade: he would evacuate Fort Sumter if Virginia would only dissolve its secession convention. "A State for a fort is no bad business," he is reported as having said. And as J. G. Randall points out, he might as well have said four states for a fort,

11. Douglas Southall Freeman, *R. E. Lee: A Biography*, 4 vols. (New York: Charles Scribner's Sons, 1934), 1:421–422.

since not only Virginia but the entire upper South was at stake.[12] But Lincoln also dispatched a relief expedition to Charleston. Without provisions, the Sumter garrison was facing evacuation, as everyone knew; the expedition was to make an attempt to reprovision the fort if the fort was still garrisoned when the expedition arrived. Only if attacked, however, was it to attempt to reinforce the garrison. If there was to be a war, Lincoln meant to have the South fire the first shot.

On April 10, General P. G. T. Beauregard, in command of Confederate forces at Charleston, got his orders to begin the bombardment when ready. In Charleston Roger A. Pryor and Edmund Ruffin of Virginia had been urging an attack as the one way of getting Virginia to secede. But when in the early predaylight of April 12 Pryor was offered the honor of firing the mortar that would signal the attack, he shook his head. "I could not fire the first gun of the war," he said.[13] Across the harbor at Cummings Point, old Edmund Ruffin had no such reservations. When the signal gun went off, he happily jerked the lanyard that sent the first shell streaking toward the fort.

On April 14, Fort Sumter surrendered. The day before, Lincoln sent out a call to the states for 75,000 militia to suppress the rebellion. Governor Letcher of Virginia promptly declined to send a single man. On April 17, while crowds demonstrated outside Metropolitan Hall in Richmond, the Virginia convention formally voted by 85 to 55 to withdraw from the Union that her statesmen had founded.

12. J. G. Randall, *Lincoln The President,* 4 vols. 1: *Springfield to Bull Run* (New York: Dodd, Mead, 1945–1955), p. 326.
13. W. A. Swanberg, *First Blood: The Story of Fort Sumter* (New York: Charles Scribner's Sons, 1957), p. 297.

8

The Civil War Era

*In which the Virginians defeat
the Yankees time after time before finally
consenting to surrender.*

ON April 25, 1861, the Commonwealth of Virginia became part of the Confederate States of America. "They say Virginia has no grievance," wrote Mary Boykin Chesnut of South Carolina as the Confederate government was being formed at Montgomery, Alabama; "she comes out on a point of honor." [1] Grievance or not, Virginia was in the war to stay. For most of the four years that followed, its soil was a battleground. The city of Richmond, to which the capital of the new nation was moved, became the principal objective of the invading Northern armies. In the west the Union spearheads probed southward down the Mississippi River and through Kentucky and Tennessee, ultimately dividing the Confederacy in two. General William T. Sherman drove southward from Chattanooga to the ocean, and up the southeastern seaboard to threaten Richmond from beneath. Not until then did the city's defenses give way. Before the depleted flank of General Robert

1. Mary Boykin Chesnut, *A Diary from Dixie*, edited by Ben Ames Williams (Boston: Houghton Mifflin, 1949), pp. 47–48.

129

E. Lee's army was finally turned at Five Forks, southwest of Petersburg, on March 31, 1865, and the retreat began that ended eight days later at Appomattox, the Army of Northern Virginia had kept the enemy from Richmond at every juncture. Beginning with the inept attack of General Irvin McDowell at First Manassas in 1861, a parade of Union generals successively directed major campaigns against the capital. George B. McClellan, John Pope, Ambrose Burnside, Joseph Hooker, and George G. Meade all led armies southward. When ultimately General U. S. Grant assumed command of the "On to Richmond" operation in the spring of 1864, he spent the better part of a summer hammering in vain at Lee's army, until he finally gave up the attempt to take Richmond by assault and settled down to siege operations south of the capital. When that happened, the end was foredoomed; the inexorable logistics of attrition made the outcome only a question of time.

Early on in the war Virginia lost its trans-Allegheny counties for good. The longtime east-west schism now brought total separation. Efforts by inadequate Confederate forces to hold the region were poorly co-ordinated and ultimately futile. By early 1862 the Union had regained the country from the Ohio River to the mountains, and in 1863 western Virginia was accepted into the Union as the State of West Virginia. Its territory included not only the country beyond the mountains but also the two northernmost counties of the Shenandoah Valley, Berkeley and Jefferson, containing the cities of Charles Town, Martinsburg, and the strategic outpost at Harpers Ferry. These counties, after more than a hundred years of being an integral part of the life of northern Virginia were subsequently known as the "lost counties," and many a diehard resident thereafter considered himself unnaturally severed from his true homeland.

Eastern Virginia was also menaced. Since the Confederacy had no navy to speak of, control of the sea and of the Chesapeake Bay was lost from the outset. Attempting to substitute ingenuity for numbers, the Confederates rebuilt the onetime steam frigate *Merrimac* into an ironclad warship, which was renamed the *Virginia*. Early in March of 1862 the *Virginia's* wheezing engines propelled it across the roadstead from Portsmouth to where a Union fleet lay at anchor off Hampton. While projectiles bounced harmlessly off its iron plating, it proceeded to sink two warships, and would have completed the job the next morning had not another equally strange ironclad vessel, the *Monitor,* arrived from New York to contest it for supremacy. After a day of vigorous but inconclusive fighting, the two ironclads broke off contact, but the roadstead remained in Union hands. Thus McClellan was enabled to move his army from northern Virginia by ship transport to the Virginia peninsula for an easier access to Richmond; soon thereafter southeastern Virginia was evacuated by the Confederacy, the *Virginia* was blown up to escape capture, and a Union force was moved in to occupy the Norfolk-Portsmouth area for the remainder of the war.

Richmond itself seemed about to fall in the late spring of 1862, following General Joseph E. Johnston's retreat up the peninsula almost to the gates of the city in the face of McClellan's superior forces. But then General Thomas J. "Stonewall" Jackson, with a small force, unleashed a lightning campaign in the Shenandoah Valley. He succeeded in defeating Union armies converging from the west and north, and penetrated to the Potomac River, so arousing the Federal government's fears for the safety of Washington that substantial forces were recalled from joining McClellan before Richmond. Given that respite, General Lee, who had succeeded Johnston after "Retreatin' Joe" was severely wounded at the inconclusive Battle of Seven Pines, called Jackson to join him and hurled his army at McClellan's flank. In seven days of confused fighting, the Union forces were driven from their base on the Pamunkey River to the James, and though the cost in Confederate casualties was high, the threat to Richmond was lifted.

In the late summer of 1862, after having routed a Union army under Pope at Manassas once again, Lee tried an invasion of his own, and crossed over into Maryland. At Sharpsburg just beyond the Potomac, however, McClellan unleashed a furious attack at the Confederates, and though it was repelled with heavy casualties, the badly mauled Army of Northern Virginia was in no condition to continue northward, and withdrew to Virginia soil. Emboldened by the results of the battle, Abraham

Lincoln now issued his Emancipation Proclamation, which, while it freed only those slaves in areas not presently under Union army control, committed the Union cause firmly and irrevocably to the goal of emancipation and made the War Between the States a war against human slavery, thus assuring that the governments of England and France would never be able to intervene on the Confederate side.

Against Federal attempts to invade Virginia, Lee's army seemed invincible. At Fredericksburg in mid-December it inflicted a crushing defeat on the enemy under Burnside, with only very light losses, while the following April, with most of General James Longstreet's corps away gathering supplies in southeast Virginia, Lee and Jackson with less than 60,000 troops executed an audacious flanking attack on Union General Hooker's invading army of 160,000 troops near the crossroads of Chancellorsville and hurled it back across the Rappahannock River. But the victory was purchased at the cost of the further services of Jackson, who was wounded by his own troops and died soon thereafter.

In the west Federal columns had penetrated deep into the Confederacy; the control of the Mississippi River was imperiled, and most of Tennessee was in Union hands. Lee and President Jefferson Davis determined upon another attempt to invade the North, and in June of 1863 the Army of Northern Virginia again crossed the Potomac. Deprived of knowledge of his enemy's whereabouts because his brilliant cavalry chief General J. E. B. Stuart had taken his cavalry on an extended swing eastward, Lee suddenly found himself engaged with his foe just south of the town of Gettysburg, in Pennsylvania. Now under command of George G. Meade, the Union army occupied a strong defensive position atop a low-lying chain of hills. Though urged by Longstreet not to attack but to maneuver toward Washington and thus force Meade to attack him, Lee determined to drive his opponent from Cemetery Ridge. In three days of fighting, climaxed by a charge, led by General George Pickett, of 11,000 Virginians, North Carolinians, Mississippians, and Tennesseans up Cemetery Ridge into the face of point-blank artillery and infantry fire, Lee failed to dislodge his opponent. "The men and officers of your command have written the name of Virginia as high today as it has ever been written before," Lee told the distraught Pickett as he moved to regroup his shattered army. "The fault is entirely my own." [2] After the most sanguinary battle in American history, in which 50,000 men in gray uniforms and blue had fallen, the Army of Northern Virginia prepared to depart for the Potomac River. The next day, July 4, 1863, in far-off Mississippi, Vicksburg fell. Although almost two more years of fighting and suffering lay ahead, the Confederate cause was now lost.

Behind the lines, in Richmond and elsewhere, food and clothing were in short supply, prices skyrocketed, Confederate paper money steadily declined in value, hospitals were crowded with wounded, desertions increased, there were shortages of everything. Flour sold for two hundred dollars a barrel when available, cornmeal at ten dollars a bushel. The Confederate congress sometimes seemed more interested in states' rights than in Confederate survival, though the harsh criticism directed at the civilian government in Richmond then and in later years was mostly the product of Southern frustration at the inability to win military victory. The Richmond press, however, in particular the *Examiner,* made a poor showing with its constant carping at Jefferson Davis. Morale among the rank and file of the populace was low. There were no more repetitions of the bread riots of the winter of 1862–1863, when a mob of angry and hungry women had looted stores and jeered at President Davis until persuaded to disband, but only the most determined optimist could really foresee Confederate victory after 1863—though few persons would publicly admit what they secretly felt.

As Sherman's army moved toward Atlanta and much of the lower South was occupied, it seemed that only Lee's army stood between the Confederacy and defeat. All knew that the campaign of 1864 would be hard fought and desperate, but Lee had proved superior to all invading strategy before, and though U. S. Grant, the Northern general who had triumphed in the west at Donelson, Shiloh, and Vicksburg, now prepared to move

2. Freeman, *R. E. Lee,* 3:129–130.

southward with an army twice the size of Lee's forces, there was still a chance. If the Union forces could be punished so severely that battlefield victory seemed too costly, then Northern disgust with the carnage might result in the defeat of Lincoln's government in the presidential elections of 1864, and a negotiated peace might be possible.

The Wilderness campaign of May-June 1864 was Lee's most masterful. Again and again he parried his opponent's thrusts and inflicted severe losses. Each time that Grant attempted to sidle southeastward around his foe, Lee was able to anticipate his moves and interpose his entrenched army between Grant and Richmond. Finally, after a desperate headlong attack by Grant at Cold Harbor was turned back at staggering cost to the invaders and minimal Confederate losses, Grant gave up trying to defeat Lee in open battle and moved south of the James to encircle· Petersburg and Richmond. As Meade wrote home, "I think Grant has had his eyes opened and is willing to admit that Virginia and Lee's army is not Tennessee and Bragg's army." [3] Yet Grant had won—for with the operation settled down into a siege, Lee lost the ability to maneuver his army. Grant could replenish his forces; there were no more recruits available for Lee to make good his losses. (*See map on page 61*)

The summer and autumn of 1864 saw the lines about Richmond drawn slowly tighter, and though a diversionary attack toward Washington by General Jubal Early got to the gates of the national capital, the Union grip on Richmond could not be broken. In retaliation for Early's attack, General Philip Sheridan introduced total war to the Shenandoah Valley, burning its barns and destroying its crops and driving off its livestock to inflict devastation similar to that being visited upon Georgia by Sherman. The Confederates were helpless to interfere.

Short of supplies and munitions, weak from lack of food, without medicines and proper clothing, the Army of Northern Virginia guarded the trenches about Petersburg through the winter. In late March a last desperate Confederate attempt to break

3. Shelby Foote, *The Civil War: A Narrative*, 3 vols. 3: *Red River to Appomattox* (New York: Random House, 1974), p. 294.

the siege failed, and there followed the disaster at Five Forks, a key road junction southwest of Petersburg. Lee's only hope now was escape to the west. Richmond was evacuated, set afire by stragglers and burned, the Confederate government fled to Danville, and what was left of Lee's army slogged westward through the red mud of the Southside, while Grant closed in for the kill. On April 9, seeing that all hope was gone and his escape was cut off, Lee asked for a meeting with Grant. On the McLean farm at Appomattox Court House the terms of surrender were drawn up, and on April 12 the Army of Northern Virginia stacked arms and furled its colors for the last time. Lee rode back to burnt-out Richmond, and the war was over in Virginia.

9

The Reconstruction Era

*In which the Virginians pick up
the pieces and resume their place in the Union,
though not as before.*

*T*HE Old Dominion was now back in the Union—by force
of arms, physically, territorially. The task now was for the state
to resume its constitutional status as a political unit of the nation, and to reconstruct its blasted economic and social life. All
this would take time. The Virginia of the year 1865 and thereafter was in certain respects a different community, and faced importantly different conditions, than the pre-Confederate state.
New economic forces, new social needs, would begin to make
themselves felt at once. The state faced a difficult task. The
guns of the Union had blasted a generation of young Virginians.
The center of Richmond was a gutted ruin. Bristol, Abingdon,
and Wytheville had been burnt almost to the ground. Fredericksburg and Petersburg had suffered heavy bombardment. In
the wide areas where armies had marched and fought, houses
stood deserted. Fields were untilled and choked with weeds.
Phil Sheridan had made of the rich farmland of the Shenandoah
Valley a wasteland. Livestock had been driven off or slaughtered for food. Railroads were virtually useless; canals were
choked with silt from caved-in banks.

The land was the source of Virginia's wealth, but the slaves who had worked much of it had been freed: more than 350,000 black Virginians were now free but largely destitute of prospects. Slave property had constituted much of the wealth; now it was wiped out. Land values plummeted; land worth $150 an acre before the war sold for two dollars now. The splitting off of West Virginia had deprived the state of almost a third of its territory and more than 300,000 of its citizens. Confederate currency was worthless; so were Confederate bonds, in which many Virginians had loyally invested their savings. In all, the total financial loss during the war and the Reconstruction period that followed was estimated in 1877 at $457 million—a staggering sum for a state with fewer than 700,000 white and 500,000 black citizens.

More than all this was the withering spiritual shock of defeat. The defeat had touched all segments of the population. An ordered society had been virtually shattered, and everywhere there was chaos. Not many Virginians had chosen to go the route of old Edmund Ruffin, who penned a defiant testament of his hatred of "the perfidious, malignant and vile Yankee race," then blew out his brains.[1] Against the example of the old secessionist was that of Robert E. Lee. "Now, more than at any other time," he told a friend, "Virginia and every other state in the South needs us. We must try and, with as little delay as possible, go to work to build up their prosperity."[2] Lee proposed to forgive, put aside animosity, and go to work; he accepted an offer to serve as president of Washington College, and went to Lexington in the Valley to live out his five remaining years. He was careful to refrain from speaking any words of hate for the conquerors. But few other Virginians could be so forgiving as Lee. Yet all knew that since life must go on, they must get to work.

During the war a nominal state government had been set up at Wheeling under Francis H. Pierpont and, following the es-

1. Avery Craven, *Edmund Ruffin, Southerner: A Study in Secession* (New York: D. Appleton and Co., 1932), p. 259.
2. Freeman, *R. E. Lee*, 4:196.

tablishment of separate statehood for West Virginia, had been moved to Alexandria, where it served as capital for that portion of Virginia under Union control. In June Pierpont transferred his government to Richmond and his "General Assembly" extended political rights to Confederates taking the amnesty oath, and called for a general election to be held in October. In the October election voters ratified an amendment to delete all political disabilities against ex-Confederates, and chose a legislature made up overwhelmingly of former Whigs and containing neither Radical Republicans nor prominent secessionists.

The delegation that Virginia now sent to Washington in accordance with President Andrew Johnson's proclamation of presidential reconstruction included two wartime Unionists as senators, and eight representatives, six of whom could take the federal test oath that they had not held important Confederate office or were not ex-Confederates worth $20,000 or more.

The Republican-dominated Congress, however, had different ideas. Disturbed by the prospect of not-so-penitent ex-Confederates joining the Democrats from the North and thus giving their opponents a majority in Congress, they feared that all the gains of the war years might now be set aside. Not all the Southern state governments were as prudent as Virginia in their choice of senators and congressmen; their delegations included four ex-Confederate generals, eight former colonels, numerous lesser officers, a member of the Confederate congress, a member of General Beauregard's staff, and the former vice-president of the Confederate States of America, Alexander H. Stephens.

Northerners, too, were disturbed at the "black codes" that the various Southern states were enacting to secure order in the laboring force. Virginia's Black Vagrancy Law imposed such emphatic restrictions upon the former slaves that its enforcement was forbidden as "slavery in all but its name" by Major General Alfred H. Terry. Such legislation provoked widespread hostility in the North. The result was the congressional elections of 1866, in which the Radical Republicans now secured a clear majority in both houses of Congress.

The Virginia General Assembly—known popularly as the

"Baldwin legislature" after Speaker of the House John B. Baldwin—had no intention of consenting to the enfranchisement of former slaves. After all, in only five of the Northern states were black men granted the ballot. When in 1866 the Fourteenth Amendment to the Constitution was passed by Congress, guaranteeing to the freedmen the right to vote upon penalty of a proportional reduction in congressional representation, Governor Pierpont had urged ratification, but the assembly declined. Not only did the legislators disapprove of the black enfranchisement, but Republicans in Congress had attached to the amendment a provision that no one could hold a federal or state office who had ever before taken an oath to protect and preserve the Constitution and had then "engaged in insurrection or rebellion against the same, or given aid or comfort to the enemies thereof." The assembly would not ratify any such restriction upon Virginia's numerous ex-Confederate officers and others who had once held military commissions or state or national office.

The response of the Republican Congress was to abolish Southern state governments and to set up five military districts, each governed by an army commander who was to register voters, including all adult black males and whites not disfranchised for having participated in "rebellion," and thereafter convene a constitutional convention. Only when Congress had approved the resulting constitution, the state legislature had ratified the Fourteenth Amendment, and the amendment had been adopted by sufficient states to become part of the Constitution, were the individual states to be readmitted to the Union. The Old Dominion now became Military District Number One, and General John M. Schofield was named commander.

In part because many white Virginians simply declined even to participate in Reconstruction politics by voting, the Republicans carried the election of October 1867, and the radical wing of the party, led by James W. Hunnicutt and U. S. District Judge John C. Underwood, was in control of the constitutional convention that met in Richmond beginning that winter. The delegates included twenty-four blacks, thirty-three whites who were not native Virginians, sixteen white Virginian Republicans, and thirty-two white Virginia Conservatives—as the traditional white element in the state, whether once Democrats or Whigs, had begun calling themselves. The constitution that was drafted was, as Raymond H. Pulley says, "the most democratic instrument of government the Old Dominion has ever known." [3] The document called for universal manhood suffrage for whites and blacks, much more liberal residence requirements for state offices, a more democratic form of state government, a statewide free public school system, taxation based on property evaluation, and a township system of local government similar to that proposed by Thomas Jefferson many years earlier, which would importantly democratize local government. It also, however, disfranchised all former federal or state officials who had served in the Confederacy, and required of all state and local officials a test oath, in which they must swear that they had never voluntarily borne arms against the United States. The constitution also called for ratification of the Fourteenth Amendment and the Fifteenth Amendment to the Constitution, guaranteeing civil rights and the franchise for blacks.

The initial reaction of most white Virginians to the Underwood constitution was bitter hostility. The newly formed Conservative party's first response was to call upon Virginians to reject ratification at the polls. But after the presidential election of 1868, in which the Republicans won a sweeping national victory and elected U. S. Grant President, cooler heads prevailed. Strident antiblack-suffrage tactics were obviously getting nowhere; the appearance of the Ku Klux Klan in certain areas not only brought undesirable violence but antagonized Northerners.

The Virginians wanted social order and a chance to rebuild, and it had become apparent that so did important financial and commercial elements in the North, including prominent and powerful Republicans. Railroad executives and promoters were particularly concerned. The Conservatives, therefore, began to reconsider their opposition to Negro suffrage and to the demo-

---

3. Raymond H. Pulley, *Old Virginia Restored: An Interpretation of the Progressive Impulse, 1870–1930* (Charlottesville: University Press of Virginia, 1968), p. 8.

cratizing features of the constitution. The lead was taken by Alexander H. H. Stuart, prewar Whig and long prominent in state politics, who proposed publicly that the Conservative party settle for "universal suffrage and universal amnesty"—i.e., black voters and no disfranchisement of ex-Confederate leaders. At Staunton a group of Virginians appointed a Committee of Nine, mostly western Virginians and businessmen, to lobby in Washington for emendation of the Underwood constitution. Responsible Virginians and allies in the North convinced President Grant that if the test act and disfranchisement provisions could be separated from the other provisions of the Underwood constitution in the ratification election of 1869, the Underwood constitution would be enacted. General Schofield himself had warned that the test-oath provision would make it next to impossible to secure competent local and county government officials. Grant set July 6, 1869, for the election, and decreed that the test-oath and disfranchisement clauses could be voted on separately from the other provisions of the constitution.

Meanwhile the election campaign for governor was under way, and here again the Virginia Conservatives adopted a compromise strategy. Railroad politics were deeply involved. The Conservatives had nominated Colonel Robert E. Withers of Lynchburg for governor. The Republicans split into two wings. The regular party nominated Governor Henry Wells, while a "True Republican" group, headed by General William Mahone, nominated Gilbert C. Walker, a New Yorker and prewar Douglas Democrat who had settled in Norfolk in 1864 and had become a prominent banker and manufacturer. Mahone, onetime Confederate hero and now a railroad promoter, also managed somehow to maneuver the Wells faction into nominating a black physician for lieutenant-governor. The Conservative party congress was persuaded to withdraw Withers's candidacy, and Conservative leaders lined up behind Walker's candidacy. Though some diehards objected, the strategy succeeded; Walker was elected governor over Wells, and the Underwood constitution was approved by all but 9,189 voters, while both the test-oath and disfranchisement provisions were solidly rejected. On January 26, 1870, Virginia's representatives were readmitted to

Congress. The years of military Reconstruction were over; by comparison with Reconstruction in some of the other Southern states, they had been mild enough. Virginia could now get back to work.

The planter element that had played so powerful a role in antebellum Virginia politics was no longer a major factor in the state's political life, and the economic policies that had been developed to safeguard the institution of slavery were now mostly irrelevant. Landed wealth, which had previously constituted a sufficient economic foundation for most Virginians, no longer sufficed. Those who now moved into positions of leadership in the Old Dominion were for the most part not the old planter leadership, but men who saw opportunity for themselves and their community in business, industrial development, railroading, finance, and who were sufficiently pragmatic to make the necessary break with the older ways of thinking about government and public service.

Wealth and material progress lay, obviously, in railroads, and politics now become a way of furthering the interests of the railroads. General William A. Mahone—no antebellum planter but a self-made man—controlled both the Norfolk and Petersburg and the South Side railroads, and wanted to consolidate them with the Virginia and Tennessee, running from Lynchburg to Bristol, into a single system that would connect the Hampton Roads area with the western trunk lines. John S. Barbour's Orange and Alexandria, principally controlled by the Baltimore & Ohio, was a rival for the trade of the southwest. The Pennsylvania Central sought control of north-south traffic, and even purchased the *Richmond Enquirer* to further its objectives. Legislators took sides and were sought after; much money changed hands. Before the war the state had invested heavily in railroad securities to further the building of new lines, and now such securities, though selling far below par because of wartime damage and economic conditions, represented a considerable source of potential future revenue. But state control of railroad securities interfered with the manipulation and maneuvering that were necessary to the forming of railroad systems, and so one of the first acts of Governor Walker's administration was to sell most of the state's railroad stock to private interests.

A battle ensued between Mahone and his forces and those of the northern-controlled lines, in particular the Pennsylvania Central; the ultimate winner was the Pennsylvania Central, which after 1873 enjoyed virtually a free hand in the state. By the 1880s northern corporations had taken over transportation in Virginia, and there were few barriers to their economic policies.

Outside money was badly needed in Virginia, and there was an automatic alliance between the financial and industrial interests of Wall Street and Philadelphia and the financial and business interests within the state. When Walker was elected governor in 1869, the *Richmond Whig* announced happily that "Virginia is now open to capitalists and immigrants," while the *Norfolk Journal* boasted that "Virginia is soon to be what Virginia never was." Not all Virginians were happy about this. "Reconstruction may make an Empire of physical Virginia— which may be great in its proportions and influential in the Councils of the Union," J. Randolph Tucker wrote to his old states-rights Democratic ally Robert M. T. Hunter. "But what can restore that social polity which constituted the Virginia of our pride?" [4] For the most part, however, the political future in Virginia lay for now in the hands of those who wanted to make the Old Dominion a business community. Richmond and Norfolk, the seats of power, had already been well along the road toward being centers of commerce and manufacture before the war. Politically they had been unionist and Whig, of the John Marshall loose-constructionist rather than the John C. Calhoun strict-constructionist ilk, as befitted communities that would like to make active use of the power of government to advance business interests. Now they were shifting into high gear, for their leaders best of all were able to join in the spirit of the capitalistic Gilded Age.

The General Assembly which convened under Governor Walker was considerably less experienced legislatively than most assemblies either before the Reconstruction or in years to come. Such an assembly was more than ordinarily vulnerable to manipulation, and so, when confronted with not only the act to

4. Allen W. Moger, *Virginia: Bourbonism to Byrd, 1870–1925* (Charlottesville: University Press of Virginia, 1968), pp. 82–85.

sell the state's railroad stocks but another measure to fund the state's prewar debt at full interest in order to sustain "the honor of Virginia," the assembly proved compliant. The result was that Virginia took on, despite what the war had done to its wealth and economy, a renewed, refunded state debt, including interest for the war years, which by 1871 amounted to some $45 million. Even West Virginia's rightful share, which should have come to about a third, was to be handled by interest-bearing certificates until that state could be persuaded to assume its proportional part (and which it did not do until forced to do so by a Supreme Court decision a half-century later). By 1871 the interest alone on the debt was so large that all the state's revenues, except for the small sum earmarked for public education, were required to meet it, and this left nothing for paying the expenses of state government, estimated at approximately one million dollars a year.

Meanwhile Virginia had a new Conservative governor, James L. Kemper, ex-Confederate hero and lawyer. Kemper was an honest man, and though racial arguments had been used to secure his election, he was determined to see that black citizens received—by his standards and those of his fellow white Conservatives—fair treatment. But Kemper was irascible, irritable, and in important ways ineffective as a leader.

The loss of revenue because of the Funding Act had increased to such an extent that money appropriated for education had to be diverted to meet interest payments. In 1877, one hundred and twenty-seven schoolhouses had to be shut down. Superintendent of Public Instruction William H. Ruffner, whose father had been a crusader for public education in antebellum days, protested bitterly. "Here we have over three thousand children remanded into semibarbarism . . . ," he declared, ". . . a costly economy, and one of the earlier bitter fruits of that spoliation of the schools." [5] Old-line Virginians had never given up their notion that public education, whether for poor whites or blacks, was a needless expenditure of funds. Only evil, declared Professor Robert Lewis Dabney of Union Theological Seminary, could come of "leveling" attempts to raise the masses,

5. Pulley, *Old Virginia Restored*, p. 33.

while black Virginians were, in his view, racially immune to education. Matthew Fontaine Maury was bitter in denunciation of "this system of common schools which had been thrust upon us." [6]

Governor Kemper, though pledging himself to support the school system, decried the notion that money for schools in any way represented an obligation superior to other governmental expenditures or the meeting of interest payments on the state debt. Business and financial interests in particular demanded that "the honor of Virginia" be maintained at all hazards, including the extinction of its school system.

Mahone had reversed his earlier support of funding, and was now engaged in an all-out campaign to force readjustment of the debt. The debt had to be readjusted and interest payments scaled down to a point that would permit the children of the Old Dominion to be educated, he declared. Such a position, declared the *Richmond Enquirer*, constituted a revolutionary menace to property. By this time Mahone had all but lost his railroad power, and his ambitions were politically focused. He wanted to run for governor, but when it became apparent that the Conservative convention of 1877 would not give him a majority, he threw his support to another ex-Confederate officer, Colonel Frederick W. M. Holliday, whom he mistakenly thought favored readjustment because he had succeeded in avoiding the issue. The extent of Mahone's error became apparent when the General Assembly passed the Barbour Bill, sponsored by delegate James Barbour, earmarking specific proportions of state revenue for government, the schools, and debt reduction, which, though not a repudiation of the debt, severely restricted the amount that could be used each year to pay it. Holliday, having previously pledged himself to respect the legislature's wishes on the matter, promptly vetoed the bill. "Free schools are not a necessity . . . ," he declared. "They are a luxury . . . to be paid for, like any other luxury, by the people who wish their benefits." [7]

---

6. Jack P. Maddex, Jr., *The Virginia Conservatives, 1867–1879: A Study in Reconstruction Politics* (Chapel Hill: University of North Carolina Press, 1970), pp. 211, 213.
7. Moger, *Bourbonism to Byrd*, p. 34.

In late February 1879 Mahone called a people's convention to meet in Richmond and there form a Readjuster party. John E. ("Parson") Massey of Albemarle, James Barbour, Harrison H. Riddleberger of the Valley, and others joined him. In the General Assembly elections that year the Readjusters swept the state, and in 1880 passed Riddleberger's bill for readjustment, which Holliday also vetoed. Mahone, elected to the United States Senate by the assembly in 1879, where he voted with the Republicans, set to work to organize the 1881 gubernatorial election, and the Readjuster candidate, William E. Cameron, was elected. In December H. H. Riddleberger was chosen for the other Senate seat. Mahone's party, now in complete control, enacted the Riddleberger debt law, which Cameron signed. The act, as Allen W. Moger says, "represented the triumph of the principle 'that the State's creditors should be compelled to share in the general loss occasioned by war and reconstruction.' " Not all provisions of the act were allowed to stand in subsequent years, but Virginia was assured a public school system, state hospitals and asylums, and the Funder concept of "Virginia's honor" was not permitted, in Moger's words, "to remain as a millstone hobbling the state's ability to serve its people in the new age." [8]

The Readjuster administration enacted a number of other socially significant measures. School funds were secured, and money diverted to pay bond interest was repaid. The poll tax was repealed. The whipping post was abolished—black Virginians insisted upon this, for by law persons punished by public whipping were disfranchised, so that conservative white courts had been quick to sentence convicted blacks to whippings. Realty taxes were reduced. Corporate revenue was increased through raising assessed valuation. Duelling was outlawed. Large appropriations were voted for state institutions of higher learning.

Mahone, however, soon had the Readjuster party deeply divided. Many of his supporters had been with him on the debt question, but were not anxious to engineer the complete over-

8. Moger, *Bourbonism to Byrd*, pp. 39–41.

haul of Virginia's established order that he had in mind. The wholesale vacating of all offices in order to fill them with his supporters alienated many; in particular the ousting of William Ruffner as state superintendent of public schools seemed unjust. Mahone's ability to manipulate the black vote not only disturbed some of his supporters but played into the hands of the Conservatives. His willingness to apply financial pressures and to require officeholders to return part of their salaries into his political chest, his ruthless use of the patronage power that his Republican affiliation gave him, ultimately proved his undoing.

Parson Massey, himself ambitious for office, broke with Mahone, as did other influential Readjusters. Elated, the Conservatives prepared for triumph; they would again "redeem" the state, they claimed, this time from Republicanism, Mahoneism, corruption, and Negro rule. (The blacks, of course, possessed little power and were in a decided minority, but that Mahone could and would rely upon black votes was argument enough.) They changed their party name from Conservative to Democratic, and they promised unqualified support of free schools for black and white. Organizing their campaign well, and ruthlessly exploiting a race riot at Danville, which some have said was deliberately staged for that purpose, they won a two-thirds majority in the General Assembly, and proceeded to revamp state government and redistrict congressional seats in order to secure their total control.

A new election law gave the Democrats near-complete mastery of the election machinery; when Governor Cameron rejected it, the assembly overrode his veto. In 1885 Fitzhugh Lee, who was a strong advocate of business and progress, was elected governor and John W. Daniel was chosen to Mahone's Senate seat. Though Mahone remained a force to reckon with in state politics for a few years more, his days of power were over.

In place of government by the planter class, Virginia was now governed by a political machine. "Railroads," as Allen Moger says, "were in the driver's seat." [9] The leading Democratic party figures were men with close ties to railroad and fi-

9. Moger, *Bourbonism to Byrd*, p. 121.

nancial interests—often enough they were attorneys for the railroads. Into a position of power soon moved Thomas Staples Martin of Scottsville, counsel for the Chesapeake and Ohio Railway. In the gubernatorial campaign of 1889, when Mahone made his last bid for power and was defeated decisively by Philip W. McKinney, Martin had shown how to use railroad money to get out the electorate and to purchase votes. In 1893 he made his move; by dint of a behind-the-scenes campaign in which railroad money was skillfully used to line up votes in the assembly, he managed to defeat the most popular of living Virginians, Fitzhugh Lee, for the United States Senate. Martin now proceeded to develop a powerful organization, with its leaders including Hal Flood, Claude A. Swanson, James Hay, Henry T. Wickham, and others, all of them closely allied with the railroads.

The spirit of the New South of commerce and manufacture was now abroad in the land. Real estate developments mushroomed; the suburbs of Richmond, Norfolk, and other cities were expanded. Collis P. Huntington brought the C&O Railroad to deep water at the little village of Newport News, spent $7 million on coal and grain terminals, and also established a shipbuilding plant, which by 1900 was valued at close to $15 million. Across Hampton Roads the Norfolk and Western Railroad created huge coaling facilities at Lambert's Point. In the mountain areas there was frantic activity. Almost overnight the city of Roanoke was created. In 1881 some four hundred persons had lived in the little village of Big Lick; then came the N&W and the Shenandoah Valley Railroad shops, manufacturing and mining companies, and by 1892, now named Roanoke, it had a population of 25,000. In towns such as Wytheville, Buena Vista, and elsewhere, developing companies moved in to create real estate booms and spread promises of overnight metamorphosis into bustling cities. Then came the financial crash of 1893, and almost everything was wiped out. Staid old Lexington, where Lee and Jackson were buried, also had a boom, only to suffer disastrously when the Bank of Lexington failed after the cashier embezzled almost $200,000. All over the state, but especially in the Valley, there were similar operations, usually followed by similar results, not so much from chicanery as from overexpansion and subsequent collapse. For years afterward one might drive through the Shenandoah Valley and the mountains and see the ghostly ruins of old hotels and factories.

By contrast, agriculture in Virginia knew no such boom cycle; even in the relatively prosperous period of the late 1880s and early 1890s, its recovery from the wartime devastation was less spectacular. Many of the old planter families who had dominated antebellum Virginia life left their plantations and moved into the cities, where the sons of country gentlemen became businessmen and attorneys. The small farmer became dominant. Rural Virginia now came to mean middle-class white landowners, getting by in a somewhat threadbare fashion. What they began coming up against more and more were the trusts—bagging trusts, fertilizer trusts, farm-equipment trusts, railroad trusts, others. The General Assembly, dominated by business and financial interests, was not at first responsive to the demand for a state railroad commission to protect against discrimination, nor was legislative relief from other trust monopolies forthcoming.

With the panic of 1893, things got much worse. Credit dried up; money was scarce. Already leading Virginia farmers had been urging united action by farmers to better their lot. The farmers' revolt that began in the southwest spread to Virginia. Even before the panic, in 1890, there were 30,000 members of the Farmers' Alliance in 94 counties. The leaders of the alliance in Virginia were men of distinction, many of them from the old antebellum planter establishment, as can be seen in their names: Colonel Robert Beverley, Mann Page, Colonel Randolph Harrison, Major A. R. Venable, Edmund Randolph Cocke, George Christman, William S. Gravely, T. Y. Allen, J. Haskins Hobson, J. M. Ruffin, the latter the grandson of the old agricultural reformer and secessionist Edmund Ruffin. The alliance founded newspapers, set up co-operative stores, sponsored farming institutes to teach scientific farming methods, and even sought to establish a factory to manufacture plows at a reasonable price. In 1891 the alliance threatened to run independent candidates for the General Assembly, but dropped the idea after a harmonizing convention in which the Democratic leadership promised faithfully to see that a full-fledged railroad regulatory commission was established. What resulted, once the assembly had been re-elected, was a weak commission arrangement, which showed the farm leaders all too clearly that the railroad influence in the party was stronger than theirs. Added to the growing agitation over free coinage of silver and the shortage of currency, the situation was ripe for agrarian revolt, and the result was the calling of a Virginia Populist party convention in 1892.

The national Democratic party had nominated Grover Cleveland, a hard-money, anti-silver man, and so at the national Populist convention some members of the Virginia Farmers' Alliance declared for the Populist candidate, James B. Weaver, a Westerner, whose running mate was James G. Field, a Virginia Confederate veteran. Cleveland, however, carried Virginia handily. U.S. Republican Senator Henry Cabot Lodge's Force Bill, calling for federal intervention in Southern elections where black voters were clearly being discriminated against, was all the weapon the Democrats needed to flaunt the race issue. The alliance rank-and-file membership disintegrated.

By the last years of the nineteenth century the Democratic party was thoroughly in control in Virginia. Republicanism was dead; so was any threat of a Populist fusion. The economic upturn of the late 1890s mollified dissident farmers, and narrowed the rural-urban schism. Virginia was a one-party state, and any opposition to Thomas S. Martin and the Democratic leadership would henceforth come from within the party.

It had taken some thirty-five years for Virginia to return to its role as a border state within the American Union. Reconstruction, Funder-Readjuster controversy, Republicanism, Fusion, Mahoneism, economic boom-or-bust, agrarian insurgency—the years had been full of tumult and disorder. The state that in antebellum times had been known for its generally placid temper, its ordered social and economic ways, its avoidance of extremes, had experienced a considerable amount of change. Virginia had had to broaden the base of its constituency to include the rural and urban white middle class, providing at least the minimum of schools, hospitals, and social institutions that such people demanded; if white supremacy was to be maintained, the yeomanry—the lower-middle-class whites—could not be excluded in such fashion. Political and social peace, in short, had required a political, social, and economic structure more closely attuned to the realities of American laissez-faire capitalism than Virginia had been willing to admit, and it had taken some time for the lesson to be learned.

Yet the weight of several hundred years of a distinctive and creative past could not be cast off so lightly; along with certain necessary readjustment went a strong and palpable impulse toward reassertion and retention of the old ways. The Virginians wanted order, stability; they were not disposed indefinitely to accept a political or social status quo which could not provide these. The extensive bribery, election fraud, and buying of votes that had been used on all sides following the readmission of the state into the Union had disgusted most voters. Whatever else might be said about the state's planter leadership in the antebellum period, there had at least been personal honesty, clean government. What had changed that, of course, was the economic and social chaos of the postwar period: not only had close to a hundred thousand black Virginians been enfranchised, but lower-class whites, no longer constrained by deference to the gentry, also became an important factor. The rush of the railroad and business interests to regain prosperity by following the successful example of the victorious capitalism of the northeast had involved the frequent and open application of money to gain political objectives. The mass of the black electorate, uneducated, unprepared for political participation, and left without any firm economic foundation to replace the shackles of slavery, was all too easily manipulated, and in no condition to resist either bribes or threats, economic or physical intimidation, by the contending interests.

In 1901, therefore, Virginia followed the lead of the Deep South states and called a constitutional convention to reform state government and disfranchise the blacks. The growing disposition in the north and west to view racial equality as a Southern rather than a national problem had resulted in black disfranchisement in state after Southern state. Free to discriminate

against its black citizens by legal means, Virginia now under-
took to remove the Underwood constitution of 1868 which had
guaranteed universal suffrage for black and white. The way to
achieve corruption-free government and to end the bribery,
stuffing of ballot boxes, intimidation, and violence that had
marked the electoral process since the war, reforming Virginians reasoned, was to remove the black man as a factor in elections. Voters must henceforth pay a poll tax, which had to be
paid up for the three preceding years, and by six months prior to
the general election. Any would-be voter who had not paid a
property tax to the state, or who was not either a Confederate or
Union veteran or the son of one, had to give a "reasonable" explanation of any section of the state constitution, with local registration boards empowered to determine what was "reasonable." After 1903 a would-be voter would have to apply for
registration in his handwriting, without aid, and so on.

Since more than half the black males of voting age were illiterate, and a poll tax of $1.50 meant a considerable outlay, black
voting declined more than ninety percent after the new constitution went into effect in 1902. But it was not only blacks who
were disfranchised; the new laws had the effect of disfranchising poor white voters as well. Particularly in the mountain districts, which not by coincidence were strongly Republican in
sentiment, large numbers of voters were henceforth denied the
suffrage. In effect Virginia now went all the way back to the
period before the constitutional convention of 1850, and restricted the franchise to "the better sort of people" in much the
same way the old property qualifications had done. How well
the new constitution succeeded in controlling the electorate can
be seen in the fact that in the next election for governor, in
1905, 88,000 fewer persons voted than in 1901.

The changes in the constitution, however, were not restricted
to voting procedures. The new constitution abolished the old
system of county courts, placed the authority to select circuit
judges and judges of the Supreme Court of Appeals in the hands
of the General Assembly, and generally gave the Democratic organization, which controlled the legislature, powers over local
government, including selection of registrars, school boards,

and clerks and judges of elections. It also established a state corporation commission to regulate railroads and other corporations, thereby heeding the demands of farming leaders and serving to minimize future possibilities of agricultural discontent. The Martin organization itself did not favor such a move, but the independent Democratic majority in the convention insisted upon it.

Along with the loss of the ballot went a series of laws enacted by the General Assembly over the next several decades which fastened upon black Virginians a segregated status in all walks of life. Streetcars, railways, public waiting rooms, theaters, eating places—all were segregated. Jim Crow laws were extended to cover all public contact between the races. As Benjamin Quarles had noted, it was "to bolster their own self-esteem" that lower-class Southern whites "insisted upon their social superiority to the Negro, and even such titles as 'Hon.' or 'Mr.' for the exceptional Negro were abandoned." [10] The continued consent of those lower-class whites—not the illiterate poor whites, but the farmers and the working people of the cities— was needed if the ordered, stable society that had now been reestablished following three decades of political chaos was to be maintained. It was the price to be paid, and it was paid willingly.

The black man was not totally disfranchised in Virginia after 1902—some 15,000 blacks continued to vote. He was, however, thoroughly removed as a political force. The scare tactics of black domination which had been employed against him had hardly been in line with the facts; once the Underwood constitution had been adopted, blacks had never constituted a majority of eligible male voters. There had never been anything close to a black majority in the General Assembly. No black Virginian had ever been elected governor, lieutenant-governor, or U. S. senator, and only one black, John Mercer Langston, had served as a congressman. Langston, former dean of the Howard University law school, U. S. minister to Haiti, and the first presi-

10. Benjamin Quarles, *The Negro in the Making of America* (New York: Collier Books, 1968), pp. 146–147.

dent of Virginia Normal and Collegiate Institute, defied Mahone's wishes and successfully campaigned for Congress in 1888. Running again in 1890, he was defeated.

The years of the 1880s and 1890s were, for black Virginians and other black Americans, what historians have since come to call the Nadir. The war had ended slavery, but had not resulted in equality before the law, and the former slave, without education or training in self-government, had been manipulated by Republicans and Democrats alike, then disfranchised as scapegoat for the corruption. To keep blacks from gaining and holding political office, violence and intimidation were regularly practiced, while white law-enforcement officers looked the other way. In prewar Virginia, slaves and free blacks had performed many of the skilled-labor jobs; now working-class whites began pushing them out of such employment, and the coming of trade unionism, from which blacks were excluded, brought further discrimination. The "forty acres and a mule," which many had been led to believe would be forthcoming from the Freedmen's Bureau, had not materialized. Without money or power, they were under a severe disadvantage. Public education was, however grudgingly, now made available for them, but the separate schools were not equal, and except for a brief time during the Readjuster period there was very little money spent on education for black Virginians.

However, a beginning at least had been made. Normal schools had been founded for black teachers after the war, and some of these were maintained. Perhaps the most important fact—and symbol, as well—of black aspirations was the Hampton Institute, founded in 1868 by General Samuel Chapman Armstrong under the auspices of the Freedmen's Bureau. Offering manual training and higher trade schooling for former slaves, it not only turned out a steady supply of teachers, but among its early graduates was the man who became the outstanding black leader of late-nineteenth- and early-twentieth-century America, Booker T. Washington. Born a slave in Franklin, Virginia, in 1856, Washington had managed to work his way through Hampton Institute, and had later gone down to head Tuskegee Institute, a new school for blacks in Alabama.

Working with almost no resources, he built Tuskegee into a leading institution, and thereafter his role became nationwide. Washington's policy of setting aside black claims to political and social equality in order to concentrate on economic goals aroused the ire of some black leaders, who felt he was acquiescing in permanent second-class citizenship, and in the years after his death he became for many black intellectuals the symbol of "Uncle Tom" subservience. Yet privately Washington worked to break down segregation and discrimination, and it must be said that given the climate of opinion in the 1890s and 1900s, he chose the only strategy that would succeed in preventing Southern white extremists from denying all support to the schools and colleges upon which eventual black hopes for better days depended. The black leaders who would spearhead the drive for an end to segregation in the 1950s and 1960s were educated at the schools that Booker T. Washington's generation built.

The constitution of 1902 not only moved to restore the political stability of the prewar years, but in its provision for a state corporation commission and its effort—which proved largely effective—to remove the potentialities for political corruption by disfranchising those who were most vulnerable to corrupting tactics, it also came to terms with the vigorous presence within the community of the forces of modern American industrial society. It was not Old Virginia that had been restored, but only so much of the older ways as could be harmonized with the economic and social realities of the new day. Richmond, Norfolk, Newport News, Petersburg, Roanoke, Lynchburg—these were not social and supply centers for life given over almost entirely to agriculture, but flourishing modern urban areas, with a vigorous industrial output and an aggressive commercial distribution into wide regions of Virginia and the southeast. By northeastern standards they were not large, but their role and importance in Virginia life was vastly greater than in the antebellum period. The state as a whole was still eighty-five percent rural, but money and power were in the cities. The Hampton Roads area was now a great ocean port; with the completion of the Virginian Railway in 1909, three major lines were steadily funneling

long trainloads of coal from the mountains to Norfolk and Newport News for shipment all over the world. Richmond in the
year 1900 was the northern terminus of the two major railroads
to the southeastern seaboard and their connection with the northeast, as well as their junction with the Chesapeake and Ohio to
the east and west. There were no less than 1,245 manufacturing
plants within the city. "Cherishing the best traditions of the past
and adopting the progressive spirit of modern enterprise," as a
tourist's guide to Richmond put it, "the city is hastening in her
advance to her destined eminence." [11]

Indeed, it was perhaps because of the rapidity of that hastening process, and the swiftness with which the city recovered
commercially and physically from the devastation of the war,
that Richmond surpassed all others in the state and even in the
entire South in the public devotion it paid to the Confederate
past. As the onetime capital of the Confederacy, it was only natural that Richmond would become a shrine, as it were, to the
memory of the Lost Cause, and since the city was financially in
rather better condition than most other Southern cities to exhibit
its homage, it lost few opportunities to do so. As the city limits
expanded steadily westward, so did a spacious boulevard, Mon-
ument Avenue, along which at intervals were erected imposing
statues of the great Confederates—Lee, Jackson, Stuart,
Matthew Fontaine Maury, and—the only non-Virginian thus
honored—Jefferson Davis. Each unveiling was the occasion for
elaborate ceremonies, with parades, speechmaking, reunions of
the veterans.

The Confederate tribute-paying was not without its political
relevance, to be sure: all the leading politicians were ex-
Confederates, and the Democratic party's regaining control of
the state was portrayed as a reassertion of the Confederate heritage by the ex-Confederates doing the controlling. Any dissent
on race or "honor" was always branded as an insult to the dead
heroes of the Confederacy.

But politics cannot explain the fervor and devotion with

    11. C. Poindexter, *Richmond, Va.: An Illustrated Hand-Book of the City and the
Battle Fields* (Richmond: The Hermitage Press, 1907), p. 122.

which the Virginians took up the memory of the Lost Cause, and converted the onetime profane and unwashed fighting men of Lee's army into the stainless chivalry of mythology. As the novelist James Branch Cabell recalled of the Richmond of the 1880s and 1890s, the Virginians addressed themselves "as to a paradise in which they had lived once upon a time, and in which there had been no imperfection, but only beauty and chivalry and contentment. They spoke of womanhood, and of the brightness of hope's rainbow, and of the tomb, and of Right upon the scaffold, and of the scroll of fame, and of stars, and of the verdict of posterity. But above all did they speak of a thin line of heroes who had warred for righteousness' sake in vain, and of four years' intrepid battling, even from the McLean farmlands at Bull Run to the McLeans' parlor at Appomattox." What they were engaged in doing, as Cabell noted—what the South was engaged in doing—was creating, "in the same instant that they lamented the Old South's extinction, an Old South which had died proudly at Appomattox without ever having been besmirched by the wear and tear of existence." [12]

It was neither coincidence nor, I think, hypocrisy that prompted Thomas Nelson Page, the state's leading author of postwar years, to compose the stories of antebellum plantation life that went to make up *In Ole Virginia,* in which aging former slaves recount in dialect tales of their white masters back in the days when, to quote one of them, "Dem was good ole times, marster—de bes' Sam ever see! . . . Dyar warn' no trouble nor nothin'." [13] Page's black retainers are entirely extensions of the white man's needs, written for a postbellum audience grappling with such problems as Funders and Readjusters, railroad regulation, white supremacy, and the Farmers' Alliance. They are eulogy and admonition, a pastoral rebuke for a people faced with making a living in a society in which white Virginians

---

12. James Branch Cabell, "Almost Touching the Confederacy," *Let Me Lie: Being in the Main an Ethnological Account of the Remarkable Commonwealth of Virginia and the Making of Its History* (New York: Farrar, Straus, 1947), pp. 145, 153–154.

13. Thomas Nelson Page, "Marse Chan," *In Ole Virginia: or, Marse Chan and Other Stories* (New York: Charles Scribner's Sons, 1887), p. 10.

were scaling down the prewar debt with three-percent Riddleberger bonds and black men were running for Congress. The
past was, at such a time, comfort, reassurance, and—equally as
importantly—model.

10

A New Era

*In which the Virginians achieve the Age
of Harry Byrd.*

*T*HE temper of Virginia's political life in the early years of
the twentieth century was marked by the reforming progressivism that characterized so much of American life during the
period. In its essence the Progressive movement represented the
development of political methods to control the economic and
social forces unleashed through modern industrialism, and most
of the political maneuverings within the Old Dominion after
1900 can be understood within that context. Greatly increased
educational expenditures—though never enough, regulation of
railroads, development of a highway network, enactment of
child-labor laws and pure-food-and-drug standards, expansion
and modernization of hospitals, asylums, reformatories, and
prisons, and creation of the agencies to oversee all these—such
were the principal accomplishments of Virginia government
during these years. There was no really important ideological
division between the state organization led by Thomas S. Martin, Henry D. ("Hal") Flood, and Claude Swanson, which controlled state government during most of the period, and the antiorganization Democrats who opposed it.

The most volatile issue of the time was Prohibition, which in
Virginia as elsewhere emerged as part of the Progressivist im-

159

pulse. The dominant Martin organization generally went along with it, and sought alliance with the Methodist minister who was Prohibition's chief mogul, James Cannon, Jr. In 1914 the General Assembly voted out Demon Run in Virginia, after one profoundly hungover statesman was routed from his alcoholic slumbers to cast the deciding ballot. For a time Cannon was the most influential force in Virginia politics; indeed, by throwing his support to Taylor Ellyson, a Dry, in the 1917 gubernatorial election, mainly because he didn't care for John Garland Pollard of Richmond, another Dry, Cannon managed to get the only avowed Wet in the field, Westmoreland Davis of Leesburg, elected governor.

Getting elected to state office in Virginia throughout the period was usually a matter of which way some eight thousand to ten thousand votes were cast. The 1902 constitution had so cut down on voting that fewer than a hundred thousand active Democrats regularly voted, and in such a situation, as Virginius Dabney says, the solid phalanx of state and federal officeholders who were beholden to the organization could deliver the necessary margin of victory.[1]

One reason why Prohibition, and not economic conditions, constituted the major political issue in the Old Dominion during the first several decades of the new century was that Virginia was generally prospering, while those elements of the population that shared least in the prosperity and so might be expected to protest—the blacks and the poorer whites—were no longer a factor in elections. Agriculture did comparatively well in these years, though with ups and downs. Except in the Southside, where tobacco was the main crop, Virginia farmers had diversified their operations, and were less vulnerable to the vicissitudes of the marketplace than in the past. More significantly, Virginia had not only continued but intensified its development of a border-state, industrial-agricultural economy; between 1910 and 1920 the value of goods produced in the state rose sixfold, and by 1920 more than half the state's population was no longer engaged in agriculture. The cities grew in population and

1. Dabney, *Virginia,* p. 457.

wealth. Richmond, the center for tobacco processing, developed a diversified industrial structure that was to stand her in good stead when the Great Depression of the 1930s came. Norfolk's overseas and coastal trade burgeoned, and the enormous expansion of the entire Hampton Roads area during the First World War brought not only much folding money but a large influx of population; government military and naval installations provided payrolls and prosperity such as had never before been known. Petersburg developed important manufactures; nearby the city of Hopewell emerged overnight from plowed fields into a munitions and chemical center. Danville had a prosperous textile industry. Towns such as Martinsville became centers for furniture building. Roanoke, the Magic City, added to its railroad operations the largest rayon plant in the world. In Northern Virginia, the long-stagnant economy of Alexandria took on new industrial life, and as the First World War expanded the operations of the national government in Washington, population began spilling over into hitherto rural Fairfax County. Virginia was indeed back in the Union, as it had not been since 1861. A Virginia-born President, Woodrow Wilson, occupied the White House, and Virginians were playing a role in national politics again such as had been denied them during all the long years since the end of the Civil War.

The South was once again influential in Washington; there were, during Wilson's two terms, twenty chairmen of congressional committees who were Southerners, seven of them Virginians. Even Martin, though passed over as majority leader, worked ably for Wilson as chairman of the Senate appropriations committee, and later on succeeded to the majority leadership. The Virginians generally supported Wilson's antitrust, tariff, and social legislation, while Carter Glass took the proposed Federal Reserve System unto himself, guided it through the House, later became Secretary of the Treasury, and ever afterward worked to further its aims, to the extent, as Allen Moger remarks, that "posterity would refer to him as the 'Father of the Federal Reserve System.' " [2]

2. Moger, *Bourbonism to Byrd*, pp. 280–281.

Woodrow Wilson enjoyed immense popularity throughout Virginia, as the organization knew very well. His economic reforms were generally popular; his idealism struck a note that had been missing in Virginia politics for many years; and in bearing, attitude, and way of language he exemplified the gentleman in politics. Black Virginians, to be sure, soon came to take a somewhat different view, because the Southern-born President did not make room for them in his New Freedom. Instead, his administration saw massive segregation introduced in all governmental activities, discrimination in civil-service appointments, and a general willingness to let Southern notions of race relations serve as national policy. But this, of course, did not at all diminish Wilson's popularity with most white Virginians, who supported him as progressive, as war leader, and as postwar crusader for a League of Nations, and for whom he ever afterward remained the ideal of what an American President should be.

When the United States entered the First World War, the long-suppressed patriotic and martial ardor of Virginia expressed itself in an enthusiastic flocking to the colors. Some 1,200 Virginians were killed during the war. On the home front the influenza epidemic that ravaged the United States took a far greater toll, with 11,641 dying in Virginia.

In 1919 Tom Martin died. Conservative, personally honest, a shrewd organizer, he had controlled Democratic politics in the Old Dominion for three decades. Governor Davis now had the right to appoint his successor, and after an interview with Carter Glass in which that longtime independent, now Secretary of the Treasury, reiterated his opposition to the Democratic machine and his intention to battle against it for the rest of his life, Davis named Glass to the Senate. The organization, now led by Hal Flood, Claude Swanson, and Rorer A. James, thereupon set out successfully to cultivate Carter Glass. Within a few years' time Glass was solidly within the fold, and remained so for the rest of his days.

It was the 1921 gubernatorial primary that first saw the emergence of the man who was to oversee its operations for almost half a century. State Senator Harry Flood Byrd, son of

House Speaker Richard Evelyn Byrd and nephew and namesake of Hal Flood, played a leading part in the election of the organization's candidate, E. Lee Trinkle of Wytheville. Trinkle was relatively little known in Virginia, but the organization valued his attempt, fruitless though it was, to defeat longtime incumbent C. Bascom Slemp for the Ninth District congressional seat in 1916. No Democrat, it appeared, could regain that seat from the Republican Slemp, for the Fighting Ninth, as it was called, which stretched along the counties of southwestern Virginia toward Tennessee, was strongly Republican. The Ninth was the one district with a genuine two-party system, and interestingly enough, the district in which both Democrats and Republicans were still given very much to the election frauds, vote-buying, ballot-box stealing, and the like that had largely disappeared from Virginia since the constitution of 1902. Trinkle had fought hard to capture the Ninth, and now he was rewarded with the organization endorsement for the governorship.

Young Byrd traveled over the state, speaking for Trinkle and co-ordinating the efforts of the party faithful. To the amazement of many who did not credit the organization's sustaining strength, Trinkle was elected by a comfortable margin.

When in 1922 Westmoreland Davis ran against Swanson for the Senate, Byrd, now state Democratic party chairman, demonstrated a matchless efficiency on Swanson's behalf, journeying throughout the state, and employing the aid of young men such as E. R. Combs, Howard W. Smith, and A. Willis Robertson. Swanson registered an easy triumph.

Byrd was a Virginian of Virginians, whose antecedents went directly back to that first William Byrd who had come to the colony as a merchant and land speculator in 1670. In the nineteenth century the Byrd family had fallen upon fallow times, but now, after more than two hundred years, it was to regain its prominence in Virginia. For the next forty years the names of Harry Byrd and the Virginia Democratic party were to be all but synonymous.

Byrd came onto the Virginia scene with an admiration for Tom Martin's organizational skills and with a strong belief that state government must be efficient, frugal, and honest. The key-

stone of his policy, almost from the first, was pay-as-you-go;
Virginia must not, he felt, mortgage its future by bonded indebtedness. A successful newspaper publisher and apple
grower, he wanted Virginia to be fiscally sound and responsive
to the needs of the economy. He was not, in those days, an opponent of necessary change. One of his strongest concerns was
for good roads; the era of the automobile had come, but
Virginia lagged far behind the other states in converting its dirt
wagon roads into paved highways. The Virginia Good Roads
Association favored a forty-million-dollar bond issue to finance
them. Byrd, however, had different ideas; what he proposed instead was a two-cents-a-gallon tax on gasoline. Byrd not only
worked against highway bonds, but to get the message to the
politicians the organization set out to make examples of certain
candidates for state office who opposed pay-as-you-go. The
bond issue was thoroughly defeated, with the rural voters voting
heavily against it.

When Trinkle's term ended, Byrd himself ran for governor
and won an easy victory. "I construe my election as a mandate
to me as a businessman to institute the best methods of efficiency and economy in state affairs," he declared, whereupon
he proceeded to do exactly that.[3] With the General Assembly
following his leadership and the electorate ratifying the results
in a referendum, he centralized responsibility by becoming the
administrative as well as the political head of the government.
Securing the recommendations of a management bureau, he
streamlined the sprawling state bureaucracy into twelve departments, eliminated the multiplicity of local commissioners of the
revenue, limited the number of elected state officials to three—
governor, lieutenant-governor, and attorney general—chosen by
popular vote, notably increased appropriations for roads, education, and mental hospitals, revised the tax structure to attract industry to the state but also forced the oil companies and the tele-
phone company to conform to state laws. He created a state
conservation and development commission to establish Shenandoah National Park and saw that a strong antilynching law was

3. Moger, *Bourbonism to Byrd*, p. 341.

enacted. He also obtained a constitutional amendment that all but eliminated future general-obligation bond issues by the state, and left office with a surplus of $4,250,000 in the treasury despite a tax cut.

It was an impressive performance, and it established Byrd as a leading Southern progressive. What he had done, in effect, was to bring Virginia's government into the twentieth-century, postwar world. Byrd made the changes or saw that they were made. He seemed, to Virginia voters of the middle 1920s, to exemplify what was best in their state; an honored name, an affability and dignity that were outgoing but did not condescend, a fiscal soundness and practicality that made government efficient and useful but not unnecessarily intrusive upon private interests and concerns, a rigorous honesty and intolerance of corruption, and the capacity to preserve the best of the past while living and working squarely within the present. That in the decades ahead he would devote much of his energy to keeping things as they were in the 1920s, and that such changes as he had brought about during his governorship were just about all the change he would ever be willing to accept for the rest of his life, could not then be foreseen.

Governor Byrd's seemingly secure position at the head of Virginia's political destinies very soon came under a formidable challenge, however, when in 1928, over the vigorous protests of Virginia's delegation and the other Southern delegations to the party convention, the national Democratic party selected as its candidate for President the governor of New York, Alfred E. Smith. Smith was a Wet, a Roman Catholic, a product of the Tammany organization, a Yankee, and of Irish immigrant stock to boot. As such he was anathema to the rural, Protestant, prohibitionist South, and to no one more than to the now Bishop Cannon, who in company with many another Southern churchman led a crusade against Smith and the Democratic ticket, giving his support to Herbert Hoover. Byrd and the Democratic organization, though unhappy over Smith's candidacy, stuck with the party, and Byrd himself loyally toured the state making speeches against the Republican ticket; there was no room in his politics then for the tactics being used against Al Smith. But the election saw Virginia and three other Southern states desert the Democratic ranks and go Republican for the first time since the Reconstruction.

In 1929, the Virginia Democratic party prepared to nominate a governor to succeed Harry Byrd. Cannon demanded that Byrd and the other organization leaders who had supported Smith offer a public apology for criticism of anti-Smith Democrats, made during the campaign of 1928, and such was the fear of Cannon's political might that organization Democrats pressured Byrd to give his support to someone who met with the bishop's approval. Byrd refused absolutely to bow to Cannon's dictum. The organization gave its support to John Garland Pollard. When Pollard won the August Democratic primary by a sizeable majority, Cannon joined with the Republicans in an effort to defeat him in the general election.

By this time, however, certain things were happening that did not stand the bishop in good stead. It was revealed that despite his oft-expressed denunciations of gambling in any form, he had for some time been engaged in energetic speculation on Wall Street through a "bucketshop" concern that specialized in stock gambling on margin, and which was being arraigned for fraud through the mails. The bishop suddenly took off on a lengthy ecclesiastical mission to Latin America, and John Garland Pollard won a landslide victory over the Republican-Prohibition candidate.

Cannon's disgrace symbolized the failure of the "noble experiment" in Virginia and elsewhere. Within four years the state was to vote to repeal the Eighteenth Amendment. Virginians, of course, had never stopped drinking. The Hampton Roads area displayed its customary ingenuity as the state port, for all the efforts of the Coast Guard to intercept incoming shipments from Canada and the West Indies. The rich Allegheny Mountain tradition of classic moonshine was honored amid changing times, and other rural areas were not lacking in distilling enterprise. "To make a long story short," as one Virginia-born journalist commented, "the heart of the old South is not always a sober heart; and there is probably no town in America of Richmond's size which can boast of more gulping of intoxicants nor more arrests for drunkenness per annum.'' [4]

Richmond was, in brief, like Norfolk, a busy American city, prosperous, commercial-minded, Southern in its historical allegiance but eclectic and cosmopolitan in its attitudes. It was proud of its Confederate tradition, yet was also seeing the steady demolition of its sturdy old downtown antebellum homes, while its more prosperous citizens built handsome Tudor estates out along the West End. As an antiquarian chronicler of the city wrote in the early 1920s, ''the modern Juggernaut, Business, is riding relentlessly up homelike Grace and Franklin Streets . . . business buzzes, traffic roars, skyscrapers soar to heaven, and numberless smokestacks proclaim that everything in the world, from matches to locomotives is made in Richmond.'' [5] The Jazz Age was upon the Old Dominion.

There was even, in Richmond, a ''little'' literary magazine, *The Reviewer,* which lasted for five years. Edited by Emily Clark, Mary Dallas Street, Hunter Stagg, and Margaret Freeman, and with James Branch Cabell as benevolent adviser, it managed to attract considerable attention and to publish the work of many of the major writers of the 1920s before it went under. (Norfolk had a magazine, too, *The Lyric,* edited by John Richard Moreland and Virginia Taylor McCormick, which concentrated on poetry, though it cut no such wide swath in the literary field as *The Reviewer.*)

It was during the 1920s that two important Richmond novelists, whose work heralded the noted Southern literary renascence of the postwar years, achieved their greatest distinction. During the change and flux of Virginia's transition from its old community ways into the diversified industrial and urban experience of the modern commonwealth, Ellen Glasgow and James Branch Cabell imaged the human transaction in a long shelfload of fiction. At least since the days of the *Southern Literary Messenger,* there had been literary activity in Richmond, but with

4. William J. Robertson, *The Changing South* (New York: Boni and Liveright, 1927), p. 118.
5. Mary Newton Stanard, *Richmond, Its People and Its History* (Philadelphia: J. B. Lippincott, 1923), pp. 218–224.

the advent of Ellen Glasgow's *The Descendant* (1897), something new arrived in Virginia and Southern fiction: the hero was a poor white, and illegitimate at that. During the next two decades she produced novel after novel that, drawing upon the techniques of social realism pioneered by William Dean Howells and others, explored what she later came to call "the social history of the Old Dominion"—men and women, rich and poor, aristocrats and plain folk, confronting the actualities of Virginia life in a time not notably heroic or romantic. In her culminating work of this period, *Virginia* (1913), she portrayed a Virginia gentlewoman, raised to fulfill a traditional role, forced to come to terms with a society that paid lip service to the values enshrined in that role, but was in reality moving toward a very different set of demands and expectations. In 1925 she published *Barren Ground,* in which her heroine, Dorinda Oakley, a farm girl, triumphed over her drab circumstance and romantic illusions to make a new place for herself as operator of a commercial dairy farm, a nontraditional kind of life but one that permitted her to "live without love"—without the vulnerability her society would have ordinarily decreed for her. *Barren Ground* was widely acclaimed, and Miss Glasgow followed it by three comedies of manners, wittily ironic depictions of the foibles and follies of upper-class life in Queenborough, which was her name for Richmond. Of these, *A Sheltered Life* (1932) is perhaps her masterpiece. Her last two novels before her death in 1945 were more somber. Though always sustained by a romantic note of hopefulness, sometimes very wan, her fiction as a whole is significant for the effort at ironic, unromanticized depiction, sometimes witty, more often steeped in pathos, of the doings of her time and place: Virginia and Virginians described, for almost the first time, as ordinary men and women inhabiting an everyday world.

Her somewhat younger fellow Richmonder, James Branch Cabell, like herself a member of the city's leading families, began in the early 1900s to write archly mannered romances of gallant and chivalrous gentlemen and ladies, coming very soon to set his scenes not in Lichfield—his Richmond—but in the imaginary medieval kingdom of Poictesme, apparently far removed from the tawdry concerns of the present. His art-for-art's-sake aesthetics, his fastidious mocking of High Seriousness and Good Causes, his enameled prose, made him the idol of those who, like H. L. Mencken, strove to rebuke the literary cant and hypocrisy, as they saw it, of a puritanical American culture almost wholly given over to worship of the cheap, the tawdry, the counterfeit.

Yet Cabell was no escapist. Those who examined the underlying lineaments of his eighteen-volume biography of Manuel noted that the equivocating heroes and ironic gallants of his faraway Poictesme resembled nothing so much as the enshrined heroes of the onetime capital of the Confederacy, and that—as Cabell himself pointed out—the myths that his fellow Richmonders insisted upon weaving about their flesh-and-blood forebears transformed and gilded the everyday actuality no less than did his bawdy allegories of knights and damsels of the land of Cockaigne.

Seen in this way—and it is the way he intended—the bittersweet comedy of legendary medieval Poictesme delivers up a formidably ironic commentary upon the doings of his own time.

Neither James Branch Cabell nor Ellen Glasgow was by any means the most famous Virginian of the day, however. That honor was reserved for Harry Byrd's next younger brother, Dick. Commander Richard Evelyn Byrd, USN, became a national hero when with Floyd Bennett in the aircraft *Josephine Ford* he was the first to fly over the North Pole. Following that feat with a transatlantic flight shortly after Lindbergh's famous voyage, he then headed an expedition to Antarctica, where he set up his base at Little America, and became the first man to fly over the South Pole. In an era of aviation heroes Dick Byrd was among the most eminent. His arrival back in Richmond after the Arctic expedition in 1926, where his brother the governor welcomed him home, was a notably triumphal procession.

Governor Pollard had scarcely taken office to succeed Harry Byrd when he was confronted with the impact of the Great Depression. To add to the worsening business conditions, the summer of 1930 produced a drought. In late September, after a cut in wages at the textile mills, the Danville area was hit by a strike; there was rioting, and the National Guard had to be called out. The strike finally ended in late January, with the millworkers capitulating; many, however, were not re-employed because of the business slump. Wheat was selling at the lowest price in 132 years. The tobacco farmers of the Southside were faced with minimum leaf prices. Several banks failed, and many persons were jobless. In southwest Virginia the coal-mine operations slowed to a trickle, and misery was widespread. Urban employment throughout the state dropped, until by late 1932 some nineteen percent of the state's labor force was without work. Black workers in particular were hard hit.

Governor Pollard and Harry Byrd were reluctant to take special relief measures; their response to worsening economic conditions was to cut state expenditures considerably, and to have the county highway system transferred to state control. Pay-as-you-go remained the watchword; the fact that Virginia was not burdened with a heavy state debt was helping it to weather the slump better than most states, and the economy-conscious Byrd intended to keep it that way.

When the Democrats returned to power in Washington in 1933, and President Franklin D. Roosevelt appointed Claude Swanson to be Secretary of the Navy, Byrd was named by Governor Pollard to the vacant Senate seat. Byrd supported Roosevelt's election, and at first was inclined to back the New Deal program, but once deficit spending began to be employed to provide public jobs, Byrd quickly joined his senatorial colleague Carter Glass in opposition. The enlargement of the national debt, the enactment of recovery measures of debatable constitutionality—these were not to the taste of the Virginia senators. Though the Federal Emergency Relief Administration, the Works Progress Administration, and the Public Works Administration poured millions into the state to provide jobs for the unemployed, Byrd and Glass were unyielding in their opposition. Byrd also opposed the Agricultural Adjustment Administration, with its program for help for farmers, even though a vast majority of Virginia farmers were strongly in favor of the legislation. Yet the state government itself did little or nothing on its own to combat the depression. Virginia was the last state in the Union to set up enabling legislation for federal old-age assistance, and after the General Assembly yielded to pressure by the Virginia Manufacturers' Association and declined at first to enact Social Security enabling legislation, Pollard's successor, George Perry, had to convene a special legislative session, at a cost of $70,000, to get the necessary statute passed.

The Old Dominion managed to come out of the throes of the economic collapse more rapidly than most other states. Indeed, by the late 1930s it was experiencing a genuine surge of prosperity, with Richmond now the fastest growing industrial center in the country. The conservative stance of Byrd and Glass and their opposition to latter-day concepts of the role of government in economic life did not prove a serious political liability, for though the Virginia electorate generally accepted the New Deal's emergency actions to salvage the economy, it remained strongly attached to the overall conservative social and fiscal philosophy of its junior U.S. senator—who, in spite of Carter Glass's flamboyant opposition to the national administration, was clearly the leader of the state Democratic organization. In 1940, when Roosevelt accepted a third-term nomination, Byrd played no part in the campaign against the Republican nominee, Wendell Willkie; he did not bolt the party, as some Texas and South Carolina Democrats did, but his disapproval was manifest, and members of his family believed that he himself voted for Willkie.

The state organization had to get along with an independent Democrat as governor after the 1937 election, for the statewide popularity of Lieutenant-Governor James Price of Richmond was so general that the party leadership was forced to accept him as its candidate. Price was considerably more sympathetic than Byrd to the New Deal, and an advocate of increased educational spending, public housing, aid for the disadvantaged, and other such measures. His successor as governor, Colgate W. Darden, Jr., promptly reappointed the organization men that Price had removed from office, and the organization was once again in complete control.

Harry Byrd himself always grew angry whenever anyone referred to the organization as the Byrd Machine. It wasn't a political machine at all, he and others insisted, but merely a voluntary association of like-minded individuals. And there is truth to this, so long as one remembers that this voluntary association was always ready to strike down anyone who showed signs of importantly abandoning his like-mindedness. For one thing, the Byrd organization was quite honest; any member discovered dipping into the till, or using his political clout unduly for personal gain, was swiftly purged and even prosecuted. For another—and in this respect the organization came to differ markedly under Byrd from what it had once been under Tom Martin—it didn't exist merely in order to control; it was much more of an ideological, social, even moral instrument than the usual political machine, in that it had as its principal objective *good* government. By good government was meant sound finances, efficient state services, low taxes, good roads, freedom from corruption and graft. It did not include in its definition of "good" any protection for the poor, including the blacks, against economic victimization by the wealthy and powerful; or social services designed to reduce ignorance, squalor, disease, poverty; or any attempt whatever at giving the poor and the disadvantaged a voice in the determination of public policy.

The working principle of the Byrd organization and the Virginia electorate was that the propertied, the educated, the "better sort"—including many whites and no blacks—could and should be trusted with control of government. Given that basic assumption, the Virginia organization governed quite well indeed, insofar as honesty, fiscal soundness, and low taxes were involved. Especially in the years before civil-rights legislation and the U.S. Supreme Court's decisions on desegregation and reapportionment began to menace the basic premises under which the Byrd organization could govern, there was room within the organization for a moderate amount of difference of opinion. Colgate Darden was certainly no yes-man; at one point during his term as governor he even sought to remove the poll tax as a qualification for voting. The rigidity which came to characterize the organization during the 1950s and the 1960s, when any deviation from its leader's views was swiftly punished, came about not so much because of the aging of its leadership, as some have said, as because its fundamental social premises were being menaced, as they were not during the 1930s and 1940s.

Virginians—a majority of the electorate, in any event—admired, respected, even loved Harry Flood Byrd. The senator from Winchester did not have to cheat or bribe in order to maintain his control over the state's government and get the organization to do his bidding. And it is unthinkable that he would have consented to do any of those things, for his own standard of personal integrity was so high that he once refused to accept $200,000 in federal soil-conservation payments to which he was legally entitled, merely because he had himself voted for the law under which the payment was made. His control over the organization came because its leaders were indeed "like-minded individuals," who took care to see that those who were not were kept out of power. A restricted electorate, felt Harry Byrd, was how good government was made possible; his organization agreed, and a working majority of the registered voters agreed, too.

Governor Darden's four years at the helm of Virginia state government were war years; he took office shortly after the attack on Pearl Harbor, and though his incumbency was marked by great increases in expenditures for education, much of his task was to oversee the government of a state whose economy and life were being greatly affected by the war emergency. Virginia was close to Washington; as the population of the Capital expanded to handle the administration of a nation at war, it spilled over into Northern Virginia, and Alexandria, Fairfax County, and Arlington became in effect residential suburbs of Washington. Moreover, the government itself began building many of its installations across the Potomac, in particular the Pentagon, the huge center of the military and naval command. Northern Virginia soon became one of the most populous urban areas of the state.

The Hampton Roads area, which had been considerably expanded during the First World War, now underwent incredible growth. The shipyards in Newport News began turning out aircraft carriers and other vessels of war as the United States went to work to win the Battle of the Atlantic and to rebuild its shattered Pacific fleet into the greatest naval force in all history. The spacious anchorage and protected deep-water facilities of Norfolk, Portsmouth, and Newport News not only became the key base for antisubmarine operations, but an assembly place for the convoys that carried American troops and supplies to the European theater. War industry sprang up throughout the state. There were new army and marine installations everywhere, crammed to capacity as mild weather and convenience to Hampton Roads and the northeastern ports made Virginia a central training and staging area. A new munitions plant at Radford employed 20,000 workers.

As for the native Virginians, more than 300,000 of them served in the armed forces, and some 9,000 lost their lives. Ten Virginians received the Congressional Medal of Honor. The most distinguished soldier of the war, Army Chief of Staff General George Catlett Marshall, though born in Pennsylvania, was a graduate of the Virginia Military Institute and a longtime Virginia resident. Other VMI alumni who held high command positions were Army General Leonard T. Gerow and Marine Corps Generals Lewis B. ("Chesty") Puller, Lemuel C. Shepherd, and Alexander A. Vandegrift, all natives of the state.

When this war was won, however, Virginia did not return to "normalcy" the way it had done after 1917–1918. The Byrd organization was still in control and in 1945 elected as Darden's successor William M. Tuck, a genial, tobacco-chewing conservative from Halifax County. But the population and economic balance of the state had been greatly altered. The Norfolk–Portsmouth–Virginia Beach region now became the largest urban area in the state, while Northern Virginia, as the southern end of the enormous industrial belt extending down the eastern seaboard from Boston, and known to geographers as Megalopolis, had transformed the hitherto largely rural Fairfax-Arlington area into a vast suburban community.[6] Not only had Virginia almost doubled in population since the turn of the century, but the

6. The authoritative survey of Virginia's geography and economy in the late 1940s is Jean Gottmann, *Virginia at Mid-Century* (New York: Henry Holt and Co., 1955).

period 1940–1950 alone had seen an increase of almost twenty-five percent. Virginia was now more urban than rural, though by far the larger part of its nonagricultural employment was in services and office work rather than factories.

Tourism had become a big business. In the 1920s John D. Rockefeller, Jr., had begun funding the tremendous project of restoring the ancient colonial capital of Williamsburg to its pre-Revolutionary War appearance, and in years to come millions of dollars were spent to rebuild, restore, and renew the buildings and grounds of the old town into a living museum of early American history. This in turn generated millions of dollars in income as tourists from all over the nation and even the world came to see the restoration. As the three-hundred-fiftieth anniversary of the landing at Jamestown approached, that once-deserted place became a restored museum which attracted hundreds of thousands of visitors. The Civil War battlefields, especially those around Richmond, drew tens of thousands of tourists a year, and as the years of the Centennial began drawing nearer in the 1950s, interest in the war grew throughout the nation, with a resulting boost to tourism in the state that had been the cockpit for the fighting from 1861 to 1865. Charlottesville, with Jefferson's Monticello and the university he designed, attracted large numbers of tourists, who often coupled visits there with a drive along the panoramic Blue Ridge Parkway, part of the Shenandoah National Forest that Harry Byrd and the New Deal had created. And there were numerous other attractions— Mount Vernon, the great plantation homes along the James River, Robert Porterfield's depression-born Barter Theater in Abingdon, Lexington and the Natural Bridge, and others. Where in the previous century the mineral springs in the mountains had been the mecca for Virginians and others during the summer months, now the strand at Virginia Beach was the place to go, and Virginians and non-Virginians went in great numbers.

Even though the increase in industrialization had created no major labor union faction within state politics, the huge growth of metropolitan areas did represent a new kind of political constituency, and since the Byrd organization's strength had always been based on the rural and small-town vote, one might have assumed that its control of the General Assembly would be jeopardized. As it happened, however, no such development took place for some years. Virginians who moved from the countryside and the farms to the metropolitan areas remained Virginians, and thus generally conservative in their political and social inclinations. The organization's firm control over the General Assembly was maintained in part, of course, because of the disproportionate legislative strength of the Southside and the rural counties. In particular the suburban area in Northern Virginia, with its heavy recent influx of government employees and their families, was notably under-represented in the legislature. The residents of that area were considered to be not really Virginians, and there was the general agreement that they were to be kept from upsetting Virginia politics. As State Senator Charles T. Moses of Appomattox put it, the reins of government ought to rest in the hands of those who turned the sod and slopped the hogs.[7] This was quite in line with the early views of Thomas Jefferson about virtuous husbandmen, but by the 1950s it had come to have rather different implications for democratic self-government.

The years of Franklin D. Roosevelt's presidency had seen the national Democratic party become steadily more liberal in its platform and program, and committed to social legislation and an antimonopolistic business stance. The federal government's role in national life was much greater and more pervasive. The voice of labor and of union leadership in the party was far more audible than ever before. The Fair Deal of Harry S Truman had succeeded the New Deal of his predecessor, and there was a growing disenchantment with the national party among Southern conservative Democrats. When after the war Truman, with whom Byrd had been very friendly in the Senate, proposed a program of social gains, continuing price and wage controls, and a public-housing program on a vast national scale, Byrd was outspoken in opposition. In his abhorrence of deficit financing he found himself drawn much more closely to Republicans

7. Guy Friddell, *What Is It About Virginia?* (Richmond: Dietz Press, 1966), p. 50.

such as Robert A. Taft, whose antiunion stance he also approved. The Taft-Hartley Act, forbidding secondary boycotts, jurisdictional strikes, and providing a cooling-off period for strikes affecting national health and safety, was very much to his liking. In Virginia itself, Governor Tuck not only took a strong stand against strikes by city, county, and state employees, but when employees of the Virginia Electric and Power Company prepared to go out on strike, he threatened to induct them into the state militia. He also secured passage of a right-to-work law forbidding closed-shop contracts in Virginia. Six times during his term of office Tuck seized utility companies to maintain service in the face of strikes.

All this served further to distance Harry Byrd and the Virginia Democratic organization from the national Democratic party. Moreover, the Truman administration showed unmistakable signs of favoring the improvement of the status of black Americans. In 1947 the President's Committee on Civil Rights brought in a report calling for the end of racial segregation in the armed services, schools, public transportation, and housing, along with a federal antilynching law, a federal ban on the poll tax, and federal protection for blacks voting in primaries and general elections. The President immediately proclaimed the report "an American Charter of human freedom," and urged Congress to enact its provisions into law.

The result, in Virginia, was to place the Byrd organization in a position of hardening resistance to the national Democratic party, and to convert primary election campaigns within the state, both for congressional seats and for state office, into tests of the popularity of the Byrd organization's opposition to national Democratic policies—tests which the organization could expect to win hands down. Though Byrd and Tuck stayed out of the fight at the 1948 Democratic nomination convention, Tuck attempted, with Byrd's approval, to rig the presidential ballot that fall so that the national ticket's names would not even appear on it, and the leadership of the state Democratic party would decide how the electoral votes would be cast. That was going too far even for conservative Virginians, and the move was roundly condemned; the *Richmond Times-Dispatch,* edited by Virginius Dabney, and *News Leader,* edited by Douglas S. Freeman, and the *Norfolk Virginian-Pilot,* edited by Louis Jaffé, all attacked the move as a brazen attempt to negate the democratic process. As it was, however, the Dixiecrat ticket of J. Strom Thurmond and Fielding Wright collected in the state just enough of the votes that would otherwise have gone to the Republican candidate, Thomas E. Dewey, to enable Truman to carry Virginia.

There was, particularly in the urban areas, a considerable antiorganization element within the Democratic party, and in 1949 the organization faced a stiff challenge. State Senator John Stewart Battle, of Charlottesville, was its candidate for governor, but another organization supporter, Mayor Horace Edwards of Richmond, decided to run on his own. Meanwhile an antiorganization Democrat, the colorful Colonel Francis Pickens Miller of Charlottesville, entered the campaign and began a strong attack on the organization as a "political clique of backward-looking men" controlled by an "absentee landlord" in Washington who was imposing upon Virginia an undemocratic government that denied the people of the state needed social and educational opportunities.[8] With Edwards campaigning for much greater funds for education financed by a two-percent sales tax, and Miller vigorously assailing the organization on all fronts, Byrd and his colleagues faced a crisis. Emergency measures were necessary, and the organization took them. Byrd made a major speech in which he attacked Miller as "the CIO-supported candidate," who was backed by doctrinaire liberals and labor leaders, and called for all who believed in sound government to unite behind Battle. E. R. Combs traveled throughout the state, working among the lagging faithful and using his position as chairman of the state compensation board to persuade those who were backing Edwards to switch their allegiance. Finally Henry A. Wise, leader of the state Republican party, urged his fellow Republicans to enter the Democratic party and vote for Battle, or else face a takeover of state govern-

8. J. Harvie Wilkinson III, *Harry Byrd and the Changing Face of Virginia Politics, 1945–1966* (Charlottesville: University Press of Virginia, 1968), p. 92.

ment by the liberals. Edward's support soon dropped away, and Battle won 42.8 percent of the vote as compared with Miller's 35.3. The organization had won—but only by a plurality and the skin of its teeth.

The campaign was ominous for the organization, for it revealed that the rural and small-town vote on which its strength was largely based was becoming unable to assure it of a handy majority of the voters. Edwards's presence in the race as a young, urban-oriented candidate with a commitment to public services and a sales tax, indicated that there was, in J. Harvie Wilkinson III's words, "a group of moderate citizens who were becoming disillusioned with the state's stinginess at a time of climbing local debts and needs." [9]

As governor, Battle moved decisively to secure much greater educational expenditures without demanding matching funds from the localities. A vigorous, high-minded leader, he was one more example—Darden was another, and Albertis Harrison and Lindsay Almond in the years ahead—of gentlemen with high ideals and a genuine sense of responsibility who were, as governors, forced by their political circumstance within the organization to be less than what they could have been in offering leadership to a modern, changing Virginia. The Old Dominion during the late 1940s and 1950s, as before and since, was basically conservative in its attitudes, but at the same time it needed and was generally ready to face up to the changes within its economic and social structure and to accommodate its demands for honest and efficient government to the much greater social requirements of post-World War II American life. There were, not merely without but also within the organization, men who were willing to furnish the necessary leadership and were capable of doing so. But Virginia's state government adhered to Harry Byrd's philosophy of government. For this man, who by dint of his immense personal popularity and his political skill called the turn on what happened in Virginia, the Old Dominion was still essentially the Virginia he had governed two decades and more ago, and he remained in a position to keep its state

9. Wilkinson, *Harry Byrd*, p. 98.

government from making an adequate response to the immense changes that had taken place in the war years and afterward. The result of this stance was that the organization became so dependent upon the votes of rural and especially of Southside Virginia to maintain its hegemony that when, as was soon to happen, the school-integration issue burst upon the state with full force, reasonable counsel could not prevail, and the entire state was forced to follow the lead of the Southside in insisting upon massive resistance.

Though as a Southern state Virginia still held to the one-party system that was the legacy of the Reconstruction, as an industrializing, urbanizing border state the Old Dominion moved steadily away from the national Democratic party insofar as what that party represented in its philosophy of government and its sources of strength and weakness (or, by the same token, one might just as accurately say the national Democratic party had moved away from Virginia). Thus, even though Governor Battle's stirring speech at the 1952 Democratic convention kept Virginia in the party, there was considerable doubt that even the support of various organization leaders would be able to overcome the enormous personal popularity of General Dwight D. Eisenhower, the Republican presidential candidate.

The doubt changed to the certainty that it could not when on October 17, 1952, Harry Byrd himself took to the radio to attack President Truman for his stands on civil rights, labor, and the debt, and declare that since Adlai Stevenson, the Democratic presidential candidate, had not repudiated Trumanism, he could not in good conscience endorse the national ticket since "endorsement means to recommend, and this I cannot do." [10] Virginia went overwhelmingly for Eisenhower, and thereafter, with the lone exception of the Johnson-Goldwater campaign of 1964, stayed in the Republican column.

Thus when in 1953 the Virginia Republican party nominated for governor State Senator Ted Dalton, an attractive, high-principled western Virginian who set forth a forward-looking program calling for repeal of the poll tax and an overhaul of the

10. Wilkinson, *Harry Byrd,* p. 84.

election laws, a concerted effort to seek out new industries for the state, higher teacher salaries, and greater attention to mental health services, there seemed no reason why Virginia voters who had gone for Eisenhower the year before should necessarily support the Democratic nominee for governor. The organization candidate, moreover, was a wealthy but undistinguished Henry County furniture manufacturer, Thomas B. Stanley, who was no match for Dalton's charisma and enthusiasm. Had Dalton not made the mistake, late in the campaign, of coming out for a hundred-million-dollar highway revenue bond issue, he might well have won; but no sooner did he do so than Harry Byrd came out fighting, denouncing Dalton's plan as a repudiation of pay-as-you-go financing and debt-free state government. The campaign was now one of Dalton *v.* Byrd rather than Dalton *v.* Stanley, as Harvie Wilkinson notes,[11] and the organization managed to pull through, but by the closest margin—225,878 to 182,887—in its history except for campaigns when it was divided.

Stanley was scarcely inaugurated governor before the organization ran into more trouble, in the form of a rebellion by a group of Young Turks—young legislators, primarily from urban areas, who wanted more effort made in the direction of needed public services. The Young Turks were not antiorganization; they intended to work from within it to make it more responsive to the needs of an urbanizing commonwealth. Their numbers included such able delegates as Armistead L. Boothe of Alexandria, George Cochran of Staunton, William B. Spong of Portsmouth, Stuart B. Carter of Fincastle, and Walter A. Page of Norfolk. The big fight came on State Senator Harry F. Byrd, Jr.,'s Tax Credit Act, put through by the organization several years earlier, which provided that general fund revenue surpluses be returned to individual and corporate taxpayers. What the Young Turks wanted was for the surplus tax money—$7 million in 1954—to be used instead to provide funds for the state's badly undersupported schools, colleges, hospitals, and welfare services. After a tumultuous 36-hour final session of the

11. Wilkinson, *Harry Byrd*, p. 104.

legislature, the organization gave in, to the extent of agreeing that $2,186,500 of the surplus would go to state needs and the balance refunded. For their rebellion the Young Turks were punished; in subsequent assemblies important committee assignments were denied them and organization support was largely withheld when they campaigned for re-election. The organization had managed, after a fashion, to hold its forces in line, but in closing the door on youth it severely weakened its future prospects. It became more apparent than ever that frugality, low taxes, and a balanced budget at the expense of needed public services, were going to face ever tougher going in the years ahead. Dalton's near-victory in 1953 had shown that the Republican party could and doubtless would mount challenges on just those grounds where the Democratic organization was vulnerable.

Then on May 17, 1954, the United States Supreme Court, by a 9-0 vote, declared in *Brown* v. *Board of Education* that segregation of children in public schools solely on grounds of race was unconstitutional, and thereafter all was different.

11

The Modern Era

*In which the Virginians undertake "massive resistance,"
then change their minds.*

*M*OST white Virginians liked to believe, and to assert, that race relations in the Old Dominion were good, particularly when compared to what was true in the states to the south. And no doubt they were—by comparison with the states to the south. Lynching, never much of a Virginia custom, had gone completely out of fashion; Governor Byrd's severe antilynch law in the 1920s had taken care of that. Blacks could vote if they kept their poll taxes paid up. But the single telling commentary on race relations in Virginia, from the standpoint of the blacks, lies in the steady emigration of black Virginians all during the first five decades of the twentieth century to the District of Columbia and the northeast in search of jobs, decent education, a chance to live in a society that, for all its prejudice and indifference, did not discriminate against blacks as a matter of public law and public policy.

The segregation of black Virginians during the first four decades of the century was massive and complete, and extended to all facets of their lives. There may not have been the violence that marked the color line in the Deep South; Virginians were never much on that sort of violence. But the black man was kept in his place, and his place was mostly at the bottom, politically, socially, economically. The going wage for a black domestic worker during the 1930s in Lynchburg, for example, was four dollars a week. No blacks sat on juries at trials of blacks. Municipalities excluded them from all public positions. Most newspapers, when referring to blacks, scrupulously avoided using the title of Mr. and Mrs. to characterize them. Schools for black Virginians were far poorer even than those for whites; in rural Virginia they were so primitive as almost to defy description. "No matter how carefree the outward appearance of Negroes may be," the WPA Guide stated in 1940, "behind their happy dispositions is the imprint of poverty, disease, and suffering—birthmarks of a people living precariously, but of a people wholly Virginian." [1] And in his introduction to that work, Douglas Southall Freeman, editor of the *Richmond News Leader,* distinguished Civil War historian, and no man to leap to extreme conclusions, recorded his agreement: "The backwardness described in the essay on education in this informative volume," he declared, "is not overpainted in its indigoes and blacks. . . . The choice of the Negro now lies between the extremes of overcrowded profession and underpaid common labor or domestic service. No middle class is being developed." [2]

There was, even so, a small but vigorous black middle class in the Virginia cities. Richmond, in fact, was, during the 1910s and 1920s, a mecca for black business enterprise, though by the depression there had been a considerable decline. In higher education, at Virginia Union University in Richmond, Hampton Institute in Hampton, St. Paul's College in Lawrenceville, Virginia State College at Petersburg, black teachers made the best of inadequate funds, sparse equipment, and meager library facilities. In the public schools black teachers did their best despite the handicaps against them; no Virginia educator ever achieved more with less, for example, than Virginia E. Ran-

1. Writers' Project, Works Progress Administration, *Virginia: A Guide to the Old Dominion* (New York: Oxford University Press, 1940), p. 86.
2. Douglas Southall Freeman, "The Spirit of Virginia," in *Virginia: A Guide to the Old Dominion,* p. 6.

dolph of Henrico County, whose work in industrial and domestic arts in the early years of the century was so outstanding that under the auspices of the Anna T. Jeanes Fund she was enabled to extend her inspirational supervisory teaching ideas throughout the state and far beyond its borders.

During the 1920s and in the decades thereafter there were black Virginians who earned national distinction. The historian Carter G. Woodson, Robert R. Moton, who succeeded Booker T. Washington at Tuskegee, the poets Leslie Pinckney Hill and Anne Spencer, President Charles S. Johnson of Fisk University, actor-dancer Bill ("Bojangles") Robinson, sculptor Leslie G. Bolling, painter George H. Ben Johnson, actor Charles S. Gilpin, a little later the operatic singers Dorothy Maynor and Camilla Williams—these and others were Virginians of renown, but for the most part their renown was necessarily earned elsewhere, for in their native state there was little or no place for their talents to thrive.

Changes were taking place—they were slow, they were undramatic, but they were indicative of the fact that not forever would the color line go unchallenged in Virginia. The editor of the *Richmond Times-Dispatch*, Virginius Dabney, was an articulate critic of racial injustice during the 1930s and 1940s; in 1943 he even proposed an end to Jim Crow seating in public transportation not merely for Virginia but throughout the south, as a way, he said, to ameliorate racial tensions. And in 1948 Oliver Hill, a black man, was elected to the Richmond City Council. And so on; here and there, little things—straws in the wind. Still as Harvie Wilkinson says, "the segregated school system in Virginia might have lasted millenniums had outside pressure not battered it down." [3]

So long as there was no real threat of a change in the massive segregation arrangements that had prevailed since the turn of the century, the Virginia Democratic leadership was quite willing to let white supremacy go unremarked and unagitated. With the increasing antidiscrimination stance of the Roosevelt and Truman

3. Wilkinson, *Harry Byrd*, p. 60.

administrations, however, there was unease in the Old Dominion, and when in 1952 Senator Byrd made his famous radio attack on the Stevenson-Sparkman Democratic ticket, he did not hesitate to base part of his case for opposing the national party's candidates upon the civil-rights policies of the Truman administration. There is no doubt that the Old Dominion's support of Dwight D. Eisenhower's bid for election was due in part at least to the feeling that the racial status quo was less likely to be upset with a Republican in the White House.

It was Prince Edward County, in Southside Virginia, that was to become a focal point for the battle over school desegregation that followed the *Brown* v. *Board of Education* decision. The late 1940s and early 1950s had seen a notable effort in many Virginia cities and counties to improve black school facilities, in part so that the "separate but equal" doctrine of *Plessy* v. *Ferguson* (1896), which had legalized school segregation by race, could not be used to attack segregation on grounds of actual inequality of the separate facilities. In 1951 black citizens of Prince Edward, seeking to secure a new high school building for black children, proposed to go to law about it, but lawyers of the National Association for the Advancement of Colored People were willing to take part only if the separate-but-equal doctrine itself was made the point of challenge. By May 17, 1954, when Chief Justice Earl Warren delivered the 9-0 decision of the Supreme Court declaring racial segregation itself inherently unequal, the new high school for blacks had already been built, but that was no longer the issue; the issue had become how—and also when and, as it turned out, whether—Prince Edward and other Virginia counties and cities were to comply with what was now the law of the land.

The first response of Virginia to *Brown* v. *Board of Education* was on the moderate side. The people of the state, declared Governor Stanley the following day, would receive the opinion "calmly and take time to carefully and dispassionately consider the situation before coming to conclusions on steps which should be taken." He would, he promised, call a meeting of state and local government representatives to "work toward a plan which will be acceptable to our citizens and in keeping with the edict of the court.'' And he added, ''Views of leaders of both races will be invited in the course of these studies.'' [4] Attorney General Lindsay Almond declared that ''the highest court in the land has spoken, and I trust that Virginia will approach the question realistically and endeavor to work out some rational adjustment.'' [5] The young editor of the *Richmond News Leader*, James Jackson Kilpatrick, who had succeeded Douglas Freeman several years before, called editorially for formulation of a proposal that would be approved by the Court, and suggested: ''If the court were to fix, say a ten-year period, and permit the states to integrate ten percent of their schools a year . . . a solution might be found.'' [6]

Southside Virginia, however, was distinctly of another mind—and so, it soon turned out, was Senator Harry Flood Byrd. Under the chairmanship of State Senator Garland (''Peck'') Gray of Sussex County, twenty Southside legislators convened at a fire station in Petersburg to express their ''unalterable opposition to the principle of integration of the races in the schools.'' [7] Publicly Byrd described the court decision as ''the most serious blow that has been struck against the rights of the states'' and said that Virginia faced ''a crisis of the first magnitude.'' Any state action, he said, should be ''based on our most mature judgment after sober and exhaustive consideration.'' [8] Privately he is reported to have been furious at the bland moderation of Governor Stanley's pronouncement.

It did not take long for Stanley to switch his tactics. ''I shall use every legal means at my command,'' he declared on June 25, ''to continue segregated schools in Virginia.'' [9] In late August Stanley appointed a 32-man legislative commission to come up with a plan, with Garland Gray as chairman and its membership dominated by the Southside and other areas with

4. Wilkinson, *Harry Byrd*, pp. 122–123.
5. Benjamin Muse, *Virginia's Massive Resistance* (Bloomington: Indiana University Press, 1961), p. 5.
6. Muse, *Massive Resistance*, p. 5.
7. Wilkinson, *Harry Byrd*, p. 123.
8. Muse, *Massive Resistance*, p. 5.
9. Muse, *Massive Resistance*, p. 71.

heavy black populations. The governor's "consultation" with black Virginians consisted of interviews with black leaders such as Oliver Hill, Dr. R. P. Daniel, and P. B. Young, who were asked to urge black Virginians to accept continued segregation, which they declined to do. Hill and another Richmond attorney, Spotswood Robinson, would soon be playing prominent roles in pressing the NAACP's legal attack on segregated education.

In Southside Virginia there was a new organization, known as the Defenders of State Sovereignty and Individual Liberties, which within two years had some 12,000 members throughout the state, sixty local chapters, a full-time executive director, and a monthly newsletter. Headed by a Farmville laundry owner, Robert B. Crawford, the Defenders made it plain from the start that their opposition to integration was to be whole-souled but nonviolent. Indeed, throughout the next several years of confusion, denunciation, and school closings, not a single act of mob violence was committed in Virginia. Virginia segregationists wanted to block application of the law of the land, but they never at any time sought to prevent its enforcement.

A counter-organization to the Defenders, but far less influential, was the biracial Virginia Council on Human Relations. Missing from its leadership were business and professional figures and other segments of the white power structure; in Harvie Wilkinson's apt description, "the most significant thing about this group was its impotence." [10] The way to overcome massive resistance to segregation in Virginia was not going to be by biracial groups arguing the virtues of integration and citing the baneful effects of segregation on blacks, but by the marshaling of sentiment to keep the public schools open when the state government began closing them in order to block integration. But in 1954 and 1955 nobody really thought schools would ever actually be closed.

The plan that the Gray Commission came up with the following November—after the Supreme Court had called for implementation of *Brown* v. *Board of Education* "with all deliberate speed"—was threefold in nature. There was to be a system of

10. Wilkinson, *Harry Byrd*, p. 124.

tuition grants to aid children wishing to attend private schools to avoid integration. Localities were to administer pupil assignment plans, ostensibly based on criteria other than race. The state's compulsory-school-attendance law was to be amended so that no child could be required to attend an integrated school. To put the plan in effect a constitutional referendum was necessary, since state law prohibited use of public moneys for any school not owned or exclusively controlled by the state government.

The state organization strongly supported the plan and the constitutional referendum, with Governor Stanley expressing his wholehearted concurrence. Senator Byrd likewise urged adoption of tuition grants, though significantly he declared he had nothing to say for the present about the other provisions—i.e., local option. The plan was also supported by persons such as Colgate Darden, now president of the University of Virginia, and former State Superintendent of Public Instruction Dabney S. Lancaster, who were known to favor public education at almost any cost, and even by Robert Whitehead, the colorful delegate from Lovingston who was the organization's most eloquent opponent. Almost all the state's newspapers were in favor, except for the outspoken Lenoir Chambers of the *Norfolk Virginian-Pilot,* who didn't like the use of public money for private education and wasn't sure that any plan deliberately designed to get around a Supreme Court decision would stand up.

The referendum passed by an overwhelming margin, but it soon transpired that those who, like Chambers and State Senator Armistead Boothe of Alexandria, had opposed the Gray plan were correct in their suspicions. In Washington Senator Byrd was now calling for massive resistance to integration throughout the South, and Jack Kilpatrick of the *Richmond News Leader* had developed a new strategy to supersede the Gray plan. Taking up the suggestion of William Olds, an elderly Chesterfield County lawyer, the young Virginia editor developed the doctrine of Interposition, whereby a state might interpose its sovereignty to block the assertion of unconstitutional powers by the federal government. In a long series of brilliant editorial presentations, the *News Leader* traced the doctrine of Interposition from the Virginia and Kentucky Resolutions of 1798 onward. In early 1956, despite objections by legislators such as Whitehead, who labeled the plan outright nullification, the General Assembly adopted an Interposition resolution, and so did the legislatures of most of the other Southern states. The difficulty was that nobody was quite sure what it meant, in that there was no constitutional mechanism for such interposing to be done. As Delegate Whitehead declared, in a speech that had all his opponents chuckling along with him, "the lightning flashed, the thunder struck, and a chigger died!" [11] In retrospect—and, I think, to Jack Kilpatrick even at the time—Interposition was a symbolic action, a device that enabled those who opposed the Supreme Court decision on desegregation to assert their opposition in terms of violated constitutionality and up-ended law and order rather than on racial grounds.

The practical burden of Byrd's call for massive resistance and of Interposition was soon revealed by E. Blackburn Moore, speaker of the House of Delegates and Harry Byrd's close friend and neighbor, when he introduced a resolution calling for a continuation of segregated schools throughout the state for 1956–1957. There was widespread objection by some newspapers and by men such as Darden and Lancaster, who had supported the Gray plan, for the pledge of local option given during the tuition-grant referendum was obviously not going to be honored. The Senate Rules Committee put aside Moore's plan, but the following summer, after Byrd, Governor Stanley, Southside Congressmen William Tuck and Watkins Abbitt, and others had met in Washington to plan strategy, the governor convened a special session of the General Assembly, and a concerted program for massive resistance was set forth in no less than 23 statutes and duly enacted. "Let Virginia surrender to this illegal demand and you'll find the ranks of the South broken. . . ," Byrd had declared two days earlier. "If Virginia surrenders, the rest of the South will go down too." [12] The heart of the program was House Bill No. 1, whereby state funds were to be cut

11. Dabney, *Virginia*, p. 535.
12. Muse, *Massive Resistance*, p. 29.

off from all elementary schools or all high schools in a district if any elementary or high school was integrated. Grants were to be made available to students to attend private schools, and the salaries of principals and teachers were to be continued. A State Pupil Placement Board was to have the authority to assign all pupils throughout the state.

Though the program went through the assembly without important change, it was resisted both from within and without the organization. Moderates wanted a local-option clause inserted, and Senators Ted Dalton and Armistead Boothe battled valiantly for its inclusion, while in the House of Delegates Kathryn Stone of Arlington fought the organization's program at every step of the way. The issue was never in doubt, however. Almost all those in opposition felt it expedient to express their personal disapproval of integration—though not State Senator Stuart Carter, of Botetourt County, who on September 20, 1957, declared, "I do conscientiously believe in integration." A more common attitude was that of Congressman Tuck: "There is no middle ground, no compromise. We're either for integration or against it and I'm against it. . . . If they won't stand with us then I say make 'em." [13]

So now the Old Dominion had its plan for preventing integration of any of its schools. It also had a new governor, Lindsay Almond, who in the fall of 1957 had won a decisive victory over Ted Dalton. Lindsay Almond was first and foremost a politician, and knowing what the dominant opinion in Virginia was concerning integration, he sounded the battle cry of massive resistance at his inauguration and with eloquent regularity thereafter. Still, there were those within the organization who remained skeptical of his ultimate fidelity to the cause. At the assembly session following his inauguration, no new crises arose. Even though integration suits had been entered by the NAACP and parents of black children in various communities, few people could really bring themselves to believe, as the school season of 1958–1959 approached, that the hard choice between integration and the shutting down of public schools was actually

13. Wilkinson, *Harry Byrd*, p. 119.

going to come. Then on Friday, September 12, the Warren County High School in Front Royal, faced with a court order to admit black pupils, was shut down by Governor Almond. One week later Lane High and Venable Elementary schools in Charlottesville were ordered closed. Ten days after that, the high schools of Norfolk were closed. The crisis had come, with bewildering abruptness. In all, the education of some twelve thousand Virginia white children was imperiled, and similar closings in Arlington and Richmond seemed imminent.

Now the walls closed in on Lindsay Almond. The Southside continued to urge defiance at all costs. Harry Byrd kept enjoining the governor to stand firm. But as winter approached with students going untaught, protests grew throughout the state. Parent-teacher associations, civic groups, petitions from most of the college and university teachers in the state, all voiced their disagreement with massive resistance. Committees for public schools were formed in several cities. In Richmond the Virginia Congress of Parents and Parent-Teachers blocked an attempt to substitute proponents of massive resistance for its current officers, then by a narrow margin passed a motion calling for local option. The state's newspapers, most of which had supported massive resistance, now began sounding the call for retreat. The *Richmond Times-Dispatch* and the *Norfolk Ledger-Dispatch* called for new approaches. Jack Kilpatrick of the *Richmond News Leader* told a Rotary Club meeting that new laws were now necessary "if educational opportunities are to be preserved and social calamity is to be avoided." [14] The corporate business community, always reluctant to speak out on such matters, got into the proceedings; twenty-nine businessmen, industrialists, and bankers held a dinner meeting with the governor to tell him that massive resistance and school closings were hurting the state and discouraging industrial development.

Then came two crucial court decisions. A federal district court in Norfolk ruled that school closings were in violation of the right to equal protection of the laws. And the Virginia Su-

14. Wilkinson, *Harry Byrd*, p. 143.

preme Court of Appeals—no branch of the government in Washington, but a legal entity of the Commonwealth of Virginia itself—found that the school closing and fund cut-off laws violated the state constitutional requirement for an efficient system of free schools throughout the State.

Governor Almond was in an impossible position—to which, however, his own expedient oratory had contributed. There were those—including the segregationist-dominated Norfolk city council—who wanted Almond to retaliate by closing the black schools in the affected districts, but he would have none of it. It would be, he said, "a vicious and retaliatory blow against the Negro race." [15] Nor would he use the authority of his office personally to urge the individual black parents in the segregation cases to withdraw their suits; that was no honorable use of the prestige of his office, he declared. On January 20, 1959, Almond took to the airwaves with a breakfast radio speech. We have just begun to fight, he declared, and he unleashed the full force of his rhetoric in a tirade against the civil-rights movement and the social effect, as he saw it, of integration, which he likened to the situation in the public schools of the District of Columbia, where, he said, "the livid stench of sadism, sex immorality, and juvenile pregnancy" prevailed. [16]

Eight days later, having called a special session of the General Assembly, Lindsay Almond set forth his plan for ending massive resistance in Virginia. Francis Pickens Miller has suggested that Almond's radio speech was really a calculated plan of strategy to throw the organization off guard and get the legislators in Richmond for the special session; but there is no evidence, so far as I know, to corroborate this. [17] Almond's own remorseful explanation of the radio performance seems more plausible: "I was tired and distraught. I agonized and gave vent to my feelings, which never should have been done. My un-

15. Wilkinson, *Harry Byrd,* p. 144.
16. Muse, *Massive Resistance,* p. 148.
17. Francis Pickens Miller, *Man from the Valley: Memoirs of a 20th Century Virginian* (Chapel Hill: University of North Carolina Press, 1971), p. 230.

derlying thought and motivation was to show the people that we had done everything we could do." [18] Whatever the motivations for the speech, the governor of Virginia had at last faced up to reality, and there in the House of Delegates chamber, with Blackburn Moore, who had had his suspicions all along, and other organization stalwarts such as Garland Gray, Harry Byrd, Jr., and Mills Godwin listening, he did what he had to do. It was, as Benjamin Muse says, his finest hour.[19] A few weeks later the schools reopened, with black pupils attending along with whites. There was no disorder, no threats, no violence; Virginians obeyed the law. A last-ditch legislative effort by the diehards to block the adjustment had failed, when by a 20–19 vote the senate voted to resolve itself into a committee of the whole in order to prevent the organization-dominated senate education committee from bottling up a bill for local assignment of pupils. Again the man of the hour was Stuart Carter of Fincastle, who two years before had dared to tell the senate that as a matter of conscience he believed in integration; now, recuperating from a stomach-ulcer operation, he hurried to Richmond and was brought into the senate on a stretcher so that he could cast the vote that prevented a deadlock.

Harry Byrd never forgave Lindsay Almond; the governor had betrayed Virginia to the enemy, he felt. For the remainder of his term as governor, Almond also found himself opposed by the organization when he sought to put through a retail sales tax for school funds, along with a cut in the personal income tax. But he made the most of the opportunity that the end of school closings had given him to push for greater industrial development of the state, calling a statewide industrial conference and establishing the Virginia Industrial Development Corporation. Though some disagreed, most Virginians came to feel that their orotund governor had ultimately done well for his commonwealth; however much he had roared and blustered, when the chips were down he assumed the burden and risked the obloquy to see that the schools stayed open.

18. Muse, *Massive Resistance*, pp. 146–147.
19. Muse, *Massive Resistance*, p. 121.

The school problem had not been settled for all time to come, but except in Prince Edward County things were in reasonable shape. In that county, when in May 1959 the court order came to desegregate its schools the following September, the board of supervisors abandoned public education. For the ensuing four years, with the citizens trapped by their own rhetoric into a disgraceful immobility, white children attended private schools and black children went without schooling. It was Albertis Harrison, Almond's attorney general and now governor, who brought an end to that; in 1963 he called in Colgate Darden and asked him to serve as chairman of a Prince Edward free school foundation, funded by federal grants, which got schools established for the blacks, and the next year the Supreme Court ordered the county to reopen its public schools. But as Virginius Dabney says, "there could never be full compensation for the lost school years of Prince Edward's black boys and girls." [20] Such was the final, bitter distillation of massive resistance in Virginia.

In the years that have followed, many have wondered why it was that Virginia had ever been led to put up so determined a resistance to the Supreme Court decision. The Old Dominion was, after all, a conservative commonwealth, not only in its political views but in its modes of political behavior. One might have thought that Virginians would have reluctantly accepted the necessity to integrate the schools, and with their penchant for law and order and a stable society, gone ahead and made the adjustments, however grudgingly, so as to accommodate their lives to the court's ruling with the least possible disruption. Massive resistance, school closings, children going without education—these seemed somehow uncharacteristic of what Virginia had customarily managed to do and be as a state.

Politics was certainly involved; there is little doubt that the dominant organization was on increasingly shaky grounds in the early 1950s, and massive resistance gave it, for a few years at least, a new hold on life. The urbanizing areas, with their growing suburban populations, had been showing signs of being unwilling to adhere to the organization's principles of low-cost,

20. Dabney, *Virginia*, p. 546.

minimal government, with public services held to the lowest possible level. After all, during the year before *Brown* v. *Board of Education* the Republican candidate for governor had almost won. But thenceforth, with the central issue made one of race rather than budget and social services, the Democratic organization had been able, just as in the 1880s, to keep control of the state.

But it wasn't just politics. It wasn't even that the organization had become so dependent for its continued control upon the overwhelming majorities given to its candidate in the Southside that it had been forced to go along with the Southside's diehard segregation views.

The underlying explanation, I believe, is that Harry Byrd wanted it—and not merely the senator himself, but what Byrd embodied. *Brown* v. *Board of Education* represented, for him, the culmination of more than two decades of federal encroachment upon the sovereignty of Virginia and the breaking up of the kind of tidy, orderly, stable, predominantly rural and small-town community that he had grown up in and cherished. In the middle 1920s, as governor, he had labored mightily and successfully to equip that community to accommodate the emerging business and industrial developments of the dawning twentieth century. His role had been, in the best sense, conservative. He had worked to conserve what he and many other Virginians thought was best and most valuable in the life of the community to keep it from either going to pieces through inefficient backwardness or else being swept into oblivion by the urbanizing, industrializing behemoth of change (or perhaps both, and simultaneously).

Then, with seemingly catastrophic suddenness, had come the crippling impact of the Great Depression, followed immediately by the renewed growth in industrialization, which the Second World War had vastly intensified, until industrial and urban expansion occurred which had once seemed inconceivable. And with all this had come the social, political, and governmental consequences of the change: new ways of viewing the relationship of government to people, a much enlarged conception of what elements of the population the political constituency should take in, a vastly changed and expanded notion of what a government must offer its less advantaged citizens—along with the growing awareness on the part of the less advantaged citizens that they could now expect such services and opportunities, and a determination to get them, whether through political action, unionization, litigation in federal courts, or whatever.

As all this happened, not merely in Virginia but throughout the nation, it was the federal government that, first as the New Deal and then the Fair Deal, became the political and social vehicle whereby the change was effected, and which served, however imperfectly and even inefficiently, as the rallying point for those who demanded the changes. Thus in the 1930s and 1940s Harry Byrd and those "like-minded individuals" he represented so faithfully grew more and more at odds with the conduct and leadership of the federal government, until there came an outright break with the political party that had traditionally been their home, and a hardening determination to resist, at all costs, both the political consequences of the change and the government serving to bring it about.

The segregation decision of 1954 was the crowning blow; not only did it symbolize all the changes that were being forced upon Virginia (and Southern) society, but it struck at the heart of the social and economic institutions that had seemed to make possible the old order, and which reflected the values and attitudes embodied in the old order. This was not merely economic change (though it had much of its ultimate explanation in economics); it was not even just political change (though politics was a way of enforcing it): it was social, emotional, visceral. It involved one's children, one's family. And it was not merely racial, but also an affair of caste and class: culture, standards of living, manners and morals, even language itself were involved.

To the Virginians of Harry Byrd's generation the threat of such overwhelming change was so ominous that they had been led into massive resistance against it. So intense was their affection for Virginia, in the political and social forms that they had been accustomed to think of it, that they could not conceive of its continuing to be Virginia in terms other than those they knew. So they fought to preserve it as it had been for them. But there was no way they could succeed, because the change had already taken place all around them.

That, I think, is what massive resistance was all about for Virginians like Harry Flood Byrd.

Was there any value to it all that compensated for the resentment, ill will, and stirring up of passion and prejudice that the six-year ordeal had brought? Very little, I think. Possibly the only gain was cathartic: it provided a mechanism whereby those most upset might vent their anger and frustration before settling down to work on the continuing political and social problems of a populous and expanding American commonwealth. If so, it was little enough compensation for the way in which white attitudes were hardened and black Virginians were alienated from the white political establishment and made to bear the full wrath of the state's press and political leadership. The argument that massive resistance gave the state a breathing space to get used to the change and to plan how to cope with it seems very dubious indeed, for until it was introduced, most of the state seemed to be ready to work out an orderly accommodation. That a majority of white Virginians would have preferred not to have integrated schools was obvious; but except in the Southside they appeared willing to accept necessity. Instead, their leaders raised false hopes that integration could be avoided and encouraged them to take extreme positions, with the inevitable disappointment that followed causing a bitterness which would be felt for years to come. It was an unlovely business that did little good and much harm. Harvie Wilkinson's verdict seems appropriate: "Massive resistance stands as a logical, though not an inevitable, product of the declining days of Harry Byrd's Virginia." [21]

Massive resistance may have kept the organization in power for a few years longer than might otherwise have happened, but its ultimate result was to destroy the organization. The fight over the schools had divided the membership into warring factions. The old organization won the next gubernatorial election, but though Byrd himself gained re-election to the Senate in

21. Wilkinson, *Harry Byrd*, p. 154.

1964 over minimal opposition, he was no longer the master of the state's political destiny, as was demonstrated in the Johnson-Goldwater presidential election of that year. When the "Lady Bird Special" carrying the President's wife campaigning went whistle-stopping through Virginia, Governor Harrison and Lieutenant-Governor Mills Godwin were her escorts, while Sidney Kellam, the Virginia Beach political overlord who had for long been a power in organization politics, vigorously masterminded the President's campaign in Virginia. Johnson carried the state, the first Democrat to do so since Truman in 1948.

It was not really the same organization any more, for other developments were eroding the foundations of its strength. The one-man, one-vote edict of the U.S. Supreme Court, by forcing a redistricting of the General Assembly in accordance with proportional representation, took assembly votes away from the Southside and other rural areas with relatively low populations and gave them to the populous areas in the metropolitan areas, thus severely undercutting the source of the organization's control. More importantly, the Twenty-Fourth Amendment to the U.S. Constitution banned the poll tax for federal elections, and the number of registered voters was greatly increased. Many of these new voters were blacks; some 125,000 to 150,000 black Virginians voted in the 1964 presidential election, giving Johnson his margin of victory. Two years later the poll tax was outlawed in state elections as well. No longer, therefore, could the organization depend on low voter turnout, disfranchisement of blacks and poor whites, and rural and small-town domination of the General Assembly to keep it in control of the state government. Urban Virginia now called the turn.

It was Mills E. Godwin, Jr., of Nansemond County, who recognized this. As lieutenant-governor under Albertis Harrison, he had begun revising the uncompromising anti-integration, antilabor, antipublic-services stands that had characterized his career since he first won election to the General Assembly in 1947. No organization stalwart had been more strident in his denunciation of those such as Armistead Boothe, his opponent for the lieutenant-governorship in 1961, who had dared to propose a more moderate approach to school problems. But during Al-

200   VIRGINIA

bertis Harrison's governorship, which was generally an era of calmness without much controversy, Godwin himself moved toward a much more moderate position. Not only did he back the Johnson candidacy when Byrd clearly wished the organization's leadership to remain neutral, but he even suggested that it might be time to re-examine the sacred pay-as-you-go method of financing schools and other services. Partly because of his shift in stance, and partly out of fear that Harry Byrd, Jr., might seek the governorship, Democratic moderates and even progressives and liberals got behind his candidacy. In the 1965 general election he went up against an outstanding young Roanoke Republican progressive, Linwood Holton, who called for greatly expanded public services and educational funds, directly attacked the Byrd organization's record, and made an issue of the Harrison administration's hefty financial surplus in the treasury, which he declared was "a devastating indictment of mismanagement and nonplanning if better schools, colleges, universities, roads, and other public facilities are our goals." [22] Godwin countered by pledging an all-out effort to boost educational and social-service expenditures, called for concerted planning, and made it clear that he was quite willing to re-examine the pay-as-you-go policy. So drastically had Godwin strayed from the organization's accustomed ways, indeed, that ultraconservatives formed the Virginia Conservative Party and nominated for governor William J. Story, Jr., a member of the John Birch Society, who warned that both the Democrats and Republicans were paving the way for a socialist, Communist police state in Virginia.

The result probably helped Godwin more than it hurt him, for now the AFL-CIO endorsed him, as did the two most influential black organizations in the state, the Richmond Crusade for Voters and the Independent Voters' League. Had it not been for the black votes, which went heavily for Godwin, the erstwhile massive-resistance stalwart might well have lost the election.

Albertis Harrison as governor had concentrated on attracting new industry, and had done a good job of it; 177,000 new jobs

22. Wilkinson, *Harry Byrd*, p. 270.

were added during his term. He had also secured the largest appropriations in the state's history for the public schools and colleges. One of his last acts as governor was to appoint Harry Byrd, Jr., to fill out the term of his father in the U.S. Senate when the older Byrd retired in November of 1965. Seriously ill, grown old (he was 78), and with his once-invincible political organization close to disintegration, Harry Flood Byrd went home to Berryville after a public career that had been second to that of no other Virginian since the days of Washington and Jefferson in its imprint upon the life and history of his state. He died the year following, of a malignant brain tumor.

It was just as well, perhaps, that Harry Byrd did not live to observe the changes that Mills Godwin and the General Assembly effected in Virginia state government. Taking full advantage of public sentiment, abundant revenues, and the changed political situation, fiscal and public-service reform was accomplished such as Virginia had never known. To make a massive assault on educational deficiencies, Godwin secured a two-percent sales tax and promise of another one percent, together with an optional one-percent tax for cities and counties. The foundations were laid for a statewide system of two-year, low-tuition community colleges. The pay-as-you-go system was abandoned, with existing constitutional provisions used to make possible a bond issue for schools, colleges, hospitals, and roads. A commission was appointed to revise the 1902 state constitution. Vestiges of massive resistance such as the Pupil Placement Board, tuition grants, and the Commission on Constitutional Government were eliminated. And, wonder of wonders, a local-option liquor-by-the-drink law was enacted—such was the extent to which urban Virginia now could make its political will felt.

The new dispensation in Virginia politics was evident in the 1966 primary for the United States Senate, when the old organization supported Harry Byrd, Jr., for the four remaining years of the seat vacated by his father, and longtime incumbent A. Willis Robertson; they were opposed by Armistead Boothe and State Senator William B. Spong, Jr., of Portsmouth. Boothe hit the younger Byrd hard on massive resistance; had Byrd had his way, he declared, "it is entirely possible that we might not have a public school system at all." [23] Byrd concentrated on national issues, and depicted Boothe as a socialistic liberal. Spong attacked Robertson's longtime record of opposition to progressive measures, and linked him with banking interests. If the elder Harry Byrd had not fallen into a deep coma five days before the election, so that his son hurried to his bedside and Boothe canceled his final campaigning out of respect, Harry Byrd, Jr., might have lost the primary to Boothe. As it was, he won by less than one percent of the vote—while Robertson went down to defeat before Spong by a margin of just over six hundred votes. As if Byrd's unimpressive victory and Robertson's defeat were not enough, Howard W. Smith, conservative of conservatives, lost the Democratic primary in the Eighth Congressional District to a liberal, George C. Rawlings, Jr. In the general election Spong won easily, and Byrd somewhat less so. Rawlings was defeated by conservative Republican William L. Scott, and another GOP conservative, William C. Wampler, ousted Pat Jennings from his longtime Ninth District seat.

It was obvious that the old organization was done for; Virginia would still be conservative, but in Republican form, while the future for the Democrats clearly resided in the kind of moderate urban progressivism exemplified by Mills Godwin's successful coalition for governor.

There were now, in fact, not merely two but three factions within the state Democratic party. What was left of the old organization constituted the conservative wing. A moderate wing seemed to be centered about Spong. Meanwhile the colorful State Senator Henry E. Howell, Jr., of Norfolk, emerged as leader of a powerful liberal faction, with close ties with the black community and labor unions. Virginia's voting habits now, as Ralph Eisenberg has noted, "reflected national voting patterns more than Southern patterns." [24]

---

23. Wilkinson, *Harry Byrd*, p. 316.
24. Ralph Eisenberg, "Virginia: The Emergence of Two-Party Politics," in William C. Havard ed., *The Changing Politics of the South* (Baton Rouge: Louisiana State University Press, 1972), p. 74.

In 1969 the final act came. William C. Battle of Charlottes-ville, son of former Governor John Stewart Battle, and 1960 Virginia campaign manager for John F. Kennedy, won the initial Democratic primary over Howell, the liberal candidate, and Fred G. Pollard, the organization standard bearer, and then defeated Howell by a close margin in a runoff for the nomination. In the general election in November, Linwood Holton, the Republican nominee, defeated Battle, and Virginia had a Republican governor for the first time since immediately after the Reconstruction. Battle's defeat was in an important measure due to the fact that the labor unions and the black groups endorsed Holton. The rank and file that once supported the Byrd organization now went all the way over into the Republican camp in state as well as national elections. After a century of Democratic hegemony, the Commonwealth of Virginia was now a two-party state.

12

Retrospective

*In which are set forth problems, prospects, and
a few conclusions.*

B Y the 1940s and 1950s Virginia had become less and
less a Southern community, so far as its patterns of life, its
economy, even its percentage of black population were concerned. Its ties with the Deep South were more historical and
emotional than economic and political, and its racial performance during the 1950s was a futile attempt to assert an identity
that was fast slipping away. With the collapse of massive resistance came the collapse, soon afterward, of the Byrd organization, followed by vastly increased expenditures for education,
health, and public service, the emergence of black Virginians
and big labor as important political forces, and two Republican
governors—the second of them being the selfsame Mills Godwin who had been first a diehard segregationist, then briefly a
leader of a Democratic progressive coalition, and finally a supporter of Richard Nixon. (Nixon had been so anxious to get ex-
Byrd organization conservatives behind him that he had in effect
betrayed longtime Republicans such as Holton.) Furthermore, of
the state's two United States senators, one, Harry Byrd, Jr., dis-
sociated himself from the national Democratic party and won re-
election as an Independent, while the other, William Spong,
was defeated for re-election by an ultraconservative Republican,

William J. Scott of Fairfax, in 1972, largely as a result of the McGovern candidacy. The Republicans added one congressional seat to the five they already had, and six of the ten Virginia congressmen were of the GOP. The post-Watergate atmosphere of the 1974 elections rectified the balance, bringing the election of one more Republican but the defeat of two, so that the Virginia congressional delegation was emblematic of the political makeup of a two-party border state which has traveled a long way from the era, barely three decades earlier, when except in the Fighting Ninth District of southwest Virginia, a successful Republican politician was almost as much a curio on the state political scene as a Vegetarian or a Single Taxer. As for the General Assembly, though that body is still heavily Democratic, it is a far cry from the organization monolith that did the bidding of Byrd and his associates so faithfully in years past.

This was nowhere more in evidence than in the revised state constitution drawn up during the first Godwin regime, and twice ratified by the assembly before submission to the voters in 1970. Not content with a provision for public schools, the legislators declared education a fundamental right of all Virginians, guaranteed children an education of "high quality," and made the General Assembly legally responsible for such an education being secured by state intervention if a locality should default. In short, one Prince Edward County debacle was enough. In its guarantee of civil rights for all, its provisions for periodic legislative reapportionment, its authorization of bonded indebtedness for hospitals, mental health, and education, it was the reflection of a greatly different and more realistic notion of the role and responsibility of state government to all the inhabitants of the Commonwealth in an age much changed from that of a half-century earlier. Backed by most of the state's political leaders, the new constitution won overwhelming ratification. The millennium did not arrive overnight, but the government of Virginia was now obligated and directed by its fundamental charter to come to grips with the complex actualities of what Virginia life had become in the late decades of the twentieth century.

One consequence of the election of Republican Governors

Holton and Godwin to head the government of a state whose General Assembly was still strongly Democratic was a distancing of the executive and the legislative branches of state government. With Republicans in the governor's mansion and Democrats controlling the assembly, the legislators have felt free to act independently, thus restoring, as Neal R. Pierce has pointed out, a balance between the two branches of government that had been notably lacking since the days of Byrd's governorship in the middle 1920s.[1] This development has, to an extent at least, reaffirmed what had once been very much a characteristic of Virginia government: the potentiality for an intense localism such as existed in colonial times and continued almost up to the time of the Civil War, when a powerful assembly and a relatively weak governor had resulted in a state government that very much reflected the will of the individual localities. In the 1810s, 1820s, and 1830s, this had proved to be an important factor in the decline of the state from its early position of national leadership. The rival local factions had combined and divided in a manner that had effectively paralyzed the state's ability to meet the political and economic needs of the changing times, resulting ultimately in disservice to the entire commonwealth.

In the mid-twentieth century, of course, exactly the opposite situation was true. Massive resistance was possible only because of the ability of the governor, the organization-dominated assembly, and U.S. Senator Byrd to force a single course of action upon localities that would have preferred to work matters out in terms of local needs. There seems little likelihood that the power of the governor and the assembly will ever recede and that of the localities increase to anything resembling the pre-Civil War levels, but Virginians now face one of the most pressing problems of all American states nowadays: how to control and direct urban and industrial development, without jeopardizing natural resources and the environment. In Virginia, where sweeping urbanization came so swiftly and, one might al-

1. Neal R. Pierce, *The Border South States: People, Politics, and Power in the Five Border South States* (New York: W. W. Norton, 1975), p. 78.

most say, without being particularly wanted by many Virginians, it is a problem indeed. As I write this book, for example, the entire fishing industry of the lower Chesapeake Bay, one of the world's most bounteous fishing grounds, is menaced because of kepone pollution from a chemical plant on the upper James. What creates jobs in Richmond and Hopewell is ruinous to Hampton Roads. How to make Richmond and Hopewell take the larger viewpoint? How to persuade a legislature to look out for the welfare of the entire state, when the immediate interests of only part of the constituency are involved?

In the year 1940 the population of Fairfax County, Virginia, was 40,929. In 1973 that population had risen to 533,000—a 1,200 percent increase! What were farms and crossroads before the Second World War are cities, subdivisions, and shopping malls now. It has been estimated that by the end of the 1970s the population of Northern Virginia will reach 1,300,000. Where in the 1940s a Richmond-bound airliner taking off from Washington National Airport would have been flying over woods and farmland once it cleared the city limits of Alexandria, now the high-rise apartment complexes, shopping centers, subdivisions, and malls, with their intricate network of superhighways and cross-routes, have spread fifty miles and more out into the countryside, until Prince William and Loudoun counties are becoming commuting suburbs of the metropolitan District of Columbia area, so that the airline passenger peering down would be almost to Fredericksburg before he was over any open countryside. What this has meant, and will mean, in terms of water supply, sewage, air pollution, highway construction, schools, hospitals, and municipal services, is staggering to contemplate. Worst of all, it has been, for the most part, accomplished without any overall planning concept, and with the real estate industry serving practically as the zoning authority: in Neal Pierce's words, "an example of pell-mell development gone wrong, devastating a region of great natural beauty." [2]

Or consider the Hampton Roads area. In the 1930s Virginia

2. Pierce, *Border South States,* p. 101.

Beach and Princess Anne County were a pleasant summer spa
for Virginians; a majority of the 20,000 year-round inhabitants
were in one way or another tied to the strand's vacationtime
commerce. Then came the war. The Navy and the Marine Corps
built huge installations along Lynnhaven Inlet and the Bay. Following the war the area continued expanding, as good highways
and available real estate made it an excellent place for the expanding population of the Norfolk area to live. There was no
reason, after all, why one should not dwell in a resort area all
year long. The result was that by 1970 there was no longer any
Princess Anne County; it was all the city of Virginia Beach,
with a population of 200,000 and every indication of far greater
expansion to come. Furthermore, the construction of the Chesapeake Bay Bridge-Tunnel, spanning the entrance to the Bay and
linking the area with the Eastern Shore, gave it direct motor
access to the metropolitan northeastern United States without
requiring transit through Philadelphia, Baltimore, and Washington. Virginia Beach was foresighted enough to hire a consulting
planning firm to develop a code for land use and new construction, but the problems involved in so gigantic a social, political,
and economic transaction were and are enormous. The same is
true of the countryside to the south of Norfolk and Portsmouth,
toward the North Carolina line, now become the City of Chesapeake, with close to 100,000 inhabitants. As for downtown
Norfolk, an urban-renewal program transformed the center city
into a place of imposing civic, cultural, and business centers.
Across Hampton Roads from Norfolk, and very much a separate
community by political and social tradition, Newport News and
Hampton, were also greatly expanded. All in all, there are now
something close to one million persons living in the Hampton
Roads area, and with the recent discontinuance of bridge-tunnel
tolls between Hampton and Norfolk, the area will be drawn into
an ever more unified economy. How to make the various political units within the Hampton Roads complex work together to
solve the immense social and governmental problems that un-
dreamed-of expansion has created? The task is awesome, and its
magnitude and complexity increase with each successive year.

As for the Richmond area, what has happened there, though

somewhat less dramatic, is likewise enough to disturb the most determined opponent of regional planning. Richmond's massive metropolitan population growth—more than a half-million inhabitants in 1970—was not tied to defense and other government installations, as was that of Northern Virginia and the Hampton Roads area. The city was a major manufacturing and merchandising center. Throughout the 1950s and 1960s the subdivisions fanned outward in all directions, until Henrico and Chesterfield counties were thickly populated with ranch houses while the houses of the old city were more and more the abode of black and other low-income families. Realizing belatedly what was happening to the downtown business and financial districts, Richmond began an urban-renewal campaign in the early 1960s, and numerous large office buildings have since been constructed, along with downtown apartment complexes. Nevertheless the city and the suburbs were fast becoming separate political enclaves.

As Neal Pierce shows, the influx of population into the metropolitan Richmond area during the 1940s and 1950s differed from that of the state's other areas of urban expansion in that most of its newcomers were Virginians by birth, and the Richmond area thus lacked "the leavening and often liberalizing influence of people born in other states than Harry Byrd's Virginia." [3] The integration of the city's schools greatly accelerated the white flight into the suburbs, and the suburbs were extremely conservative in political and social outlook. Meanwhile the city's black population quickly asserted its political identity, and this and the outflow of middle-class whites caused the power structure of the city to be considerably altered. Matters came to a head when the city, disturbed at the growing *de facto* school segregation of blacks in the city, secured a federal court order for consolidating the city's school districts with those of Chesterfield and Henrico counties, which would have caused massive cross-boundary busing. The resulting furore was extremely bitter. Irate parent groups marched on the capital, the Ku Klux Klan began to make inroads, while the two Richmond

3. Pierce, *Border South States,* p. 98.

newspapers conducted an all-out editorial campaign against the court edict. However, Governor Holton, who had personally chosen to enroll his own children in their assigned city public schools even though the schools were ninety-six percent black, did much to prevent the situation from getting out of hand. Ultimately the school district merger decision was reversed by the higher courts, and the issue was defused for the time being. But it was symbolic of Richmond's problems in the post-Byrd era, as it faced a downtown-suburban schism that threatened the social and political stability and the commercial health of the onetime Confederate capital and produced the kind of school-busing crisis characteristic not of Southern cities so much as of the large metropolises of the northeast and the Midwest.

Indeed, the traveler who motors southward along the Richmond-Petersburg Turnpike, once he crosses the bridge over the James River into South Richmond, enters a manufacturing area that suggests the South far less than it does the industrial belt of Delaware–eastern Pennsylvania–New Jersey. It continues for much of the way to Petersburg, while to the east the city of Hopewell, built overnight during the First World War on what had been farmland, boasts a phalanx of chemical plants and other heavy industry that has created enormous problems of water and air pollution. Such is the industrial concentration throughout the Richmond-Petersburg-Hopewell triangle that the same kind of heavy smog conditions that afflict the northern industrial cities are now an habitual part of the landscape.

Yet Richmond is *not* Newark or Detroit, and neither are Petersburg and Hopewell the equivalents of Elizabeth, N.J., or Dearborn, Michigan. Virginians, whether operating farms or motels, planting tobacco or working in steel mills, remain Virginians. The annual income of a Virginian is now so close to the national average that no longer is there left to Virginians even that once-distinctive characteristic of Southern experience—poverty. But Virginians do not tend to measure their lives exclusively by economic patterns any more today than in the past. The one social talent of Virginians that underlies all the others, and that has marked their lives almost from Jamestown Island onward, is probably their capacity for keeping to the middle, civilized way, and investing their experience with grace and dignity. They may not get sufficiently alarmed about matters such as pollution and public education and urban sprawl to avoid the problems through foresight and planning, but at the same time they also refuse to be dominated by them and kept from living decently and comfortably, and when they do face up to the need for action, they usually act effectively.

Virginians never have particularly cared for change; they resist it as a matter of course and principle. Yet when the time comes that change must be made, the Virginians do it, and usually with a minimum of confusion and with good manners. In all the excitement over massive resistance, there was not a single incident of mob violence, rock throwing, dynamiting of churches, schools, and homes, or physical intimidation. And I have the hunch that the General Assembly, the governor, and the people, whether white or black, Republican or Democratic, will ultimately find a way to control industrialization and urbanization and make these into something distinctively and recognizably Virginian, rather than allow Virginia to become northeastern New Jersey or Cook County, Illinois.

When one looks at the History and Present State of Virginia, to use the phrase of old Robert Beverley in 1705, certain patterns and traits do emerge. The localism that pervaded colonial government has by no means died out yet. Even the Byrd organization, for all that it managed to force the entire state into a brief but costly statewide policy of school closing in 1957–1958, was built on the courthouse, the county government, the adherence and participation of the rank and file. The Word sometimes came down from Richmond—or Berryville— and it was heeded, but only because Richmond and Berryville spent a considerable amount of time and effort in finding out how the constituency in Gloucester Court House, Accomack, Amelia, Warrenton, and Strasburg felt about things. There have been times when the wishes and needs of this area or that of the state have been insufficiently heeded, and division has resulted, but the only time when such neglect caused irreparable cleavage was during the pre-Civil War period, when the east's failure to heed the problems of trans-Allegheny Virginia brought about the eventual secession of West Virginia.

Otherwise the history of the Old Dominion reveals few occasions when it has not seemed more important to the inhabitants of all regions of Virginia, no matter how diverse, to remain Virginians, and like it, than to insist upon their specific regional grievances being heeded at no matter what cost. An inhabitant of Grundy, Virginia, out in the southwestern extremity of the state, may live geographically closer to the capitals of Tennessee, Kentucky, and West Virginia than to Richmond, but he is nonetheless just as determinedly a Virginian in habit and attitude as the inhabitant of Hanover or Charles City County, and if you have any doubts concerning the matter, he will promptly disabuse you of them. This is not merely because Grundy is politically in Virginia, but because in his opinion the maintenance of the corporate, historical, and cultural entity that is Virginia is as much his own responsibility as it is anyone's. No one who has ever covered a session of the General Assembly for a newspaper could fail to mark the assurance, the entire absence of timidity with which the elected delegates and senators of the various and far-flung localities comport themselves in Richmond in carrying on the business of the commonwealth; it is *their* capitol, which Thomas Jefferson himself designed for them to use, and as far as they are concerned, what is good for Eastville and Galax is good for Virginia, and vice versa. And no one who ever heard the late Lovick P. Law, sergeant-at-arms of the House of Delegates, stand at center aisle and announce majestically, "Mr. Speaker, a Message from the Senate of Virginia!" could fail to grasp the transcendent importance that the General Assembly of Virginia attaches to the transactions of the General Assembly of Virginia.

Localism, of course, is not necessarily democracy—and in Virginia it often hasn't been particularly democratic. Thomas Nelson Page, in one of his nostalgic tales of the Golden Age before the Civil War, has a faithful black retainer recount proudly that "'didn' nuttin' but gent'mens vote den.'' [4] Which was largely true—though what the faithful black retainers privately thought about it is another matter. Not until the 1960s did Virginia become a genuine political democracy again, and no

4. Thomas Nelson Page, "Unc' Edinburg's Drowndin'," *In Ole Virginia*, p. 58.

one, viewing the flux and change in Virginia politics during the last decade or so, can say for sure what this will eventually come to mean in Virginia politics.

Yet it must be said that if the Virginians have, since colonial times, shown a distinct mistrust of unrestricted popular democracy, they have also registered a distinctly above average performance in providing disinterested public servants and attaining a level of governmental integrity that has been remarkably free of economic buccaneering and personal self-aggrandisement. In the late nineteenth century it required the impact of war, Reconstruction, and a belated and confusing entry into the milieu and mores of the late-nineteenth-century commercial capitalism to shatter for a time the traditional rectitude of the conduct of governmental affairs in Virginia. Thereafter, with few exceptions, Virginians have enjoyed honest leadership. No one, whatever his quarrel with the Byrd organization, ever validly accused it of corruption or lack of high personal integrity among its leadership.

Thus we have the continuation of a paradox which has existed in one form or another throughout most of the Old Dominion's history. The quality and integrity of Virginia political leadership has been possible, to a large extent, because of the restricted franchise, and the assumption that only the "better sort" were qualified to choose the state's leaders and determine the state's governmental policies: i.e., government by and in the interests of a class—honest, upright government, but not socially responsible government. Given the choice between an orderly, stable society—which is to say, not merely a political and economic association of people but a genuine human community whereby a citizen can define his identity through his membership and position within it—and a society open to all and fully responsive to the needs and aspirations of all the human beings dwelling within it, Virginia has usually come down upon the side of order and stability, at the expense of social responsibility and opportunity.

Now events have once more, as they did in the 1850s and 1860s, caught up with it, so that once again the Virginians face an old problem. How to retain the Virginia community—

the sense of pride, the decency and stability and honesty that have made possible a way of life that rises above mere economics and, in the words of the redoubtable H. L. Mencken, "got beyond and above the state of a mere infliction and became an exhilarating experience" [5]—while accepting the social responsibility and bringing into it those formerly ignored, left out, and merely *used:* the blacks, the poor whites, all those Virginians who were made to contribute to the comfort and economic and social well-being of the "better sort" without getting in return more than provision for a marginal existence? How to make Virginia be for *all* Virginians what in previous years it has been for only some of them?

To achieve this the Virginians will need leadership. In the late 1920s Harry Byrd came along to give Virginians the guidance they needed to get moving in the right direction. Later on, Colgate Darden saw to it that Virginia's schools were given the impetus they required, and had the energies and concerns of the state not been diverted into the requirements of the war effort, Darden's accomplishments might well have been even more impressive. Lindsay Almond, for all his early blustering, had the integrity to face up to the needs of the state during the school crisis. Mills Godwin read the times correctly and acted. Linwood Holton, despite being the first Republican governor in a century and confronting a Democratic General Assembly, showed courage, determination, and tact in getting the state to incorporate the participation of a greatly enlarged electorate into its political and economic life. The question now is whether the Virginians can come up with leadership strong enough and imaginative enough to persuade them to tackle the enormous problems of environmental protection and population growth on a concerted statewide basis, in order to preserve and enhance the quality of Virginia life while providing for the state's economic needs.

Consider, for example, the state song as it was until recently bowdlerized:

5. H. L. Mencken, "The Sahara of the Bozart," in Huntington Cairns, ed., *The American Scene: A Reader,* (New York: Alfred A. Knopf, 1965), p. 158.

Carry me back to old Virginny,
There's where the cotton and the corn and 'tatoes grow.
There's where the birds warble sweetly in the springtime,
There's where the old darkey's heart am longed to go.

Virginia today does considerably more than raise cotton, corn, and potatoes; it also produces space rockets and atomic reactors—but the birds do tend to warble in the springtime as always, even in the subdivisions, and what Robert Beverley wrote about the Virginians more than 250 years ago still applies:

The clearness and brightness of the sky add new vigor to their spirits and perfectly remove all sullen and splenetic thoughts. Here they enjoy all the benefits of a warm sun, and by their shady groves are protected from its inconvenience. Here their senses are entertained with an endless succession of native pleasures. Their eyes are ravaged with the beauties of naked nature. Their ears are serenaded with the perpetual murmur of brooks and the thorough bass which the wind plays when it wantons through the trees. The merry birds, too, join their pleasing notes to this rural consort, especially the mock birds, who love society so well that whenever they see mankind they will perch upon a twig very near them and sing the sweetest wild airs in the world.[6]

Such, I think, is still true for much of Virginia, and even though the smog over Richmond often spoils that "clearness and brightness of the sky," and the rush-hour traffic along the Shirley Highway and Virginia Beach Boulevard makes it next to impossible to hear that "thorough bass which the wind plays when it wantons through the trees," I have every confidence that the Virginians will retain not only a sufficient supply of the "endless succession of native pleasures" but, more importantly, the long-demonstrated Virginia habit of taking time out to savor and relish them.

But though the state song, "Carry Me Back to Old Virginny," was written by a black man, a native of New York, it was designed for the edification of a white audience and not for black Virginians, who would have been extremely skeptical

6. Robert Beverley, *The History and Present State of Virginia,* edited by David Freeman Hawke (Indianapolis, Ind.: Bobbs-Merrill, 1971), p. 157.

of the sincerity of the old darkey's lament. I have no doubt that Bland was privately more than a little ironic about the authenticity of the nostalgia for a place where a black man "labored so hard for old Massa, / Day after day in the field of yellow corn . . ." And until the Virginians can make that nostalgia genuine for its black citizens as well as for all its white citizens, and until Virginians realize that the gracefulness and comfort and decency have been purchased in part at the price of squalor, degradation and want for too many of its people, Virginians will not have truly earned the right to sing the state song that a black man wrote for them.

I have been very critical, at various points in this narrative, of the failure of the Virginians to live up to the social, political, and cultural ideals set forth by their own leaders and spokesmen. At the same time, however, it seems important not to undervalue what the Virginians have been, and what they therefore can be. It is not only that Virginia provided the nation with its early champions of liberty and helped create the new republic. It is not only that Virginians set forth the finest aspirations of the new republic in words which even two centuries later are as challenging and as demanding as when they were first expressed. It is also, I believe, that the Virginians, not merely in spite of, but in part because of, what they have been and not been, have given the nation something perhaps as useful as the ideal of political freedom nowadays, though without political freedom it would not be either real or lasting. This is the ideal of the elegant life: the community of grace, self-respect, gentleness, honor; of men and women who are where they want to be, and who love the place they inhabit. To the swift-paced confusion and frantic bustle of American life, the Virginians have said, "Where are you going? Why are you in such a hurry to get there? Stop a while and think about it." However much this attitude may have involved laziness, and however much it may smack of self-satisfaction and selfishness, it has also served at times as a valuable corrective and a needed rebuke to the materialism of a notably successful acquisitive American society. To a nation that is still very much on the move, there are many worse things to offer than Williamsburg—provided, of course, that one shows the slave quarters as well as the Governor's Palace, and also that one remembers that the money to restore the colonial capital came from the judicious development of oil wells. But if it required a Rockefeller to restore Williamsburg, it took Virginians to cherish what was left of it through all those years so that much of it was still there to be restored.

Virginia came late to urbanization, and tardily and reluctantly to democracy for all its people. It may be, however, that her very dilatoriness will work to her ultimate advantage. For the Virginians have a history to show them where they have been, what they did well and where they failed, and they have not been in so great a hurry that they have obliterated their history. They have a state that, however rapidly it is being urbanized, has retained much of the friendliness of a leisured mode of existence. They have a pride and sureness in their identity that can provide anchor and definition in change. They have marvelous human resources, and a tradition of individuality that can save them from submergence in the massive conformity of modern urban experience. They have an instinct for accommodation—for finding the middle ground, and getting along with each other. They have a heritage of honest government and high-principled leadership that, whatever the present turmoil of shifting party allegiances and maneuverings as the political image of a greatly expanded electorate is brought into clearer focus, shows few signs thus far of yielding to influence-peddling, bribe-taking, and the other ills which too often have characterized politics in so many states. However much the leaders of Virginia government have differed on what is best for Virginia, and whatever shortcomings one might identify in their judgment, few can question the devotion and personal integrity which they have brought to their task, and the resoluteness of their dedication to the state they have loved.

I find this love of and pride in Virginia the most pervasive and striking characteristic of her people, and to a degree almost unique in American experience. One sees it in governors, legislators, businessmen, newspapermen, industrial workers, labor leaders, college presidents, ministers of the church, housewives, men and women in all walks of life, of high and low degree.

Her writers have been full of it. Think of the manner in which, for example a novelist such as William Styron of Newport News has conducted his passionate exploration of Virginia experience in the past and in contemporary times. Or the variety of ways in which Clifford Dowdey of Richmond has described Virginians from the earliest colonial times onward. Or the painstaking accuracy with which a historian such as the late Carter G. Woodson of Buckingham County delineated the struggle of black Virginians for human dignity. Or the lifelong devotion with which Virginius Dabney of Richmond has chronicled, interpreted, and criticized the Virginia scene. Or the humor and wisdom that Guy Friddell of Norfolk has brought to bear on his ever-continuing analysis of why Virginia behaves the way she does. Was ever a state so much written about, or so much worth writing about?

So I do not believe that the changes which have come to Virginia in recent years are likely to overwhelm the Virginians, or that their newfound prosperity will cause them to be the less Virginian in the things they cherish. I think of something that Robert Russa Moton wrote in his autobiography, published in 1920, in describing the decision he had faced about his future career when, as a young black man, he began his senior year at Hampton Institute in 1889:

> My heart was pretty definitely set on going back to Prince Edward County, and the little town of Farmville was to me an ideal place. Something about the atmosphere of the locality appealed very strongly to me. I had been in Philadelphia, Washington, and Baltimore, and had seen a little of Norfolk, Richmond, and Petersburg, but somehow they did not compare in importance to my mind with Farmville, nor seem nearly so attractive as a place to live in as this little town on the Appomattox River.[7]

Can any good Virginian read that without recognizing how he too has felt? And can a white Virginian, knowing what happened, read it without wincing a little? If to that love of the land can be added a determination to preserve the loveliness for future Virginians, and to make a place within the community for all Virginians, then the Old Dominion will prevail.

---

7. Robert Russa Moton, *Finding a Way Out: An Autobiography* (Garden City, N.Y.: Doubleday, Page and Co., 1920), p. 107.

Suggestions for Further Reading

Writing an informal historical essay such as this was possible only because the writer could draw upon the research and insights of so many good chroniclers and interpreters of Virginia. Here I can cite only a few of them.

At every point along the way I was able to turn to Virginius Dabney's excellent history, *Virginia: The New Dominion* (Garden City, N.Y.: Doubleday and Company, 1971). Anyone working in Southern history has at his disposal the excellent period studies in the Louisiana State University Press's History of the South. For the colonial period there is Wesley Frank Craven, *The Southern Colonies in the Seventeenth Century, 1607–1689* (Baton Rouge, 1949). For the Revolutionary Period, there is John Richard Alden, *The South in the Revolution, 1763–1789* (Baton Rouge, 1957). For the period between independence and secession there are Thomas Perkins Abernethy, *The South in the New Nation, 1789–1819* (Baton Rouge, 1961); Charles S. Sydnor, *The Development of Southern Sectionalism, 1819–1848* (Baton Rouge, 1948); and Avery O. Craven, *The Growth of Southern Nationalism, 1848–1861* (Baton Rouge, 1953). The post-Reconstruction, New South period is delineated in C. Vann Woodward, *Origins of the New South, 1877–1913* (Baton Rouge, 1951); the twentieth-century South is ably handled in George Brown Tindall, *The Emergence of the New South, 1913–1945* (Baton Rouge, 1969).

The colonial Virginia scene is especially rich in historical scholarship. Richard L. Morton's two-volume *Colonial Virginia* (Chapel Hill: University of North Carolina Press, 1960), is thorough and detailed. An important recent reinterpretation is Edmund S. Morgan, *American Slavery, American Freedom: The Ordeal of Colonial Virginia* (New York: W. W. Norton, 1975). Other studies to which I am heavily indebted are Thomas J. Wertenbaker, *The Planters of Colonial Virginia* (Princeton, N.J.: Princeton University Press, 1918); Louis B. Wright, *The First Gentlemen of Virginia* (Charlottesville: University Press of

Virginia, 1964); Parke Rouse, Jr., *James Blair of Virginia* (Chapel Hill: University of North Carolina Press, 1971); Wesley Frank Craven, *The Colonies in Transition, 1660–1713* (New York: Harper and Row, 1968); Clifford Dowdey, *The Virginia Dynasties* (Boston: Little, Brown, 1969); Charles S. Sydnor, *Gentleman Freeholders: Political Practices in Washington's Virginia* (Chapel Hill: University of North Carolina Press, 1952); and the excellent editorial commentaries as well as the documents in Warren M. Billings ed., *The Old Dominion in the Seventeenth Century: A Documentary History of Virginia, 1606–1689* (Chapel Hill: University of North Carolina Press, 1975).

David John Mays's two-volume biography, *Edmund Pendleton 1721–1803: A Biography* (Cambridge, Mass.: Harvard University Press, 1952) is an authoritative account of mid-eighteenth-century Virginia political and social history. Dumas Malone's multivolume *Jefferson and His Time* (Boston: Little, Brown, 1948—) is detailed and definitive. Merrill Jensen, *The New Nation: A History of the United States During the Confederation, 1781–1789* (New York: Vintage Books, 1950) is an excellent account of the post-Revolutionary period. Two books by Noble E. Cunningham, Jr., *The Jeffersonian Republicans: The Formation of Party Organization, 1789–1801* (Chapel Hill, University of North Carolina Press, 1957) and *The Jeffersonian Republicans in Power, 1801–1809* (Chapel Hill: University of North Carolina Press, 1963), are filled with material on Virginia politics. Richard Beale Davis's *Intellectual Life in Jefferson's Virginia, 1790–1830* (Chapel Hill: University of North Carolina Press, 1964) is a definitive study.

The intellectual history of the antebellum period is well chronicled in Clement Eaton, *The Mind of the Old South* (Baton Rouge: Louisiana State University Press, 1967) and Carl N. Degler, *The Other South: Southern Dissenters in the Nineteenth Century* (New York: Harper and Row, 1974).

The most useful account of late-nineteenth- and early-twentieth-century politics in Virginia is Allen W. Moger, *Virginia: Bourbonism to Byrd, 1870–1925* (Charlottesville: University Press of Virginia, 1968). Other valuable studies include Jack P. Maddex, Jr., *The Virginia Conservatives, 1867–1879* (Chapel Hill: University of North Carolina Press, 1970); and Raymond H. Pulley, *Old Virginia Re-*

stored: An Interpretation of the Progressive Impulse, 1870–1930 (Charlottesville: University Press of Virginia, 1968).

By far the best account of Senator Harry Flood Byrd's career is J. Harvie Wilkinson, III, *Harry Byrd and the Changing Face of Virginia Politics, 1945–1966* (Charlottesville: University Press of Virginia, 1968). For the black Virginian's situation during the period see Andrew Buni, *The Negro in Virginia Politics, 1902–1965* (Charlottesville: University Press of Virginia, 1967). Benjamin Muse, *Virginia's Massive Resistance* (Bloomington: Indiana University Press, 1961) is an account of the rise and fall of massive resistance to educational integration. James Jackson Kilpatrick's *The Sovereign States: Notes of a Citizen of Virginia* (Chicago: Henry Regnery, 1957) is an articulate statement. Post-Byrdian developments are detailed in Ralph Eisenberg, "Virginia: The Emergence of Two-Party Politics," in William C. Havard, ed., *The Changing Politics of the South* (Baton Rouge: Louisiana State University Press, 1972) and Neal R. Pierce, *The Border South States: People, Politics and Power in the Five Border South States* (New York: W. W. Norton, 1975). Jean Gottmann, *Virginia at Mid-Century* (New York: Henry Holt, 1955) is a valuable geographical and social examination.

There are numerous other works that might be cited, and which I have used. I have been permitted to list only a few. I could not, however, compile any such checklist as this, no matter how selective, without calling attention to the several delightful books on present-day Virginia and Virginians by Guy Friddell, unsurpassed connoisseur of *Homo sapiens Virginiensis* both *Major* and *Minor*.

Index

Adams, John, 67, 82, 84, 99
Agriculture: as basis of economy, 94–95, 100–101, 102; in early and mid-1800s, 97–98, 121; in late 1800s, 149–150; in early 1900s, 160. *See also* Plantations; Tobacco
Alexandria, 96, 106, 138, 161, 173
Alien and Sedition acts, 82–84
Almond, Lindsay, 179, 187, 191–194 *passim*
American Revolution, 49–63
Anglican Church: and dissenters, 18, 36, 40, 59; clergy of, 29, 30; and Two-Penny Act, 45, 46

Bacon, Nathaniel, 21–27 *passim*
Bacon's Rebellion, 23–27, 28, 107
Battle, John Stewart, 178–179, 180, 203
Berkeley, Sir William, 15–16, 17
Blacks: first in Virginia, 9; status of, 64, 65, 115, 145; free, 86, 113; after Civil War, 137–138; in late 1800s, 154; in mid-1900s, 183–185; education of, 154–155, 184–185; in Richmond, 209–210; mentioned, 10, 170, 214, 216. *See also* Civil Rights; Segregation; Slaves; Voting—of blacks
Blair, Rev. James, 29–31, 40
Board of Trade (British), 29–31, 37, 45
Booth, Armistead, 181, 189, 191, 199, 201–202
Breckinridge, John, 84, 125, 126
Brown, John, 124–125
Burr, Aaron, 84–85, 88–89
Business interests: and politics, 142, 143, 188, 192
Byrd, Harry Flood: as state senator, 162–163; as governor, 164–165; as U.S. senator, 170, 171, 176–181 *passim;* and desegregation, 170–198 *passim;* decline

and death, 198–201; mentioned, 175, 186, 205, 206, 214
Byrd, Harry F., Jr., 181, 200–204
Byrd organization, 171–182, 194–200, 211, 213

Cabell, James Branch, 157, 167–169
Calhoun, John C., 92, 117, 118
Cannon, James, Jr., 160, 165, 166
Carter, Robert ("King"), 31, 33–34
Carter, Stuart, 181, 191, 194
Chesapeake Bay: in period of settlement, 3, 13; at present, 207, 208; mentioned, 72, 79, 93, 130
Civil rights: and Fifteenth Amendment, 140; and Truman, 177, 180, 186; and blacks, 184; and constitution of 1970, 205. *See also* Blacks; Segregation; Supreme Court
Civil War, 129–135. *See also* Confederacy
Clark, George Rogers, 56–57, 65
Clay, Henry, 92, 116–120 *passim*
Commerce: in Richmond and Norfolk, 79, 106, 156, 161; Jefferson's embargo on, 90, 92; collapse of in 1893, 148–149; mentioned, 70, 93, 94, 148, 155. *See also* Business interests; Tobacco
Confederacy: formation of, 126; military forces of, 128, 129–135; romanticization of, 156–157
Confederation, 70–71, 73
Conservative party, 140–141, 144–147
Constitution (U.S.): and debts to English merchants, 67; and interests of Virginia, 70–71; Jefferson and, 71–72; Constitutional Convention, 72–74; ratification of, 74–76, 80
—interpretation of: federalism vs. decentralization, 79–89 *passim,* 91; and state government, 95; and slave property,

223

Governor's council (*Cont.*)
21; under Board of Trade, 28, 30, 36; abolished, 122; mentioned, 101
Grant, Ulysses S., 130, 133, 134, 140
Gray, Garland, 187–190 *passim*, 194

Hamilton, Alexander, 72, 76, 79–85 *passim*
Hampton Roads: in War of 1812, 93; as seaport, 94, 155; in Civil War, 131; expansion of during World War I, 161; in World War II, 173–174; recent development of area, 207–208; mentioned, 10, 12, 56, 60, 96, 142
Harrison, Albertis, 179, 195, 199–201
Henry, Patrick: in General Assembly, 46–50 *passim*, 62; as governor, 57; and Constitution, 72, 75, 76, 77; mentioned, 38, 106
Holton, Linwood, 200, 203, 206, 210, 214
House of Burgesses: in early colonial era, 8, 9; election of, 14, 16, 32, 36, 52; in pre-Revolutionary period, 43, 45, 48. *See also* General Assembly

Immigration: English, 13, 17; German, 31, 33, 38–39, 105; French, 31; Scotch-Irish, 33, 36, 39, 105; Scottish, 39–40
Indentured servants, 7, 9, 11, 13, 29
Indians: and early settlers, 4, 5, 7; conflict with whites, 6, 10–11, 20–25 *passim*; in French and Indian War, 44, 49; mentioned, 26, 30, 31, 65, 88, 93
Industrial development: early iron industry, 31; in mid-1900s, 194, 196, 200, 206, 211; mentioned, 175. *See also* Manufacturing

Jackson, Andrew, 115, 116, 118
Jackson, Thomas J. ("Stonewall"), 131, 132, 156
James River: and early settlements, 3, 6, 13; in Revolution, 60; in Civil War, 134; mentioned, 31, 33, 34, 35, 38, 175, 210
Jamestown: settlement of, 3–12; and Bacon's Rebellion, 22, 23, 24; and tourism, 175; mentioned, 29
Jefferson, Thomas: and Declaration of Independence, 32, 50–51, 52–53; on slavery, 32, 63–65, 66, 86; forebears of, 34, 38; as governor, 57–66 *passim;* and

entail, 58, 96; on religious freedom, 58–59, 68, 84; on education, 68; and individual freedom, 72, 92; in France, 67, 72; as secretary of state, 76, 81; as architect, 79; as leader of Jeffersonian Republicans, 80–81, 83; on Washington, 82; and Alien and Sedition acts, 83–84; election to presidency, 84–85; as president, 86–90; in retirement, 91–92, 99–100; mentioned, 51, 60, 67, 68, 92, 94, 100, 101, 175, 176
Jeffersonian Republicans, 79–89 *passim*, 91, 101

Kentucky, 66, 69, 70, 75, 78
Kilpatrick, James Jackson, 187, 189–190, 192

Labor: strikes, 169–170, 177; political activity of, 176, 200, 202, 203. *See also* Slave labor
Land: as attraction for colonists, 12; speculation in, 38, 65–66; as investment for planters, 95; values, 121, 137
—distribution of: in early colonial period, 7, 8, 16, 17; in later colonial period, 31, 37, 43, 65–66
—as voting qualification: in early colonial period, 14, 15, 19; in later colonial period, 32, 33, 37; in early national period, 97
Lee, Richard Henry, 34, 48, 50, 77
Lee, Robert E., 34, 127, 129–135, 137, 156
Lincoln, Abraham, 125, 126, 127, 132
Literature: and westward migration of Virginians, 98; in antebellum era, 104, 106–109; during Reconstruction, 157–158; of 1900s, 167–169
Local option (and desegregation), 189–192 *passim*
Loyalists (in Revolution). *See* Tories

Madison, James: in Virginia politics, 67–68; and Constitution, 71, 73, 74, 77; as congressman, 77; as Jeffersonian Republican, 80, 83; as president, 90, 92; mentioned, 51, 59, 64, 71, 72, 94, 99, 100
Mahone, William A., 141–147 *passim*, 154
Manufacturing: in Richmond, 79, 93, 121, 156; of cotton goods, 94, 121; in Jeffer-